ESSAYS OF YESTERDAY AND TODAY

EDITED BY JOHN A. LESTER

HILL SCHOOL, POTTSTOWN, PENNSYLVANIA

Illustrated by Susanne Suba

HARCOURT, BRACE & WORLD, INC.

NEW YORK   CHICAGO   ATLANTA

DALLAS   BURLINGAME

A NOTE TO TEACHERS

This collection seeks to give students and teachers a good time as they read and study together the great essayists of yesterday and today. A good balance has been preserved between yesterday and today; about one third of the essays were written before 1900 and two thirds since. This collection is unique in that it reaches clear back to ancient Greece and Rome. Some of the most exciting essays in the book are among the oldest. There is Plato's moving narrative of Socrates drinking the hemlock and Pliny's vivid description of his uncle's death beneath the ashes of the erupting Vesuvius. The young student will inevitably compare the drama of these older essays written centuries ago with what is happening today.

Though this volume represents a time span of more than twenty-two centuries, nearly fifty per cent of the essays were written during the life time of the students who will read them.

The purpose of the teaching helps is twofold: first to motivate the reading of the essays, second to lead the student to do something with them. The short introduction to each essay creates in the student a wish, or at least a readiness to read it; it supplies a short biography of the author and mentions his chief writings; it anticipates the hard spots and prepares the young reader to get over them. Following each essay is a set of Things to Do. These are put down in a list without definite labels, but with a well considered sequence. First come comprehension questions, to help the student to understand the essay; next, some questions to aid him in discussing its implications; third, two or three suggestions for related activities; fourth, some possible titles for themes; and fifth, suggestions for further reading in the same author or in related authors.

There are two additional and novel features in this volume. To sharpen the appeal of the book to young readers, Miss Susanne Suba has prepared some twenty-three informal sketches for *Essays of Yesterday and Today*. These drawings, by the artist whose work we have enjoyed regularly in *The New Yorker,* have caught with uncanny penetration the central themes of the essays, grave or gay. In addition to these drawings we have used a total of fifty or sixty epigrams, anecdotes, or student " boners " as fillers after many of the essays. The student may sometimes discover a relation between the filler and the preceding essay.

The wise teacher will use this book as a new experience in group reading. The essays should be presented simply as a series of short prose pieces by able writers, on topics of interest to boys and girls. Attempts to explain the nature of the essay, to classify or to define it, may well be postponed until the student knows, through the experience of reading, what it is he is trying to classify or define — until he has read a sampling of essays wide enough for him to feel differences and make comparisons. Indeed, the teacher will usually find that the best occasions for criticism and comparison arise by the way, spontaneously from the group, in the process of reading.

In what order shall these essays be read? So widely does the reading ability of different high school groups differ that only the teacher of each individual group can wisely answer this question, and then only after he has thoroughly acquainted himself with what the book contains. The essays are organized by themes or interest centers, with a foreword to each of these sections. There is an element of unity in each section, and they are arranged roughly in the order of difficulty. Teachers who prefer to use a different order of presentation may do so by consulting the table of contents; those who prefer to read in chronological order may consult the second table of contents (page x).

After the teacher has established that group attitude of eagerness and curiosity necessary for classroom reading, he may be able to enlist the students in forming a co-operative plan for the use of the book, and utilize the great range in interest and power to read with appreciation which is present in every classroom. With some groups the appointment or election of a few rapid and sensitive readers as "tasters" to collaborate with the teacher in the planning of the reading has been found most successful. Certain essays possess a peculiar appeal for certain students, and a versatile teacher can use this fact to encourage such persons to become class "experts" in a certain type of essay, for instance the essay on sport, science, music, wild life, or the book review. This spirit of exploration will quickly spread beyond the book itself. Some students may become interested in the essays of a certain period, for instance the early nineteenth century, American essays of the last half of the nineteenth century, American or English essays of today.

The teacher should provide for this extension of interest before the reading begins. The school or town librarian will be eager to co-operate in providing references and in reserving a shelf of selected books. No list of essayists or of selections is appended to this volume because it is believed that this self-propelled exploration is a better incentive. A practice which has been found very successful where it is possible is the co-operative formation on the part of teacher and students of a classroom library of essays, brought from home for the use of the group while the reading is in progress. It is best to have the group select one of their number as class librarian in charge of the books. Before the reading begins the teacher will have provided bound volumes of the recent issues of *The Reader's Digest, The Atlantic Monthly,* and *Harper's Magazine;* and as the reading proceeds some students are likely to volunteer as reporters on current issues of these magazines, and of *Scholastic* with its leads to essays published elsewhere.

After the reading is finished the teacher and his group may wish to arrange the essays by types; for instance, in such categories as personal, reflective, critical, expository, didactic, humorous, biographical, etc. However the number of categories may be enlarged it will be found that a lively debate will ensue about the placement of some fifteen of these essays, for the reason that they have right of entry to several pigeon-holes. None the less this effort to classify is useful. It entails a comprehensive review; it requires hard thinking about the main purpose or nature of each essay; and it inevitably leads us to realize that we are not sorting marbles.

Though the average reading difficulty of this volume is about that of the second year of high school, it includes some frankly difficult pieces. A book of essays offered for high school reading today needs no apology for the inclusion of some hard reading. The tasks and problems confronting America are hard. Their solutions will have to be approved by future citizens now in school. Indeed every high school student is now perforce tragically aware of the importance of national and international events, and it follows that high school teachers, and particularly teachers of English have now an unusual opportunity and duty. The situation strengthens the hands of all those teachers who have been trying to get their students to see in the writing of an essay, not so much a polite exercise in literary urbanity, as a dynamic expression of informed and timely judgment. There are included in this volume notable essays dealing with the foundations of the future, and they can be used as springboards for the thinking and writing of high school students about what they now know to be their own vital interests.

Two final words. All the essays included in this collection deserve to be *read*. The teacher should aim at careful and thorough reading, and should discourage smattering and skimming. Before the group is asked to undertake a new reading assignment, the teacher should take time to create the anticipation, the readiness, and the attitude of mind essential for full success. This preliminary survey of the essay next to be read is especially necessary to obtain the full benefit from the reading of the later units.

For their critical advice the editor wishes to thank Dr. Clara A. Molendyk, Chairman of the English Department, Lafayette High School, Brooklyn, New York, and Mr. Francis W. Griffith, Chairman of the English Department, James Madison High School, Brooklyn, New York. To Miss Susanne Suba he is grateful for her care in designing the typography as well as for her skillful pen and ink sketches.

JOHN A. LESTER

February, 1943

CONTENTS

CHRONOLOGICAL ORDER

Some teachers may not care to use the essays in the groupings by subject matter. For the benefit of those who prefer a historical approach the following list is given. Here the essays are named in the order of their dates of publication.

A WORD TO STUDENTS

THE FORTY-SIX essays which follow were chosen in order that in reading them you might share the pleasure which the authors had in writing them. The wide variety of interests represented in a room full of high school students has governed the selection. The authors are of seven different nationalities, and, though they represent a time span of more than twenty-three centuries, considerably more than half the essays were written during your lifetime.

Bring to this reading all your power to understand and to appreciate; your sense of the whimsical and the humorous, for there is plenty to laugh over; bring all your information and independence of judgment, for there are views expressed with which you may disagree and will want to thrash out in class discussion. Emerson says, " 'Tis the good reader that makes the good book," and it is only fair to an author to understand him before you differ with him. Whatever the class plan for the use of this book may be, get to the bottom of the message the author of an essay has written for you. Hard words are explained at the foot of the page, and it will help you to be certain that you have got the author's full message if after reading an essay, you will carry out the Appreciation Hints printed at the end of each selection.

As you read this book you will come on some essay which particularly appeals to you, and sets you off in search of more like it. The suggestions of further reading at the end of each essay will be helpful, and both you and the rest of the class will benefit from the report you may make about your explorations in more extensive reading. For this collection is only a sampling of a rich field of literature which contains some of the most interesting writing in our language. It is designed to be a gateway leading to a wider landscape and to a greater sensitivity to its beauties.

FUN ᐧIN SCHOOL AND OUT

BUSINESS and pleasure, work and play, drill and fun — these things won't stay separate. A boy came to class one day and repeated the names of all the islands in the West Indies beginning off the coast of Florida and going all the way to Trinidad. And when he was asked what on earth he had done that for, he said, " Just for fun." Many of the most successful people find their diversion and their work wrapped up in the same package.

The essays in this group illustrate in various ways that fun is where you find it. In the first essay, the sisters worked hard at their bird lore in order to spring that knavish trick on their instructor in nature study. Every one who can play a game well will feel the truth of " Who's Catching " because he knows that the fun we get from playing well is spread out over the hard work of training. Stephen Leacock gets fun out of his recollections of the little red schoolhouse, where urchins figured out problems with slate and pencil. To them the tasks at which A, B, and C pumped and dug and rowed were no laughing matter. And William Saroyan was thinking of his own schooldays when he tells us how Aram and Joey simply had to break out of the classroom and beat it for the circus. James Thurber gets his fun from the grown-up Joeys and Arams — the adult truants who want to make up for lost time overnight. James Thurber's sparkling satire at this education by magic makes excellent reading. Every trout-fisher knows that hard work may be fun, and Walton's scholar experienced both pain and pleasure when he went forth for his first day with the trouts.

These writers would find the boundary line between their work and their fun hard to draw; and that is true in school and out. Einstein must get great fun in finding the equation that satisfies, and so does the student when he has at last worked out the right answer to his problem. Perhaps this sense of satisfaction is part of the quest; at any rate fun is where you find it.

RUTH McKENNEY 1911– IF WE can trust Ruth McKenney, there is plenty of adventure in modern life for the growing girl. She affirms that, with her inseparable sister, Eileen, she "spent a whole summer in a deserted monastery in Columbus, Ohio, fighting a brood of oversized and somewhat insane bats which flew round our beds making nasty whirring sounds." Indeed if we read much about the carryings on of these two girls, we get the impression that Ruth and her sister in their teens were tomboys so full of life that they *had* to find adventure, and unusual adventure, in life in order to be satisfied with it. So outrageous were some of their acts that the author tells us that *My Sister Eileen,* the book in which they are recorded, is "a considerably censored account of the awful things my sister Eileen and I lived through when we were growing up." And the reason it is censored is that "nobody would believe the very worst things that happened to Eileen and me during our tender years." One might think from the title that it was Eileen who was the ringleader, but they are usually partners in crime. Whatever they might have been at the time, these happenings become, in the telling, not tragedies, but comedies of youth, and like the play *My Sister Eileen* are full of fun and laughter.

All of us can think of some escapade or adventure of our early youth. Some of them cause us to smile as we recall them, others may even bring on our faces the semblance of a blush, but probably all of them have gained in vividness with the passing of the years. We may be sure that this is true of the escapades of the two McKenneys.

At fourteen Ruth McKenney held a night job as printer's devil in a Cleveland print shop. She worked her way, partly by reporting and waiting on table, through Ohio State University, gained wide recognition as a journalist in Ohio, and then, with her sister, migrated to New York. Ruth began to write for the New York *Post,* and later for *The New Yorker.* It was in this magazine that the stories collected in *My Sister Eileen* first appeared. Her volume entitled *Industrial Valley* reflects her experiences of a very different sort in Akron, Ohio.

Ruth McKenney really is Mrs. Richard Bransten. Her latest book is entitled *McKenneys Carry On,* published in 1940.

A Loud Sneer for Our Feathered Friends

FROM childhood, my sister and
I have had a well-grounded dislike for our friends the birds. We came
to hate them when she was ten and I was eleven. We had been exiled
by what we considered an unfeeling family to one of those loathsome
girls' camps where Indian lore is rife and the management puts up
neatly lettered signs reminding the clients to be Good Sports. From
the moment Eileen and I arrived at dismal old Camp Hi-Wah, we
were Bad Sports, and we liked it.

We refused to get out of bed when the bugle blew in the morning, we fought against scrubbing our teeth in public to music, we
sneered when the flag was ceremoniously lowered at sunset, we
avoided doing a good deed a day, we complained loudly about the
food, which was terrible, and we bought some chalk once and wrote
all over the Recreation Cabin, "We hate Camp Hi-Wah." It made a
wonderful scandal, although unfortunately we were immediately ac-
cused of the crime. All the other little campers *loved* dear old Camp
Hi-Wah, which shows you what kind of people they were.

The first two weeks Eileen and I were at Camp Hi-Wah, we sat
in our cabin grinding our teeth at our councilor and writing letters to
distant relatives. These letters were, if I say so myself, real masterpieces of double dealing and heartless chicanery. In our childish and,
we hoped, appealing scrawl, we explained to Great-Aunt Mary Farrel
and Second Cousin Joe Murphy that we were having such fun at dear
Camp Hi-Wah making Indian pocketbooks.

"We would simply L-O-V-E to make you a pocketbook, dear Aunt Mary," we wrote, "only the leather costs $1 for a small pocketbook or $1.67 for a large size pocketbook, which is much nicer because you can carry more things in it, and the rawhide you sew it up with, just exactly the way the Indians did, costs 40 cents more. We burn pictures on the leather but that doesn't cost anything. If we O-N-L-Y had $1 or $1.67 and 40 cents for the rawhide, we could make you the S-W-E-L-L-E-S-T pocketbook."

As soon as we had enough orders for Indian pocketbooks with pictures burnt on them, we planned to abscond with the funds sent by our trusting relatives and run away to New York City, where, as we used to explain dramatically to our cabin-mates, we intended to live a life of sin. After a few days, our exciting plans for our immediate future were bruited all over the camp, and admirers came from as far away as Cabin Minnehaha, which was way down at the end of Hiawatha Alley, just to hear us tell about New York and sin.

Fame had its price, however. One of the sweet little girls who lived in our cabin turned out to be such a Good Citizen ("Camp Hi-Wah Girls Learn to Be Good Citizens") that she told our dreadful secret to our councilor. Our mail was impounded for weeks, and worst of all, we actually had to make several Indian pocketbooks with pictures burnt on them. My pictures were all supposed to be snakes, although they were pretty blurred. Eileen specialized in what she believed to be the likeness of a werewolf, but Cousin Joe, who had generously ordered three pocketbooks, wrote a nice letter thanking Eileen for his pretty pocketbooks with the pretty pictures of Abraham Lincoln on them. We were terribly disgusted by the whole thing.

It was in this mood that we turned to birds. The handicraft hour at Camp Hi-Wah, heralded by the ten-thirty A.M. bugle, competed for popularity with the bird walks at the same hour. You could, as Eileen had already somewhat precociously learned how to say, name your own poison. After three weeks of burning pictures on leather, we were ready for anything, even our feathered friends.

So one hot morning in July, the two McKenney sisters, big and bad and fierce for their age, answered the bird-walk bugle call, leaving the Indian-pocketbook teacher to mourn her two most backward pupils. We were dressed, somewhat reluctantly, to be sure, in the required heavy stockings for poison ivy and brambles, and carried, each of us, in our dirty hands a copy of a guide to bird lore called *Bird Life for Children.*

Bird Life for Children was a volume that all the Good Citizens in Camp Hi-Wah pretended to find engrossing. Eileen and I thought it was stupefyingly dull. Our favorite literary character at the time was Dumas' Marguerite de Valois, who took her decapitated lover's head home in a big handkerchief for old times' sake. Eileen, in those days, was always going to name her first girl child Marguerite de Valois.

Bird Life for Children was full of horrid pictures in full color of robins and pigeons and redbirds. Under each picture was a loathsomely whimsical paragraph describing how the bird in question spent his spare time, what he ate, and why children should love him. Eileen and I hated the book so, we were quite prepared to despise birds when we started off that morning on our first bird walk, but we had no idea of what we were going to suffer, that whole awful summer, because of our feathered friends. In the first place, since we had started off making leather pocketbooks, we were three weeks behind the rest of the Hi-Wah bird-lovers. They had been tramping through blackberry bushes for days and days and had already got the hang of the more ordinary bird life around camp, whereas the only bird I could identify at the time was the vulture. Cousin Joe took me to a zoo once, and there was a fine vulture there, a big, fat one. They fed him six live rats every day in lieu of human flesh. I kept a sharp eye out for a vulture all summer, but one never turned up at Camp Hi-Wah. Nothing interesting ever happened around that place.

On that first bird walk, Eileen and I trotted anxiously along behind the little band of serious-minded bird-lovers, trying desperately to see, or at least hear, even one bird, even one robin. But alas, while other bird-walkers saw, or pretended to see — for Eileen and I never believed them for a moment — all kinds of hummingbirds and hawks and owls and whatnot, we never saw or heard a single, solitary feathered friend, not one.

By the time we staggered into camp for lunch, with stubbed

toes, scratched faces, and tangled hair, Eileen and I were soured for life on birds. Our bird logs, which we carried strapped to our belts along with the *Guide,* were still chaste and bare, while all the other little bird-lovers had fulsome entries, such as " Saw and heard redbird at 10:37 A.M. Molting."

Still, for the next three days we stayed honest and suffered. For three terrible mornings we endured being dolts among bird-walkers, the laughingstock of Camp Hi-Wah. After six incredibly tiresome hours, our bird logs were still blank. Then we cracked under the strain. The fourth morning we got up feeling grim but determined. We sharpened our pencils before we started off on the now-familiar trail through the second-growth forest.

When we got well into the woods and Mary Mahoney, the premier bird-walker of Camp Hi-Wah, had already spotted and logged her first redbird of the morning, Eileen suddenly stopped dead in her tracks. " Hark! " she cried. She had read that somewhere in a book. " Quiet! " I echoed instantly.

The bird-walkers drew to a halt respectfully and stood in silence. They stood and stood. It was not good form even to whisper while fellow bird-walkers were logging a victim, but after quite a long time the Leader, whose feet were flat and often hurt her, whispered impatiently, " Haven't you got him logged yet? "

" You drove him away," Eileen replied sternly. " It was a yellow-billed cuckoo."

" A yellow-billed cuckoo? " cried the Leader incredulously.

" Well," Eileen said modestly, " at least *I* think it was." Then, with many a pretty hesitation and thoughtful pause, she recited the leading features of the yellow-billed cuckoo, as recorded in *Bird Life for Children.*
The Leader was ter-

ribly impressed. Later on that morning I logged a kingfisher, a red-headed woodpecker, and a yellow-bellied sapsucker, which was all I could remember at the moment. Each time, I kept the bird-walkers standing around for an interminable period, gaping into blank space and listening desperately to the rustle of the wind in the trees and the creak of their shoes as they went from one foot to another.

In a few days Eileen and I were the apple of our Leader's eye, the modest heroes of the Camp Hi-Wah bird walks. Naturally, there were base children around camp, former leading bird-walkers, who spread foul rumors up and down Hiawatha Alley that Eileen and I were frauds. We soon stopped this ugly talk, however. Eileen was the pitcher, and a very good one, too, of the Red Bird ball team and I was the first base. When Elouise Pritchard, the worst gossip in Cabin Sitting Bull, came up to bat, she got a pitched ball right in the stomach. Of course it was only a soft ball, but Eileen could throw it pretty hard. To vary this routine, I tagged Mary Mahoney, former head bird-walker, out at first base, and Mary had a bruise on her thigh for weeks. The rumors stopped abruptly.

We had begun to get pretty bored with logging rare birds when the game took on a new angle. Mary Mahoney and several other bird-walkers began to see the same birds we did on our morning jaunts into the forest. This made us pretty mad, but there wasn't much we could do about it. Next, Mary Mahoney began to see birds we weren't logging. The third week after we joined the Camp Hi-Wah Bird Study Circle, everybody except the poor, dumb Leader and a few backward but honest bird-lovers was logging the rarest birds seen around Camp Hi-Wah in twenty years. Bird walks developed into a race to see who could shout "Hark!" first and keep the rest of the little party in fidgety silence for the next five minutes.

The poor bird-walk Leader was in agony. Her reputation as a bird-lover was in shreds. Her talented pupils were seeing rare birds right and left, while the best she could log for herself would be a few crummy old redbirds and a robin or so. At last our Leader's morale collapsed. It was the day when nearly everybody in the study circle swore that she saw and heard a bona-fide nightingale.

"Where?" cried our Leader desperately, after the fourth night-

ingale had been triumphantly logged in the short space of five minutes. Heartless fingers pointed to a vague bush. The Leader strained
her honest eyes. No notion of our duplicity crossed her innocent, un-
worldly mind.

"I can't see any nightingale," our Leader cried, and burst into
tears. Then, full of shame, she sped back to camp, leaving the Camp
Hi-Wah bird-lovers to their nightingales and guilty thoughts.

Eileen and I ate a hearty lunch that noon because we thought we
would need it. Then we strolled down Hiawatha Alley and hunted up
Mary Mahoney.

"We will put the Iron Cross on you if you tell," Eileen started
off, as soon as we found Mary.

"What's the Iron Cross?" Mary squeaked, startled out of her
usual haughty poise.

"Never mind," I growled. "You'll find out if you tell."

We walked past Cabin Sitting Bull, past the flagpole, into the
tall grass beyond the ball field.

"She'll tell," Eileen said finally.

"What'll we do?" I replied mournfully. "They'll try us at camp-
fire tonight."

They did, too. It was terrible. We denied everything, but the
Head of Camp, a mean old lady who wore middy blouses and pleated
serge bloomers, sentenced us to no desserts and eight-o'clock bedtime
for two weeks. We thought over what to do to Mary Mahoney for
four whole days. Nothing seemed sufficiently frightful, but in the
end we put the wart curse on her. The wart curse was simple but horrible. We dropped around to Cabin Sitting Bull one evening and in
the presence of Mary and her allies we drew ourselves up to our full
height and said solemnly in unison, "We put the wart curse on you,
Mary Mahoney." Then we stalked away.

We didn't believe for a moment in the wart curse, but we hoped
Mary would. At first she was openly contemptuous, but to our delight, on the fourth evening she developed a horrible sty in her eye.
We told everybody a sty was a kind of a wart and that we had Mary in
our power. The next day Mary broke down and came around to our
cabin and apologized in choked accents. She gave Eileen her best

hair ribbon and me a little barrel that had a picture of Niagara Falls inside it, if you looked hard enough. We were satisfied.

APPRECIATION HINTS

1. What features of camp life did the girls especially dislike?
2. What was their first punishment, and what was it for?
3. How did the class study birds?
4. What bird did Eileen identify? What did Ruth identify?
5. How were the suspicions of other campers discouraged?
6. How were the girls betrayed and punished?
7. How did they get even with their betrayer?
8. Where do you find evidence that the author understood young girls?
9. Usually of two sisters one is the leader. Can you find any evidence to show which was the leader here?
10. Write a letter to a promising person for money — a letter which you think will bring results — or a composition on "The Gentle Touch."
11. Write a composition about your training in Indian lore, or about your early studies in flowers (butterflies, fish, rabbits, shells, mice, coins, stamps).
12. Other amusing essays in *My Sister Eileen* are "Guinea Pig," "La Scandale Internationale" (what came of school correspondence with French students), and "The Sock Hunt."
13. Other adventures are recorded in *The McKenneys Carry On*.

I once talked to an old cannibal who, hearing of the Great War raging then in Europe, was most curious to know how we Europeans managed to eat such enormous quantities of human flesh. When I told him that Europeans do not eat their slain foes, he looked at me in shocked horror and asked what sort of barbarians we were, to kill without any real object.

Bronislaw Malinowski

JOHN R. TUNIS 1889- WHATEVER is your favorite game, you ought to be able to play and to watch it better after reading this essay on inside baseball. It is far more than just a bit of baseball reporting. To be sure we have the story of two innings, but we have besides a sort of diary of a big league catcher's day; a description of his technique, his responsibilities, his relation with his pitchers; we go in and out of the Yankee stadium; and yet all this is woven together to make a unified picture of what lies behind a league baseball game. We shall get more fun out of watching good games when we are more conscious of what is going on behind the scenes.

Next best to playing a game well is appreciating good play and what makes it so. The crowd stands up and yells as the tape is broken in nine and seven-tenths seconds, but only a few of them know anything of all the training which made the feat possible. Do you know what to look for in a well played game of field or ice hockey, basketball, soccer, football or baseball? In reporting a game for the school paper do you give credit to what lies behind and makes possible the spectacular play and the victory? For the better the play, the more of preparation, and planning, and practice lies behind it. A good sports broadcaster knows this; his eyes notice the sweeping end run, but they don't miss the blocking that makes it possible.

It is rare to find a real expert in sport who has also the skill and sensitiveness to write vividly about it. But the two skills sometimes go together; Heywood Broun was once a baseball reporter. You will recognize that the author of "Who's Catching?" knows baseball and makes even the technical side of it intensely interesting.

John R. Tunis graduated at Harvard in 1911. He was an athlete, a first rate tennis player, and became short-story writer, journalist, and sports critic. Among his recent volumes may be mentioned three books which appeared in 1940: *Champion's Choice, Kid from Tomkinsville,* and *Sport for the Fun of It.* The latter is a sort of handbook of information on twenty different sports. *All American* (1942) is an exciting story of principles of democracy worked out as problems of everyday life in a large high school. Some of his best writing has been done, like the following essay, for the magazines.

Who's Catching?

THE COACH spat copiously and ejected tobacco juice on the grass behind third base. He was a man who had lived hard and played hard, with a face tanned and reddened by the sun of fifty ball parks, and a nose reddened by something besides nature.

"If you had a team of perfect players out there on that field and offered me my pick, I'd choose the catcher. Every time."

Football stars are occasionally beautiful but dumb. Baseball demands intelligence, especially behind the plate — because the catcher is the quarterback of baseball. He runs the team and is the only man who sees every player on the field and every move that takes place. He calls the pitches and sometimes directs much of the defensive play. He is the one person on the team who can never for a moment relax, whether his team is in the field or at bat. He must know wind conditions in every ball park, and his duties vary from studying the opposing batteries, the mental condition of his own pitcher, and the spacing of the outfielders, watching runners on base, keeping track of the tactical situation and seeing that the rest of the team knows it also, to backing up third and first except when a runner is in a scoring position.

All the spectators at a ball game watch the pitcher. Pitchers get the headlines. The Ruffings and Grissoms and Vander Meers attract the publicity, but the Dickeys, Mancusos, and Hartnetts can make them or break them.

Probably there is no such animal as a typical big-league catcher, but J. Luther Sewell of the Cleveland Indians comes fairly close to it, despite the fact that he is a graduate of the University of Alabama and that only one man in four in the National League ever attended college. If you saw Luke sitting in the lobby of the Hotel New Yorker reading the *Times,* you'd place him as a successful businessman. That's precisely what he is, too. Top salaries for catchers in the big leagues range around $18,000. Dickey of the Yanks, generally considered the best catcher in baseball, receives this, while Gabby Hartnett of Chicago makes $17,835. Sewell is paid over $10,000 this year. But Luke has other than financial distinctions.

He is the oldest active player in the game today, with a major-league catching record that is likely to last. Starting with Cleveland in 1921, he has played with Chicago, Washington, and Brooklyn, has averaged ninety games a year, and is now playing his nineteenth season, outdating Hartnett by a year and Lou Gehrig, of the Yanks, by four. Now he's back where he broke into baseball in 1921. A reserve, but still liable for duty.

II

Let us suppose Luke has had a sleepless night. Cleveland is playing the Yankees, and – well, you know New York in late June. The temperature has been around 95 or 96 all night, and sleep was impossible. He rose at eight-thirty, bathed, shaved, and dressed, and then came downstairs. As a rule ball players eat only two good meals a day, so he must have enough to carry him through until after the game. Orange juice, coffee, toast, eggs and bacon, are his breakfast.

It's hot in the lobby of the hotel and hotter still in his inside room on the tenth floor. The sweat is dripping from his forehead, but he stays there for several hours talking with Mel Harder, whom he'll catch that afternoon. They are discussing the batters on the Yankee team. Sewell can tell you the weakness of every hitter in the league, just what sort of ball he will bite on, and what kind of ball he will " powder." Furthermore he knows just what pitches are effective in certain ball parks and how to pitch to each man in the different grounds. Down South, last spring, Bill Dickey of the Yanks was telling newspaper men one day that at the Yankee Stadium he would never let Jimmy Foxx of the Red Sox, a right-handed hitter, have a low ball. But at Fenway Park in Boston, where the left-field fence is short, he feeds him nothing but low balls. All this is part of the catcher's job. It's the result of years of study and observation.

The temperature has gone up, not down, when Sewell and his teammates hop into taxis for the ride to the Yankee Stadium. It's at least two degrees hotter there. Once at the field, he starts getting dressed. In spite of the heat he puts on about twenty pounds of equipment. He leans over to lace his shoes when Harder, who has also been dressing, comes over and sits on the bench before his locker.

Harder isn't so sure about that high inside ball to Henrich, the Yankee right fielder. Last year he had better luck pitching low and inside to him. Sewell instantly agrees. He knows it's better to have the pitcher feel easy in his mind than to start an argument before the game, although he may not agree. One of the reasons for Sewell's success has been his ability to keep his pitchers contented and relaxed. Some pitchers are bad with men on base because they aren't relaxed; they tighten up. Feller of Cleveland keeps his mind on the base runner so much that he is apt to turn and throw a pitch that is murdered.

Oscar Vitt, the manager, comes up and the three men go carefully over the Yankee batting list. They take up each man in turn: Crosetti, Rolfe, Henrich, DiMaggio, Dickey, Selkirk, Gordon, and Dahlgren. This talk between batteries goes on all the time; in hotel rooms, at meals, in trains and buses, they are always thinking about and analyzing the opposing batters. But it's just before game time that they dissect them most minutely. " Now this man Dickey is the best pull hitter in baseball. Keep it away and outside. Rolfe — well, a change of pace sometimes fools him. DiMaggio — we got him out for three games by pitching low when I was with Chicago. Then one day Dietrich was pitching, and suddenly DiMaggio got to a low ball and hit it into the back of the Yankee bullpen, longest hit I ever saw. I'd keep 'em high and inside to him now — and pray." " Okay," says the pitcher. Should DiMaggio get a couple of hits, they'll switch to something else. Baseball is a game of guessing, the pitcher trying to throw to the batter's weakness and the batters trying to outsmart the pitchers.

The Yanks take the field. The heat is terrific, but the whole squad warms up, tossing the ball around and engaging in a " pepper game." Everyone is out except Sewell, who sits watching the New York team at batting practice. If a new man comes up who bats left-handed with a free swing and hits to left field, he makes a mental note to call for a pitch to his hands. If the player hits to right, he'll have his pitchers throw high and away from the batter. Suppose it's a newcomer to the league? Every pitcher immediately starts trying different kinds of balls on him until finally someone discovers his weakness. This soon gets known round the circuit. Then the only trouble is to get the pitcher to put the ball in the slot.

III

At two-thirty the bell rings, and the two Cleveland pitchers likely to start, Drake and Harder, go out to warm up. Sewell catches Harder. At first he comes within fifty feet of the pitcher to ease up on his pitching arm, but as it loosens a little he goes back to sixty-one feet, the regulation distance. The two umpires appear with masks and chest protectors under their arms. The bell rings again, New York takes the field, and the game is on.

While the Indians are batting, take a look at Sewell's hands. You'd expect them to be knotty and broken, but they are smallish, rather sensitive, and well formed. Sewell never had a serious injury and believes no catcher need expect broken thumbs and fingers if he has the right technique. Most injuries come from not holding the fingers of the throwing hand together and relaxed. When the ball leaves the pitcher's hand Sewell cups his fingers slightly, then claps them over the ball as it strikes the mitt. The most dangerous pitch for a catcher is the low ball off the right knee that is so often foul-tipped. This ball, on which 90 per cent of hand injuries occur, is often tipped and swings out, hitting one of the first two fingers of the right hand. After studying this pitch Sewell discovered a position which prevents injury. He goes down with the left elbow up, twisting his left wrist and turning the mitt over, placing the right hand underneath it to protect the fingers.

Now the Yanks come in and the Indians take the field. While they're tossing the ball around, let's see how Sewell gives his signals. There are signals in baseball for pitching, batting, and fielding, but the pitching signals are always given by the catcher. He uses the fingers of the right hand, although occasionally he signals by touching his mask or placing his free hand on his leg or hips. Each pitcher on the squad has his own signals, so that a big-league catcher must know six or seven different sets. The important thing is to have the pitcher concentrating upon the batter, so the simplest signals are best — for instance, one finger for a fast ball and two for a curve.

The catcher gives the signals by extending his finger down his leg while crouching, so that the opposing coaches on first and third cannot see. Some players are adept at stealing signals. The greatest signal stealer in the major leagues is Del Baker of Detroit. Charlie Dressen, Brooklyn coach and former manager at Cincinnati, is another. When the National League team played the American League in the All Star game of 1937, Dressen was coaching the National side. There were men from eight National League clubs on the team, and the night before the game some discussion rose as to what signals should be used. Dressen told them to use their own signals and said he would understand each set.

For this reason signals must be changed every few innings. In fact, some catchers have a different set for odd and even innings, or for the first five and the last four of the game. There are catchers who use the ball-and-strike count. If it's one ball and one strike, the signal is the third one flashed. Whenever he thinks the batters are getting his signals from their own coaches, the catcher calls for a switch. That is, he may call for a fast ball and then, by tapping his knee with his mitt, indicate that he wants a curve. Some pitchers cross up their catchers and aren't overpopular on that account. I know one sensational star who nearly annihilated several catchers last season by tossing a curve when a fast ball was called, or shooting over a fast one when the catcher expected a change of pace.

Obviously when a player is traded to another team in the league
the whole system of signaling must be overhauled. There have been
catchers who betrayed the pitch to the batter by their stance. When
a catcher stands upright, it is evident a fast ball is coming — hence the
necessity for a uniform stance on every pitch. Some pitchers betray
the pitch by little movements such as sticking out their tongue or lift-
ing their left leg higher on certain balls. Infielders also betray the
pitch by shifting position too soon. One such move cost the Brooklyn
team victory in the World's Series of 1920. Burleigh Grimes, the famous spitball pitcher, won the second game 3–0. But the Cleveland
scouts got a tip on his throwing: each time he pitched a spitball Kil-
duff, the second baseman, would scoop up a little dirt into his glove
so that the wet ball wouldn't slip if a grounder came his way. By
watching carefully, Cleveland beat Grimes 8–1 in the fifth game and
3–0 in the last one.

Signals are also intended to help fielders get the jump on a hit
ball. To know where the ball is likely to be hit, every infielder has to
know what the pitch is and therefore watch the signals carefully. But
the third and first basemen cannot see the catcher's fingers, so the
second baseman and shortstop usually relay it with a word. " Heads
up," " Look out, Jim," or some tip gives them the pitch and an indication which way to start for the ball.

I V

Back at the Yankee Stadium the game has been going on, coming
into the eighth with the Indians leading 1–0. As he enters the dugout,
wiping the sweat from his face, Sewell glances at a thermometer hung
on the wall. It's 118, and in the shade, too. But the game is nearly
over. Finally New York comes to bat for its last chance in the ninth.
Dickey, the first batter, works the count to two and two, and then hits
a stinging grounder between first and second. Shilling, the second
baseman, is over fast, makes a one-handed stop, and steadies himself
for the throw. Meanwhile Sewell, flinging aside his mask, has run
down behind first in line with the throw. The man on the bag grabs
it — a fine stop, a good throw — and one man is out.

Sewell comes back wearily to the plate. He's tired, and so is the pitcher. That's why Selkirk, the next batter, tries to work him — good strategy toward the end of a game on a hot afternoon. He gets a base on balls. Sewell, taking off his mask, stands before the plate holding up one finger and shouting round the diamond: " One out . . . one man down." Then he goes back, gets into the crouch, and calls for a pitch-out. The situation is set for a hit-and-run play which he wishes to stop.

Ball one. Quickly he snaps the ball to first in a vain attempt to nail the runner. This is also done to prevent his taking a lead from first, although keeping the runner on the bag is really up to Harder. If pitchers kept every runner flat-footed, there would be no base stealing. That's why it is usually considered the fault of the pitcher when runners steal bases. Ball two. Then Gordon, the batter, reaches out and smacks a single to right field. The runner has a good lead, and Sewell knows he will reach third, so he shouts to Webb, the shortstop, " Cut it off! Cut it off! " Webb, in line with the throw to third, cuts it off, snaps the ball to second, but Selkirk slides safely into third. One out, men on first and third.

Sewell calls for a curve, because curves are low and an infield ball will do less damage than a high fly to the outfield on which Selkirk might score from third after the catch. Ball one. Notice how he snaps that throw back to the pitcher as hard as he can. He wants to wake Mel up. Ball two. Now he walks down the path to his pitcher and hands him the ball. What's he saying?

Just a word or two of confidence and a suggestion to pass the batter. Harder is doing this, because, with a man on first, there's a better chance for a double play. Watch how slow Sewell is in getting back to position. He scoops up some dirt with his finger, he fumbles round with his mask, he pulls on the straps of his protector before he finally gets down. From the corner of his eye he has noticed John Drake, the relief pitcher, warming up in the bullpen, and he wants to give him as much time as possible. Sometimes when he goes down the path it may be to give a signal, of course. And sometimes the pitcher may be the one to say a word to the catcher in these conferences.

Years ago Eddie Mahan, Harvard's great halfback, was pitching

against Holy Cross and leading two to one in the last of the ninth.
Holy Cross got three men on base with two out. The stands at
Worcester were in an uproar, and Mahan saw that his catcher was
rattled. He called him out. Their heads went together. " Hey, Dick,
how about going on a party to-night? " The catcher nodded seriously,
returned to the plate. Mahan went into the box and struck out the
batter.

Sewell stands for a minute before the plate watching his infielders come on to the grass and waving his outfielders about, for Ruffing,
pinch-hitting for Pearson, is at bat. He signals for a high ball to prevent a squeeze play, because it's harder to bunt a high ball. But Ruffing is content to wait the pitcher out. Ball one. Strike one. Ball two.
The next is high and inside. Then strike two. He swings at the fifth
pitch and hits it into the air. Instantly Sewell's mask is off and his
head is up. Where is it?

Everyone is calling: " Luke! Luke! " He sees it behind him,
dodges Crosetti, the next Yankee batter, jumps over the row of bats
before the dugout, swerves to the right, looks down a second, and —
holds out his mitt as the ball falls. " Home . . . home . . . home! "
the whole diamond is calling, fearing the man from third will try to
come home. But Sewell's reflexes are instantaneous. He turns, whirls,
and throws to the plate all in one movement. Harder is waiting there
to cut off the runner, who retreats to third without attempting to
come home.

Two men out. Sewell again comes before the plate and holds up
two fingers. Crosetti, the next man, must hit. He swings at the first
ball. Strike one. Harder is putting everything he has into this one.
Strike two. Ball one. Then Crosetti swings at the next pitch, tops it,
and the ball rolls weakly toward third. This is one of the most difficult
plays in the game, because the ball might roll foul. Sewell is looking
down the line and is in the best position to judge, so he calls, " First,
first! " Harder, running over, must stop, recover balance, turn, and
throw to first. He does it — and the man is out by a nose. The game
is over.

The crowds pour out of the stands, disappointed that the rally
was nipped, but feeling that they've seen a good game and had their

money's worth. The two teams run or walk to the lockers, the day's work over — an hour and fifty minutes of concentrated strain in a temperature over 100 all afternoon. Sewell is exhausted as he staggers into the dressing room and removes his steaming clothes. So too is the rest of the team. There is no hilarity, horseplay, or singing, as there usually is when they have won a close game. They dry off, dress slowly, and taxi back to the hotel. Dinner will be their first meal since breakfast, and they'll need it.

V

The one important thing in a pitcher is control. All catchers agree that the easiest man to handle is the pitcher who has control. That's what veteran receivers like Sewell always try to make rookie pitchers realize. Without control you cannot "build up the hitter," as the catchers say. You can't keep him in a hole. Therefore anything that increases the pitcher's control helps, and this is why not the least part of the catcher's work is keeping the pitcher relaxed and contented. In this way much can be done to add to his effectiveness. Teams always do better with pitchers who have control. They call a man who doesn't throw many balls and get the team in trouble "a ball player's ball player." The good catcher makes him one.

Some pitchers prefer certain catchers and insist on having that man catch them and no one else. Bob Feller of Cleveland always wants to be caught by Ral Hemsley. When Dizzy Dean joined the Cubs he refused to let anyone but Hartnett catch him. It was this confidence he had in Gabby which enabled him to pitch winning ball, once beating the Giants with Hartnett behind the plate by throwing only 88 balls in nine innings.

The catcher gives all the signals to the pitcher, but offensive signals are usually given by the coach behind third, who is seldom an active player. Jack Coombs, the old Athletic pitcher now coaching at Duke, explains why someone not in the game should direct offensive strategy. Once he decided to let a boy on his squad act as coach at third. This lad was to hold his cap in his left hand as the signal for a hit-and-run, and take his cap off his head as a signal for a steal. When three men had all hit safely and all stolen second, third, and home, Coombs rushed to the players' bench. He discovered the boy at third had taken off his cap and forgotten to put it back on again.

Catchers have many tricks to influence umpires, none of which, needless to say, are oversuccessful. They try to block an umpire's vision on bad balls, but the umpire who knows his business sees each ball as it comes across the plate. One favorite trick is to swing the ball over the center of the plate as it strikes the mitt to make it appear a strike. Often when there are two strikes on the batter and the next pitch is close the catcher will hurl the ball to third as if it were a strike and the man were out. These gestures influence the fans more than the umpire.

Everyone, including the manager of the Cubs, admits that Gabby Hartnett is one of the best catchers in the big leagues today. One player even goes so far as to call him the greatest catcher baseball has ever seen. That man should know. He was once Gabby's manager on the Cubs, and has had pretty fair success since. His name is Joe McCarthy. Hartnett, who has also worked for Bill Killefer, George Gibson, Rogers Hornsby, Rabbit Maranville, and Charlie Grimm, reciprocates by nominating McCarthy as the greatest all-round manager in the game. Statistics seem to bear him out.

There's eternally something different in baseball, which is one reason it has lasted one hundred years from the time when Abner Doubleday laid out the first diamond at Cooperstown, New York. Sewell, a catcher with twenty-five years' experience in college and big-league baseball, puts it this way: "I try to learn something different every afternoon. That's what makes baseball so interesting. There's a different problem coming up in every game."

Speaking of Sewell, what was he doing that steaming evening after Cleveland's 1–0 defeat of the Yanks in New York? The majority of the boys had gone to an air-conditioned movie, the only place in town to keep cool. Not Sewell. He was in his room with Manager Vitt, going over the hitters on the St. Louis Browns. The following night the team was to entrain for a three-game series in St. Louis, and there were new batters coming up to the plate.

"Now this fella Don Heffner — if I were you I'd feed him . . ."

APPRECIATION HINTS

1. Why is the catcher the one man on the team who can never relax?
2. How did Sewell spend the morning before the game?
3. How did Sewell give signals? Why and how are signals sometimes changed?
4. Describe the ninth inning of the game.
5. Explain the importance of control in pitching.
6. Give reasons for having some one not in the game give the offensive signals. Who is in the best position to give them?
7. Tell about the strategy of attack in field hockey.
8. Tell about team defense in basketball.
9. Write a composition based on a wrong, or a mistaken, or a foolish signal.
10. Write a composition based on "luck" or "a break" in a game; for example, A Critical Fumble, The Basket That Counted.
11. Read "Twenty-Fifth Reunion" in *Scribner's Magazine* for June, 1936, the story of the Harvard class of 1911 as Tunis found it 25 years after graduation.
12. Look up and report on another sport and its background. Consult *Sport for the Fun of It* by Tunis.
13. Read "More Pay for College Football Stars," *Review of Reviews* for December, 1936.
14. If you care for tennis read the article by Tunis on Borotra, "the bounding Basque," in *The Saturday Evening Post*, July 25, 1936.

CUCKOOS IN THE CLASSROOM

Miss Jones asked, "Can any one tell us about the habits of the cuckoo?"

"I can, Miss Jones," said a bright little girl. "In the first place the cuckoo builds its own nest, but never lays its own eggs. The cuckoo lays other birds' eggs in its own nest, and viva voce.*"*

BIRD LORE

He understood the speech of birds
As well as they themselves do words.

Samuel Butler: *Hudibras*

STEPHEN LEACOCK 1869–

REFERRING to one of the serious books of Stephen Leacock, *The Unsolved Riddle of Social Justice*, Christopher Morley writes, "one of the unsolved riddles of social injustice is why Professor Leacock is so much more amusing than most people." Why indeed? The early events of Stephen Leacock's life did not point to success in the field of humor. In the first place, he was born in England; then he became a doctor of philosophy, and humorists are not common among Ph.D.'s; and finally he emerged as a professor of the "dismal science," political economy. In 1907–08 he made a trip throughout the British empire, giving lectures on imperial organization under the Cecil Rhodes Trust.

Then came 1910, a year of wonders, including Halley's comet. In this year Mr. John Lane, the London publisher, got hold of a volume entitled *Literary Lapses*, published in Canada and written by a Stephen Leacock very different from the brilliant professor. No doubt it had been thrown off as a holiday joke. Mr. Lane promptly reissued it, and at once the whole English-speaking world was set aroar. The success was so great that Mr. Leacock had to go on writing funny books, and he did so with such sidesplitting skill that nobody would believe that this laughter-raising fellow and the learned man at McGill were the same person.

Since 1910 Mr. Leacock has continued to live the double life of professor and humorist very successfully. In this respect he resembles his famous predecessor Lewis Carroll; indeed, he once stated that he would rather have written *Alice in Wonderland* than the *Encyclopaedia Britannica*. *Literary Lapses* was soon followed by *Nonsense Novels, Further Foolishness,* and *Frenzied Fiction.* His latest book *Too Much College,* 1939, contains a chapter called "Has Economics Gone to Seed?" which happily combines his wisdom and humor.

Like Mark Twain Mr. Leacock is a delightful speaker. The following lines were written about him after he had spoken at the Coffee House Club in New York:

> The frank, blithe face, ruddy with twinkling zest,
>   With self-inflicted laughter brimming o'er —
> He lays the fuse and touches off the jest,
>   And then the table bursting, roar on roar.

A, B, and C — The Human Element in Mathematics

THE STUDENT of arithmetic who has mastered the first four rules of his art and successfully striven with money sums and fractions finds himself confronted by an unbroken expanse of questions known as problems. These are short stories of adventure and industry with the end omitted, and though betraying a strong family resemblance, are not without a certain element of romance.

The characters in the plot of a problem are three people called A, B, and C; the form of the question is generally of this sort:

"A, B, and C do a certain piece of work. A can do as much work in one hour as B in two, or C in four. Find how long they work at it."

Or thus: "A, B, and C are employed to dig a ditch. A can dig as much in one hour as B can dig in two, and B can dig twice as fast as C. Find how long, etc., etc."

Or after this wise: "A lays a wager that he can walk faster than B or C. A can walk half as fast again as B, and C is only an indifferent walker. Find how far, and so forth."

The occupations of A, B, and C are many and varied. In the older arithmetics they contented themselves with doing a "certain piece of work." This statement of the case, however, was found too sly and mysterious, or possibly lacking in romantic charm. It became the fashion to define the job more clearly and to set them at walking matches, ditch-digging, regattas, and piling cordwood. At times, they became commercial and entered into partnership, having, with their old mystery, a "certain" capital. Above all they revel in motion. When they tire of walking matches, A rides on horseback, or borrows a bicycle and competes with his weaker-minded associates on foot. Now they race on locomotives; now they row; or again they become historical and engage stagecoaches; or at times they are aquatic and swim. If their occupation is actual work, they prefer to pump water into cisterns, two of which leak through holes in the bottom and one of which is watertight. A, of course, has the good one; he also takes the bicycle, and the best locomotive, and the right of swimming with the current. Whatever they do they put money on it, being all three sports. A always wins.

In the early chapters of the arithmetic, their identity is concealed under the names of John, William, and Henry, and they wrangle over the division of marbles. In algebra they are often called X, Y, Z. But these are only their Christian names, and they are really the same people.

Now to one who has followed the history of these men through countless pages of problems, watched them in their leisure hours dallying with cordwood, and seen their panting sides heave in the full frenzy of filling a cistern with a leak in it, they become something more than mere symbols. They appear as creatures of flesh and blood, living men with their own passions, ambitions, and aspirations like the rest of us.

A is full-blooded, hot-headed and strong-willed. It is he who proposes everything, challenges B to work, makes the bets, and bends the others to his will. He is a man of great physical strength and phenomenal endurance. He has been known to walk forty-eight hours at a stretch, and to pump ninety-six. His life is arduous and full of peril. A mistake in the working of a sum may keep him digging a fortnight without sleep. A repeating decimal in the answer might kill him.

B is a quiet, easy-going fellow, afraid of A and bullied by him, but very gentle and brotherly to little C, the weakling. He is quite in A's power, having lost all his money in bets.

Poor C is an undersized, frail man, with a plaintive face. Constant walking, digging, and pumping has broken his health and ruined his nervous system. His joyless life has driven him to drink and smoke more than is good for him, and his hand often shakes as he digs ditches. He has not the strength to work as the others do, in fact, as Hamlin Smith has said, " A can do more work in one hour than C in four."

The first time that ever I saw these men was one evening after a regatta. They had all been rowing in it, and it had transpired that A could row as much in one hour as B in two, or C in four. B and C had come in dead fagged and C was coughing badly. " Never mind, old fellow," I heard B say, " I'll fix you up on the sofa and get you some hot tea." Just then A came blustering in and shouted, " I say, you fellows, Hamlin Smith has shown me three cisterns in his garden and he says we can pump them until tomorrow night. I bet I can beat you both. Come on. You can pump in your rowing things, you know. Your cistern leaks a little, I think, C." I heard B growl that it was a dirty shame and that C was used up now, but they went and presently I could tell from the sound of the water that A was pumping four times as fast as C.

For years after that I used to see them constantly about the town and always busy. I never heard of any of them eating or sleeping. After that, owing to a long absence from home, I lost sight of them. On my return I was surprised to find A, B, and C no longer at their old tasks; on inquiry I heard that work in this line was now done by N, M, and O, and that some people were employing for algebraical jobs four foreigners called Alpha, Beta, Gamma, and Delta.

Now it chanced one day that I stumbled upon old D, in the little garden in front of his cottage, hoeing in the sun. D is an aged laboring man who used occasionally to be called in to help A, B, and C. " Did I know 'em, sir? " he answered. " Why I knowed 'em ever since they was little fellows in brackets. Master A, he were a fine-hearted lad, sir, though I always said, give me Master B for kind-heartedness-like. Many's the job as we've been on together, sir, though I never did no racing nor aught of that, but just the plain labor, as you might say. I'm getting a bit too old and stiff for it nowadays, sir — just scratch about in the garden here and grow a bit of a logarithm, or raise a common denominator or two. But Mr. Euclid he uses me still for propositions, he do."

From the garrulous old man I learned the melancholy end of my former acquaintances. Soon after I left town, he told me, C had been ill. It seems that A and B had been rowing on the river for a wager, and C had been running on the bank and then sat in a draught. Of course the bank had refused the draught and C was taken ill. A and B came home and found C lying helpless in bed. A shook him roughly and said, " Get up, C, we're going to pile wood." C looked so worn and pitiful that B said, " Look here, A, I won't stand this, he isn't fit to pile wood tonight." C smiled feebly and said, " Perhaps I might pile a little if I sat up in bed." Then B, thoroughly alarmed, said, " See here, A, I'm going to fetch a doctor; he's dying." A flared up and answered, " You've got no money to fetch a doctor." " I'll reduce him to his lowest terms," B said firmly, " that'll fetch him." C's life might even then have been saved but they made a mistake about the medicine. It stood at the head of the bed on a bracket, and the nurse accidentally removed it from the bracket without changing the sign. After the fatal blunder C seems to have sunk rapidly. On the evening of the next day, it was clear, as the shadows deepened, that the end was near. I think that even A was affected at the last as he stood with bowed head, aimlessly offering to bet with the doctor on C's labored breathing. " A," whispered C, " I think I'm going fast." " How fast do you think you'll go, old man? " murmured A. " I don't know," said C, " but I'm going at any rate." The end came soon after that. C rallied for a moment and asked for a certain piece of work that he had left downstairs. A put it in his arms and he expired. As his soul sped heavenward, A watched its flight with melancholy admiration. B burst into a passionate flood of tears and sobbed, " Put away his little cistern and the rowing clothes he used to wear, I feel as if I could hardly ever dig again." — The funeral was plain and unostentatious. It differed in nothing from the ordinary, except that out of deference to sporting men, and mathematicians, A engaged two hearses. Both vehicles started at the same time, B driving the one which bore the sable parallelopiped containing the last remains of his ill-fated friend. A on the box of the empty hearse generously consented to a handicap of a hundred years, but arrived first at the cemetery by driving four times as fast as B. (Find the distance to the cemetery.) As the sarcophagus was lowered, the grave was surrounded by the broken figures of the first book of Euclid.

It was noticed that after the death of C, A became a changed man. He lost interest in racing with B, and dug but languidly. He finally gave up his work and settled down to live on the interest of his bets. — B never recovered from the shock of C's death; his grief preyed upon his intellect and it became deranged. He grew moody and spoke only in monosyllables. His disease became rapidly aggravated, and he presently spoke in words whose spelling was regular and which presented no difficulty to the beginner. Realizing his precarious condition he voluntarily submitted to be incarcerated in an asylum, where he abjured mathematics and devoted himself to writing the History of the Swiss Family Robinson in words of one syllable.

APPRECIATION HINTS

1. What are the jobs usually assigned to A, B, and C?
2. What names do they assume in algebra?
3. What are the characteristics of A?
4. What are the characteristics of C?
5. On what occasion did the author first meet A, B, and C?
6. Who was D?
7. What was the immediate cause of C's death?
8. Describe his funeral.
9. Trace the subsequent histories of A and B.
10. Find in your mathematics text some "short stories of adventure and industry with the end omitted."
11. Ask several of the oldest persons you know who Hamlin Smith was.
12. Write a playful paper on one of your own school books.
13. Write on the human element in some other study; e.g., English grammar, the orchestra, chemistry in the laboratory.
14. Discover if you can, from the attic or storeroom, some texts used by your father and mother. Study all the marginal notes, and then write a sketch of father and mother when they were young.
15. Read other essays by Leacock in *Literary Lapses* and *Behind the Beyond*.

WILLIAM SAROYAN 1908– PERHAPS it would be unwise even to suggest that Aram and his pal Joey in the following essay got some "education" by playing hooky and spending the day with the circus. But so far they had not learned much from school; they were only fifth graders and probably had not yet reached the classrooms where pupils were taught "correct English." And if the circus was "everything everything else they knew wasn't," we might expect that they would learn something from this glorious day which shines out in Saroyan's memories of his early boyhood. You must decide for yourself whether this was "education." As you read the essay, see if you can spot any "learning situations," as the educators call them, in the day's happenings. You may find when you have finished it that there are two sides to the proposition that, to promote the education of the pupils at the Emerson School, old man Dawson should have closed up for the day on condition that everyone attend the circus. And a discussion of this proposition would depend on what we mean by education; it would lead us to what Hayakawa says in a later essay about "words that don't inform."

This essay shows that the man who wrote it had a deep tenderness for small boyhood's turbulent mistakes. It is a safe bet that Aram Garoghlanian is William Saroyan when he was growing up in the Armenian colony of Fresno, California. The sketches collected in *My Name Is Aram* originally appeared in magazines, and all of them are about events in a boy's life, trivial, droll or dramatic — snapshots of moments in the life of a young Armenian as he is gradually becoming an American. They show how puzzling a problem to his teachers, and especially to his parents, is the child of the foreign born.

A well-known critic has called Saroyan "the Whirling Dervish of Fresno," and likens him to an Italian actor who could jump behind the screen every other minute and emerge as a different person. Saroyan likewise changes his costume, but what reappears is always recognizable as Saroyan. His plays — for example *The Time of Your Life,* 1939 — and his sketches are always abounding in life, and his characters usually slightly crazy. Like Aram and Joey in this sketch, they are often a combination of bravado and humility.

The Circus

ANY TIME a circus used to come to town, that was all me and my old pal Joey Renna needed to make us run hog-wild, as the saying is. All we needed to do was see the signs on the fences and in the empty store windows to start going to the dogs and neglecting our educations. All we needed to know was that a circus was on its way to town for me and Joey to start wanting to know what good a little education ever did anybody anyway.

After the circus *reached* town we were just no good at all. We spent all our time down at the trains, watching them unload the animals, walking out Ventura Avenue with the wagons with lions and tigers in them and hanging around the grounds, trying to win the favor of the animal men, the workers, the acrobats, and the clowns.

The circus was everything everything else we knew wasn't. It was adventure, travel, danger, skill, grace, romance, comedy, peanuts, popcorn, chewing gum and soda water. We used to carry water to the elephants and stand around afterwards and try to seem associated with the whole magnificent affair, the putting up of the big tent, the getting everything in order, and the worldly-wise waiting for the people to come and spend their money.

One day Joey came tearing into the classroom of the fifth grade

at Emerson School ten minutes late, and without so much as remov-
ing his hat or trying to explain his being late, shouted, Hey, Aram,
what the hell are you doing here? The circus is in town.

And sure enough I'd forgotten. I jumped up and ran out of the
room with poor old Miss Flibety screaming after me, Aram Garoghlanian, you stay in this room. Do you hear me, Aram Garoghlanian?

I heard her all right and I knew what my not staying would
mean. It would mean another powerful strapping from old man
Dawson. But I couldn't help it. I was just crazy about a circus.

I been looking all over for you, Joey said in the street. What
happened?

I forgot, I said. I knew it was coming all right, but I forgot it was
today. How far along are they?

I was at the trains at five, Joey said. I been out at the grounds
since seven. I had breakfast at the circus table. Boy, it was good.

Honest, Joey? I said. How were they?

They're all swell, Joey said. Couple more years, they told me, and
I'll be ready to go away with them.

As what? I said. Lion tamer, or something like that?

I guess maybe not as a lion tamer, Joey said. I figure more like
a workman till I learn about being a clown or something, I guess. I
don't figure I could work with lions right away.

We were out on Ventura Avenue, headed for the circus grounds,
out near the County Fairgrounds, just north of the County Hospital.

Boy, what a breakfast, Joey said. Hot cakes, ham and eggs, sau-
sages, coffee. Boy.

Why didn't you tell me? I said.

I thought you knew, Joey said. I thought you'd be down at the
trains same as last year. I would have told you if I knew you'd forgotten. What made you forget?

I don't know, I said. Nothing, I guess.

I was wrong there, but I didn't know it at the time. I hadn't
really forgotten. What I'd done was *remembered*. I'd gone to work
and remembered the strapping Dawson gave me last year for staying
out of school the day the circus was in town. That was the thing that
had kind of kept me sleeping after four-thirty in the morning when

by rights I should have been up and dressing and on my way to the trains. It was the memory of that strapping old man Dawson had given me, but I didn't know it at the time. We used to take them strappings kind of for granted, me and Joey, on account of we wanted to be fair and square with the Board of Education and if it was against the rules to stay out of school when you weren't sick, and if you were supposed to get strapped for doing it, well, there we were, we'd done it, so let the Board of Education balance things the best way they knew how. They did that with a strapping. They used to threaten to send me and Joey to Reform School but they never did it.

Circus? old man Dawson used to say. I see. *Circus*. Well, bend down, boy.

So, first Joey, then me, would bend down and old man Dawson would get some powerful shoulder exercise while we tried not to to howl. We wouldn't howl for five or six licks, but after that we'd howl like Indians coming. They used to be able to hear us all over the school and old man Dawson, after our visits got to be kind of regular, urged us politely to try to make a little less noise, inasmuch as it was a school and people were trying to study.

It ain't fair to the others, old man Dawson said. They're trying to learn something for themselves.

We can't help it, Joey said. It hurts.

That I know, old man Dawson said, but it seems to me there's such a thing as modulation. I believe a lad can overdo his howling if he ain't thoughtful of others. Just try to modulate that awful howl a little. I think you can do it.

Then he gave Joey a strapping of twenty and Joey tried his best not to howl so loud. After the strapping his face was very red and old man Dawson was very tired.

How was that? Joey said.

That was better, old man Dawson said. By far the most courteous you've managed yet.

I did my best, Joey said.

I'm grateful to you, old man Dawson said.

He was tired and out of breath. I moved up to the chair in front of him that he furnished during these matters to help us suffer the stinging pain. I got in the right position and he said, Wait a minute, Aram. Give a man a chance to get his breath. I'm not twenty-three years old. I'm *sixty*-three. Let me rest a minute.

All right, I said, but I sure would like to get this over with.

Don't howl too loud, he said. Folks passing by in the street are liable to think this is a veritable chamber of tortures. Does it really hurt that much?

You can ask Joey, I said.

How about it, Joey? old man Dawson said. Aren't you lads exaggerating just a little? Perhaps to impress someone in your room? Some girl, perhaps?

We don't howl to impress anybody, Mr. Dawson, Joey said. We wouldn't howl if we could help it. Howling makes us feel ashamed, doesn't it, Aram?

It's awfully embarrassing to go back to our seats in our room after howling that way, I said. We'd rather not howl if we could help it.

Well, old man Dawson said, I'll not be unreasonable. I'll only ask you to try to modulate it a little.

I'll do my best, Mr. Dawson, I said. Got your breath back?

Give me just a moment longer, Aram, Mr. Dawson said.

When he got his breath back he gave me my twenty and I howled a little louder than Joey and then we went back to class. It was awfully embarrassing. Everybody was looking at us.

Well, Joey said, what did you expect? The rest of you would fall down and die if you got twenty. You wouldn't howl *a little,* you'd die.

That'll be enough out of you, Miss Flibety said.

Well, it's true, Joey said. They're all scared. A circus comes to town and what do they do? They come to school. They don't go out to the circus.

That'll be enough, Miss Flibety said.

Who do they think they are, giving us dirty looks? Joey said.

Miss Flibety lifted her hand, hushing Joey.

Now the circus was back in town, another year had gone by, it was April again, and we were on our way out to the grounds. Only this time it was worse than ever because they'd seen us at school and knew we were going out to the circus.

Do you think they'll send Stafford after us? I said.

Stafford was truant officer.

We can always run, Joey said. If he comes, I'll go one way, you go another. He can't chase *both* of us. At least one of us will get away.

All right, I said. Suppose one of us gets caught?

Well, let's see, Joey said. Should the one who isn't caught give himself up or should he wreck Stafford's Ford?

I vote for wreck, I said.

So do I, Joey said, so wreck it is.

When we got out to the grounds a couple of the little tents were up, and the big one was going up. We stood around and watched. It was great the way they did it. Just a handful of guys who looked like tramps doing work you'd think no less than a hundred men could do. Doing it with style, too.

All of a sudden a man everybody called Red hollered at me and Joey.

Here, you Arabs, he said, give us a hand.

Me and Joey ran over to him.

Yes, sir, I said.

He was a small man with very broad shoulders, and very big hands. You didn't feel that he was small, because he seemed so power-ful and because he had so much thick red hair on his head. You thought he was practically a giant.

He handed me and Joey a rope. The rope was attached to some canvas that was lying on the ground.

This is going to be easy, Red said. As the boys lift the pole and get it in place you keep pulling the rope, so the canvas will go up with the pole.

Yes, sir, Joey said.

Everybody was busy when we saw Stafford.

We can't run now, I said.

Let him come, Joey said. We told Red we'd give him a hand and we're going to do it.

I'll tell you what, I said. We'll tell him we'll go with him after we get the canvas up; then we'll run.

All right, Joey said.

Stafford was a big fellow in a business suit who had a beef-red face and looked as if he ought to be a lawyer or something. He came over and said, All right, you hooligans, come along with me.

We promised to give Red a hand, Joey said. We'll come just as soon as we get this canvas up.

We were pulling for all we were worth, slipping and falling. The men were all working hard. Red was hollering orders, and then the whole thing was over and we had done our part.

We didn't even get a chance to find out what Red was going to say to us, or if he was going to invite us to sit at the table for lunch, or what.

Joey busted loose and ran one way and I ran the other and Stafford came after *me*. I heard the circus men laughing and Red hollering, Run, boy, run. He can't catch *you*. He's soft. Give him a good run. He needs the exercise.

I could hear Stafford, too. He was very sore and he was cussing.

I got away, though, and stayed low until I saw him drive off in his Ford. Then I went back to the big tent and found Joey.

We'll get it this time, Joey said.

I guess it'll be Reform School this time, I said.

No, Joey said. I guess it'll be thirty. We're going to do some awful howling if it is. Thirty's a lot of whacks even if he *is* sixty-three years old. He ain't exactly a weakling.

Thirty? I said. Ouch. That's liable to make me cry.

Maybe, Joey said. Me too, maybe. Seems like ten can make you cry, then you hold off till it's eleven, then twelve, and you think you'll start crying on the next one, but you don't. We haven't so far, anyway. Maybe we will when it's thirty.

Oh, well, I said, that's tomorrow.

Red give us some more work to do around the grounds and let us sit next to him at lunch. It was swell. We talked to some acrobats who were Spanish, and to a family of Italians who worked with horses. We saw both shows, the afternoon one and the evening one, and then we helped with the work, taking the circus to pieces again; then we went down to the trains, and then home. I got home real late. In the morning I was sleepy when I had to get up for school.

They were waiting for us. Miss Flibety didn't even let us sit down for the roll call. She just told us to go to the office. Old man Dawson was waiting for us, too. Stafford was there, too, and very sore.

I figured, Well, here's where we go to Reform School.

Here they are, Mr. Dawson said to Stafford. Take them away, if you like.

It was easy to tell they'd been talking for some time and hadn't been getting along any too well. Old man Dawson seemed irritated and Stafford seemed sore at him.

In *this* school, old man Dawson said, I do any punishing that's got to be done. Nobody else. I can't stop you from taking them to Reform School, though.

Stafford didn't say anything. He just left the office.

Well, lads, old man Dawson said. How was it?

We had lunch with them, Joey said.

Let's see now, old man Dawson said. What offense is this, the sixteenth or the seventeenth?

It ain't that many, Joey said. Must be eleven or twelve.

Well, old man Dawson said, I'm sure of one thing. This is the time I'm supposed to make it thirty.

I think the next one is the one you're supposed to make thirty, Joey said.

No, Mr. Dawson said, we've lost track somewhere, but I'm sure this is the time it goes up to thirty. Who's going to be first?

Me, I said.

All right, Aram, Mr. Dawson said. Take a good hold on the chair, brace yourself, and try to modulate your howl.

Yes, sir, I said. I'll do my best, but thirty's an awful lot.

Well, a funny thing happened. He gave me thirty all right and I howled all right, but it *was* a modulated howl. It was the most modulated howl I ever howled; because it was the *easiest* strapping I ever got. I counted them and there were thirty all right, but they didn't hurt, so I didn't cry as I was afraid I might.

It was the same with Joey. We stood together waiting to be dismissed.

I'm awfully grateful to you boys, old man Dawson said, for modulating your howls so nicely this time. I don't want people to think I'm killing you.

We wanted to thank him for giving us such easy strappings, but we couldn't say it. I think he knew the way we felt, though, because he smiled in a way that gave us an idea he knew.

Then we went back to class.

It was swell because we knew everything would be all right till the County Fair opened in September.

APPRECIATION HINTS

1. What was it about the circus which made Joey and Aram go wild?
2. What was the real reason that Aram had not been down to meet the circus?
3. Why had the boys "taken their strappings for granted"?
4. What kind of an agreement did the boys have with old man Dawson when they were strapped?
5. What was the boys' plan in regard to Stafford?
6. Why didn't the boys run when Stafford appeared?

7. How were the boys occupied after Stafford drove off?
8. Tell how old man Dawson gave them thirty.
9. What admirable qualities do you find in the two truants?
10. Collect evidence to show that Aram had not mastered English grammar at the Emerson School.
11. Who was the better judge of boys, Miss Fliberty or old man Dawson? Why do you think so?
12. Write a composition on your experience at a circus or fair. Suggestions: The Big Tent; Here Come the Clowns; The Lion Tamer; Peanuts, Popcorn and Chewing Gum; My First Circus; The Genuine Sign of Spring.
13. Write a composition based on corporal punishment. Suggestions: The Barrel-stave and the Woodshed; Spare the Rod and Spoil the Child; But It's Soon Over; Self-Discipline and How to Learn It.
14. Read in *My Name Is Aram,* by Saroyan, the sketches entitled " The Fifty Yard Dash," " The Journey to Hanford," and " Old Country Advice to American Travelers."
15. Read " The Daring Young Man on the Flying Trapeze," by Saroyan.

SPARE THE ROD . . .

There is now less flogging in our great schools than formerly, but then less is learned there; so that what the boys gain at one end they lose at the other.

Samuel Johnson

LEAVE IT TO FATHER

A father wrote to the headmaster of the school attended by his son: " Sir, I must strictly forbid you to administer punishment to Thomas again. We never do so ourselves except in self-defence."

JAMES THURBER 1894– "YOU HAVE to enjoy humorous writing while you're doing it." That's what James Thurber wrote, and he ought to know, because his essays in *The New Yorker,* and the quaint drawings which illustrate them, have brought merriment into countless homes. When you read the following essay, you will have no doubt that the author was having fun while he was writing it. Though Mr. Thurber loves to ridicule fashionable literary fads, especially when they strike a pose, his satire is never ill-tempered. It is the internal laughter of the writer of humor, he believes, which communicates itself to the reader. Human dignity may be " silly and a little sad," but you can't be "mad, or bitter," when you show up its defects.

James Thurber grew up in Columbus, Ohio, "with a fondness for peppering passing legislators with electric light bulbs dropped from the State House dome." He began to write at 10 and to draw at 14. After studying at Ohio State University, he became a code clerk in Washington, and in 1918–20 served at the American Embassy in Paris. The loss of sight in one eye kept him from active participation in the World War. After the armistice he became managing editor of *The New Yorker,* and supervised the department called " Talk of the Town."

Mr. Thurber was known as a writer of humor before his name became associated with the drawings of mournful hounds and dejected men and women which have become his trade-mark. He is a wholesome corrective to the herd instinct among readers. His reaction to the books on sex is seen in his *Is Sex Necessary?* 1929, and the flood of books telling us how to use our minds produced *Let Your Mind Alone,* 1937. Other well-known " works " of James Thurber are *The Owl in the Attic,* 1931; *The Seal in the Bedroom,* 1932; and *The Middle-Aged Man on the Flying Trapeze,* 1935. *My Life and Hard Times,* 1934, tells of his grandfather's brother, Texas, who died of the same disease that was killing the chestnut trees. Ernest Hemingway called this book superior to *The Autobiography of Henry Adams.*

The Thurbers live in reverse, sleeping by day and working by night.

Wake Up and Live, Eh?

NOW MRS. DOROTHEA BRANDE
has written a book and Simon & Schuster have published it, with the grim purpose in mind of getting me and all the other woolgatherers mentally organized so that, in a world which is going to pieces, we can be right up on our toes. I have no doubt that the book, which is called "Wake Up and Live! ", will sell some two hundred thousand copies, because there are at least that many people in the United States who want to face the final crack-up in the pink of mental condition. I am not one of these. I don't want a copy of the book; in fact, I don't need one. I have got the gist of the idea of "Wake Up and Live! " from reading an advertisement for it in the Sunday *Times* book section. The writer of the ad said that Mrs. Brande in her inspirational volume suggests "twelve specific disciplines," and he names these, in abbreviated form. I'll take them up in order and show why it is no use for Mrs. Brande to try to save me if these disciplines are all she has to offer:

"1. Spend one hour a day without speaking except in answer to direct questions."

No hour of the day goes by that I am not in some minor difficulty which could easily become major if I did not shout for help. Just a few hours ago, for example, I found myself in a dilemma that has become rather familiar about my house: I had got tied up in a typewriter ribbon. The whole thing had come unwound from the spool and was wound around me. What started as an unfortunate slip of the hand slowly grew into an enormous involvement. To have gone a whole hour waiting for someone to show up and ask me a question could not conceivably have improved my mind. Two minutes of silence now and then is all right, but that is as far as I will go.

"2. Think one hour a day about one subject exclusively."

Such as what, for example? At forty-two, I have spent a great many hours thinking about all sorts of subjects, and there is not one of them that I want to go back to for a whole solid hour. I can pretty well cover as much of any subject as I want to in fifteen minutes. Sometimes in six. Furthermore, it would be impossible for me, or for Mrs. Brande, or for Simon & Schuster to think for an hour exclusively on one subject. What is known as "psychological association" would be bound to come into the thing. For instance, let us say that I decide to think for a solid hour about General Grant's horse (as good a subject as any at a time when practically all subjects are in an unsettled state). The fact that it is General Grant's horse would remind me of General Grant's beard and that would remind me of Charles Evans Hughes and that would remind me of the NRA. And so it would go. If I resolutely went back to General Grant's horse again, I would, by association, begin thinking about General Lee's horse, which was a much more famous horse, a horse named Traveller. I doubt if Mrs. Brande even knows the name of General Grant's horse, much less enough about it to keep her mind occupied for sixty minutes. I mean sixty minutes of real constructive thinking that would get her somewhere. Sixty minutes of thinking of any kind is bound to lead to confusion and unhappiness.

"3. Write a letter without using the first person singular."

What for? To whom? About what? All I could possibly think of to write would be a letter to a little boy telling him how to build a rabbit hutch, and I don't know how to build a rabbit hutch very well. I never knew a little boy who couldn't tell me more about building a rabbit hutch than I could tell him. Nobody in my family was ever good at building rabbit hutches, although a lot of us raised rabbits. I have sometimes wondered how we managed it. I remember the time that my father offered to help me and my two brothers build a rabbit hutch out of planks and close-meshed chicken wire. Somehow or other he got inside of the cage after the wire had been put up around the sides and over the top, and he began to monkey with the stout door. I don't know exactly what happened, but he shut the door and it latched securely and he was locked in with the rabbits. The place was a shambles before he got out, because nobody was home at the time and he couldn't get his hand through the wire to unlatch the door. He had his derby on in the hutch all during his captivity and that added to his discomfiture. I remember, too, that we boys (we were not yet in our teens) didn't at first know what the word "hutch" meant, but we had got hold of a pamphlet on the subject, which my brother Herman read with great care. One sentence in the pamphlet read, "The rabbits' hutches should be cleaned thoroughly once a week." It was this admonition which caused my brother one day to get each of the astonished rabbits down in turn and wash its haunches thoroughly with soap and water.

No, I do not think that anybody can write a letter without using the first person singular. Even if it could be done, I see no reason to do it.

"4. Talk fifteen minutes without using the first person."

No can do. No going to *try* to do, either. You can't teach an old egoist new persons.

"5. Write a letter in a placid, successful tone, sticking to facts about yourself."

Now we're getting somewhere, except that nothing is more stuffy and conceited-sounding than a "placid, successful tone." The way to write about yourself is to let yourself go. Build it up, exaggerate, make yourself out a person of importance. Fantasy is the food for the mind, not facts. Are we going to wake up and live or are we going to sit around writing factual letters in a placid, successful tone?

"6. Pause before you enter any crowded room and consider your relations with the people in it."

Now, Mrs. Brande, if I did that there would be only about one out of every thirty-two crowded rooms I approached that I would ever enter. I always shut my mind and plunge into a crowded room as if it were a cold bath. That gives me and everybody in the room a clean break, a fresh starting point. There is no good in rehashing a lot of old relations with people. The longer I paused outside a crowded room and thought about my relations with the people in it, the more inclined I would be to go back to the checkroom and get my hat and coat and go home. That's the best place for a person, anyway — home.

"7. Keep a new acquaintance talking exclusively about himself."

And then tiptoe quietly away. He'll never notice the difference.

"8. Talk exclusively about yourself for fifteen minutes."

And see what happens.

"9. Eliminate the phrases 'I mean' and 'As a matter of fact' from your conversation."

Okie-dokie.

"10. Plan to live two hours a day according to a rigid time schedule."

Well, I usually wake up at nine in the morning and lie there till eleven, if that would do. Of course, I could *plan* to do a lot of different things over a period of two hours, but if I actually started out to accomplish them I would instantly begin to worry about whether I was going to come out on the dot in the end and I wouldn't do any of them right. It would be like waiting for the pistol shot during the last quarter of a close football game. This rule seems to me to be devised simply to make men irritable and jumpy.

"11. Set yourself twelve instructions on pieces of paper, shuffle them, and follow the one you draw. Here are a few samples: 'Go twelve hours without food.' 'Stay up all night and work.' 'Say nothing all day except in answer to questions.'"

In that going twelve hours without food, do you mean I can have drinks? Because if I can have drinks, I can do it easily. As for staying up all night and working, I know all about that: that simply turns night into day and day into night. I once got myself into such a state staying up all night that I was always having orange juice and boiled eggs at twilight and was just ready for lunch after everybody else had gone to bed. I had to go away to a sanitarium to get turned around. As for saying nothing all day except in answer to questions, what am I to do if a genial colleague comes into my office and says, "I think your mother is one of the nicest people I ever met" or "I was thinking about giving you that twenty dollars you lent me"? Do I just stare at him and walk out of the room? I lose enough friends, and money, the way it is.

"12. Say 'Yes' to every reasonable request made of you in the course of one day."

All right, start making some. I can't think of a single one off-hand. The word "reasonable" has taken a terrible tossing around in my life — both personal and business. If you mean watering the geraniums, I'll do that. If you mean walking around Central Park with you for the fresh air and exercise, you are crazy.

Has anybody got any more sets of specific disciplines? If any-body has, they've got to be pretty easy ones if I am going to wake up and live. It's mighty comfortable dozing here and waiting for the end.

APPRECIATION HINTS

1. What was it that started with a slip of the hand and "grew into an enormous involvement."
2. What are the objections to concentrating on one subject for an hour?
3. Explain how psychological association works in Thurber's case.
4. What is the train of thought which leads to the discussion of rabbit hutches?
5. What is the author's preparation for entering a crowded room?
6. What is it that he compares with waiting for the pistol shot that ends a close football game?
7. What is the difficulty in staying up all night and working next day?
8. "Two hundred thousand copies." Name some recent best sellers which deal with increasing our personal effectiveness, and explain their popularity.
9. What part of this essay do you think the author had most fun in writing?
10. Write a description based on some discipline which has given you trouble. Suggestions: Rules of Conduct That Won't Work; Good

Resolutions; Finger Nails in Mourning; We're Going to Have Company; Now, John, Concentrate on Your Work!
11. Write a composition based on the vogue for books and newspaper columns devoted to etiquette. Suggestions: The Girl's Own Guide to Etiquette, How to Lose Friends, Manners at the Dance, Manners at the Court of King Arthur.
12. Read *Let Your Mind Alone*, by James Thurber.
13. Read *My Life and Hard Times* and *The Middle-Aged Man on the Flying Trapeze*, by James Thurber.

THE SPIDER

What shall I compare it to, this fantastic thing I call my Mind? To a waste-paper basket, to a sieve choked with sediment, or to a barrel full of floating froth and refuse?

No, what it is really most like is a spider's web, insecurely hung on leaves and twigs, quivering in every wind, and sprinkled with dewdrops and dead flies. And at its center, pondering for ever the problem of Existence, sits motionless the spider-like and uncanny Soul.

IN CHURCH

What a bore it is, waking up in the morning always the same person. I wish I were unflinching and emphatic, and had big bushy eyebrows and a Message for the Age. I wish I were a deep Thinker, or a great Ventriloquist.

AIMS

There are two things to aim at in life: first, to get what you want; and, after that, to enjoy it. Only the wisest of mankind achieve the second.

Logan Pearsall Smith

IZAAK WALTON 1593-1683

THINK over some fishing experience of yours, and ask yourself whether *all* the pleasure of the trip was represented in the catch you brought home — if there was one to bring. Surely not, even if you brought home a goodly string of trout. Count the catch against the money expended for tackle and equipment by the millions of Americans who go fishing, and the price per pound of the fish caught is staggering. What is this urge in our blood which drives us to our rods and tackle boxes every April?

The old angler gives us the answer in the following essay. While he is giving this first lesson in trout fishing to his " scholar," he insists that they are practicing an art. If you have ever wet a fly or watched a fly-casting competition between experts, you will agree. Fetch the rod from the attic; dust it off; test its delicate balance with your wrist; the feel is like the feel of the bat to the home-run slugger.

"Praise God, be quiet, and go a-fishing." If Izaak Walton's immortal book can be put in seven words, there it is. *The Compleat Angler* has been the bible of all true fishermen for almost three hundred years. There are many better guidebooks if you want just to kill fish; there are none if you want to enjoy fishing. The book reflects the fisherman's superstitions, and its facts and technical advice are not always reliable. As a boy, fishing for trout in the English Lake District, I tried Walton's recipe for making the worms irresistible by " anointing the bait box with oil of ivy berries." But the Lord was still on the side of the trout.

Piscator, a fisherman, Venator, a huntsman, and Auceps, a falconer, chance to meet one fresh May morning on the road to Ware in old England, and discourse of their several arts. Piscator promises to join Venator for an otter hunt next day, on condition that on the day after that they go fishing together; the result is that the huntsman becomes a confirmed disciple of Piscator. It is from the fourth day that the following essay is taken.

Izaak Walton, "the father of angling," was a shopkeeper in London until Cromwell and his Ironsides took the field against the Stuarts. *The Compleat Angler* was published in 1653, and ran through five editions in Walton's lifetime.

A Day with the Trouts

Piscator. Good-morrow, good hostess! I see my brother Peter is still in bed; come, give my scholar and me a morning drink, and a bit of meat to breakfast; and be sure to get a good dish of meat or two against supper, for we shall come home as hungry as hawks. Come, scholar, let's be going.

Venator. Well now, good master, as we walk towards the river give me direction, according to your promise, how I shall fish for a trout. . . .

Pisc. My honest scholar, it it now past five of the clock, we will fish till nine, and then go to breakfast. Go you to yon sycamore-tree and hide your bottle of drink under the hollow root of it; for about that time and in that place, we will make a brave breakfast with a piece of powdered beef [1] and a radish or two that I have in my fish-bag; we shall, I warrant you make a good, honest, wholesome, hungry breakfast, and I will then give you direction for the making and using of your flies; and in the meantime there is your rod and line, and my advice is, that you fish as you see me do, and let's try which can catch the first fish.

Ven. I thank you, master, I will observe and practice your direction as far as I am able.

Pisc. Look you, scholar, you see I have hold of a good fish: I now

[1] Beef which has been dried and seasoned.

see it is a trout, I pray you put that net under him, and touch not my line, for if you do, then we break all. Well done, scholar, I thank you.

Now for another. Trust me, I have another bite; come, scholar, come lay down your rod, and help me to land this as you did the other. So now we shall be sure to have a good dish of fish for supper.

Ven. I am glad of that; but I have no fortune: sure, master, yours is a better rod and better tackling.

Pisc. Nay, then, take mine, and I will fish with yours. Look you, scholar, I have another. Come, do as you did before. And now I have a bite at another. Oh me! he has broke all: there's half a line and a good hook lost.

Ven. Ay, and a good trout too.

Pisc. Nay, the trout is not lost; for pray take notice, no man can lose what he never had.

Ven. Master, I can neither catch with the first nor second angle: I have no fortune.

Pisc. Look you, scholar, I have yet another. And now, having caught three brace of trouts, I will tell you a short tale as we walk towards our breakfast. A scholar (a preacher I should say) that was to preach to procure the approbation of a parish, that he might be their lecturer, had got from his fellow pupil the copy of a sermon that was first preached with great commendation by him that composed it; and though the borrower of it preached it, word for word, as it was at first, yet it was utterly disliked as it was preached by the second to his congregation; which the sermon-borrower complained of to the lender of it, and thus was answered: " I lent you, indeed, my fiddle, but not my fiddlestick; for you are to know that every-one cannot make music with my words, which are fitted to my own mouth." And so, my scholar, you are to know, that as the ill pronunciation or ill accenting of words in a sermon spoils it, so the ill carriage of your line, or not fishing even to a foot in a right place makes you lose your labour; and you are to know that though you have my fiddle, that is, my very good rod and tacklings with which you see I catch fish, yet you have not my fiddlestick, that is, you yet have not the skill to know how to carry your hand and line, or how to guide it to a right place: and this must be taught you (for you are to remember, I told you angling is an art) either by practice or by a long observation, or both. But take this for a rule, when you fish for a trout with a worm, let your line have so much, and not more lead than will fit the stream in which you fish; that is to say, more in a great troublesome stream than in a smaller that is quieter; as near as may be, so much as will sink the bait to the bottom, and keep it in motion, and not more.

But now, let's say grace and fall to breakfast; what say you, scholar, to the providence of an old angler? Does not this meat taste well? and was not this place well chosen to eat it? for this sycamore-tree will shade us from the sun's heat.

Ven. All excellent good, and my stomach excellent good too. And now I remember and find that true which devout Lessius says: " That poor men, and those that fast often have much more pleasure in eating than rich men and gluttons, that always feed before their stomachs are empty of their last meal, and call for more; for by that means they rob themselves of that pleasure that hunger brings to poor men." And I do seriously approve of that saying of yours " that you would rather be a civil, well-governed, well-grounded, temperate, poor angler than a drunken lord." But I hope there is none such; however, I am certain of this, that I have been at very many costly dinners that have not afforded me half the content that this has done, for which I thank God and you.

Pisc. And now, scholar, I think it will be time to repair to our angle-rods, which we left in the water to fish for themselves; and you shall choose which shall be yours; and it is an even lay which of them catches.

And, let me tell you, this kind of fishing with a dead rod, and laying night-hooks, are like putting money to use; for they both work for the owners when they do nothing but eat, sleep or rejoice, as you know we have done this last hour, and sat as quietly and as free from cares under the sycamore as Virgil's Tityrus and his Meliboeus did under their broad beech-tree. No life, my honest scholar, no life so happy and so pleasant as the life of the well-governed angler, for when the lawyer is swallowed up with business, and the statesman is preventing or contriving plots, then we sit on cowslip banks, hear the birds sing, and possess ourselves in as much quietness as these silent silver streams, which we now see glide so quietly by us. Indeed, my good scholar, we may say of angling, as Dr. Boteler said of strawberries, " Doubtless, God could have made a better berry, but doubtless God never did "; and so (if I might be judge) " God never did make a more calm, quiet, innocent recreation than angling."

But, I pray, forget not the catch which you promised to make against night; for our countryman, honest Corydon will expect your catch, and my song, which I must be forced to patch up, for it is so long since I learned it that I have forgotten a part of it. But come, now it hath done raining, let's stretch our legs a little in a gentle walk to the river, and try what interest our angles will pay us for lending them so long to be used by the trout; lent them, indeed, like usurers, for our profit and their destruction.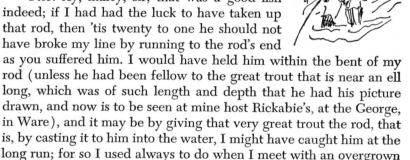

Ven. Oh me! Look you, master, a fish! a fish! Oh, alas, master, I have lost her!

Pisc. Ay, marry, sir, that was a good fish indeed; if I had had the luck to have taken up that rod, then 'tis twenty to one he should not have broke my line by running to the rod's end as you suffered him. I would have held him within the bent of my rod (unless he had been fellow to the great trout that is near an ell long, which was of such length and depth that he had his picture drawn, and now is to be seen at mine host Rickabie's, at the George, in Ware), and it may be by giving that very great trout the rod, that is, by casting it to him into the water, I might have caught him at the long run; for so I used always to do when I meet with an overgrown fish; and you will learn to do so too hereafter; for I tell you, fishing is an art; or, at least, it is an art to catch fish. . . .

Ven. But, master, will this trout which I had hold of die? for it is like he hath the hook in his belly.

Pisc. I will tell you, scholar, that unless the hook be fast in his very gorge, 'tis more than probable he will live; and a little time, with the help of the water, will rust the hook, and it will in time wear away; as the gravel doth in the horse-hoof, which only leaves a false quarter.

And now, scholar, let's go to my rod. Look you, scholar, I have a fish too, but it proves a logger-headed chub; and this is not much amiss, for this will pleasure some poor body, as we go to our lodging to meet our brother Peter and honest Corydon. Come, now bait your hook again, and lay it into the water, for it rains again; and we will even retire to the sycamore-tree, and there I will give you more directions concerning fishing; for I would fain make you an artist.

APPRECIATION HINTS

1. What tackle, bait, and equipment were these fishermen using?
2. What did Venator catch? What did he lose, and how? What did he help to catch?
3. What illustration did Piscator use to explain to Venator that good fishing does not depend merely on good tackle?
4. What else, besides catching fish, made the morning agreeable?
5. On what grounds does Piscator prefer the life of the fisherman to the life of the lawyer?
6. How was the great trout "near an ell long" caught?
7. Think of reasons that the hunter or the trapper might give for preferring their own sports to fishing.
8. *The Compleat Angler* was written only forty years after the King James version of the Bible. Collect from the essay you have just read examples of words and expressions that differ from modern usage.
9. Write a composition about some trip on fresh or salt water. Suggestions: My Fishing Trip, Fishing from the Wharf, Up the River, Canoeing, On the Bay, Hunting with the Camera.
10. Write a description of some one who loves sports. Suggestions: The Old Trapper, Our Guide, The Boy Who Showed Us How to Catch Fish, Captain Bob.
11. Read in *Little Rivers*, by Henry van Dyke, "An Angler's Wish in Town."
12. Read in *Fisherman's Luck*, by Henry van Dyke, "The Thrilling Moment."
13. Look over *Tales of Fishing Virgin Seas*, by Zane Grey.

THE SCIENTIST EXPLORES

THE WORD *explorer* suggests such names as Columbus and Peary, and the host of others who enlarged men's knowledge of the geography of the world. Though the opportunity for that kind of discovery and adventure has not passed, and vast areas of land are still unmapped and almost unknown, men more and more have begun to explore above the land and below the water. William Beebe, represented by one of the essays which follow, is an explorer, in part at least, of this type, for he has been the first to give us glimpses of the hitherto unseen world of deep water.

But the most important discoveries of modern times have been made at home. No more influential essay has been written in the last twenty-five years than the briefest, and to most of us, the least comprehensible. It is the few pages of formulae in which Einstein wrote down his theory of relativity. Like Alan Devoe's speculations upon the mystery of migration in this section, it did not depend on ships of sea or air. The mind explored regions infinitely beyond their reach.

The essays which follow give five examples of scientific exploring. They are all by men who could not only observe with the scientist's accuracy, but also report about what they saw and found with the skill of the writer. Alan Devoe speculates about what has been an unsolved mystery ever since the prophet Jeremiah observed that "the stork and the crane and the swallow observe the time of their coming." William Beebe describes one of the strangest, and clumsiest, and apparently best adapted of God's creatures, and Pliny reports from his personal experience one of the greatest historic cataclysms of nature. H. J. Muller vividly represents to us the brief span of man's dominance on the planet, and describes the processes which have produced changes in the forms of life. Donald Culross Peattie calls attention to the beauty of the world which the facts of science help to reveal.

ALAN DEVOE 1909– LOOK through a telescope or a pair of field glasses at the full moon on a clear September night, and you will notice little black specks occasionally dart across the field of vision. They are migrating birds, sometimes as much as three miles above the earth. On foggy nights they lose their way and are attracted to any beacon or lighthouse which they see shining out. One of these, in the direct path of birds migrating down the Hudson River, is the Statue of Liberty. After a storm no less than 1400 dead birds have been picked up at its base. But you can watch birds migrating during the day at many vantage points and bird sanctuaries. For instance at Hawk Mountain in Pennsylvania on a " good " day — that is, a calm day after a storm further north — it is not unusual to count 40,000 hawks of various species coasting south on the wind currents.

But you may be one of those " practical " people who take no interest in such things as birds. But you will soon be interested in taxes. In 1885 the state of Pennsylvania passed the " scalp act " which provided a bounty of fifty cents on each hawk or owl killed. After the act had been in force for eighteen months, ornithologists showed that the state had been throwing away annually $2105 for every dollar saved in young chickens, and had involved the taxpayers in a total loss of about $4,000,000 per annum. The field mice, normally kept in check by owls and hawks, had so increased that they damaged the grain crops by that amount. We had better be well enough informed about the value of birds at least to check up on our legislators; for Frank M. Chapman, one of the greatest of American ornithologists, writes " it is not too much to say that without birds the earth would not long be habitable."

Alan Devoe was " nature columnist " for the Montclair *Times* and later for the Brooklyn *Daily Eagle*. In 1934 he made over a chicken house into a residence on Phudd Hill in upstate New York, five miles from the nearest town. His first book, *Phudd Hill*, appeared in 1937. He has contributed regularly to *The American Mercury*, conducting a department called " Down to Earth." This is the title of his last book, from which the following essay is taken.

The Mystery of Migration

THEY are gone now. No robins carol from the fence posts; no medley of catbird tunes issues from the blackberry tangles; no woodcocks rise on whirring wings from our swamplands and marshes. The populace of birds is now meager and tuneless. Once again the annual mystery has come about. Once again the Summer birds have vanished.

It is a phenomenon older than the memory of man. Ages ago Ojibways and Pequots tilted bronze faces to the sun to watch the wild geese go honking southward, and tribal storytellers invented legends to explain the mystery. White men of science wrote solemn monographs asserting that in Winter the birds retired to hollow trees, to hibernate until Spring like woodchucks, and so erudite a man as Dr. Samuel Johnson supposed that the English swallows spent the Winter sleeping in the river-mud of the Thames. The theories were innumerable and unconfirmed. They still are. We are not now quite so naïve, of course, as to fancy that the birds spend the Winter asleep in caves or river-bottoms, and we know quite well that they migrate to warmer climates. We have checked their routes, and clocked their arrivals and departures, and graphed their journeyings with great accuracy. And, having done this, we can still only stand awed and wondering. What impulse is abroad on Autumn nights, to tell these orioles and phoebes and sandpipers that the time for traveling is at hand? What secret inner knowledge guides these millions of wings on their long intricate courses? It is not known.

The preparations for migration begin long before the coming of the Fall. They begin, in a real sense, with the molt, in latter Summer when the care of the fledglings is over; for it is then that worn, frayed feathers are replaced by new ones and the bird's light-boned body acquires fresh buoyancy. Like many another happening in fields and forests, the molting of the birds is so casual and unspectacular an event that hardly one man in a thousand even remarks its occurrence, but it deserves rank among the minor miracles. Two feathers, and two feathers only, are shed at one time, and they are shed with perfect symmetry. The middle feather of each wing is the first to go. When the new replacement-feathers for these gaps have achieved half their growth, another pair of quills loosens and is shed. With perfect precision the process continues, until a whole new plumage has come into being. So gradual is the process, so nicely contrived, that at no time is more than a single pair of feathers missing; at no time is the bird's flight-mechanism unbalanced or impaired. And in the case of certain of our species the miracle is of an even more arresting kind. There is the metamorphosis, for instance, which the male scarlet tanagers undergo. Before the molting-time their flame-red plumage affords one of the gaudiest colors in our countryside. When the molt has ended, they are arrayed in dingy green. It will hide them, on their southward flight, from the sharp preying eyes of hawks.

There is a second preparation for the great Autumn flight, and it consists of smaller flights in the nature of trials. Ever since July the adult male robins have been leading their fledglings to communal roosting-places, usually deep-hidden in the leafy woods, and the grackles and swallows and starlings have similarly massed together in tremendous hordes. At every daybreak the great flocks issue forth, and all day they wheel and veer together through the Autumn sky, returning at nightfall to the place of their communal sleep. This is the time when wings are trained and strengthened, when flight-patterns are established and co-ordinated, when there is perfected that deep and subtle mass-harmony of motion which no scientist can pretend to understand. Uncountable thousands of gulls, of swifts, of cowbirds are learning one of the most ancient and most unfathomable techniques in nature.

There is a third and final preparation. It is the same preparation which skunks and bears and woodchucks make before their Winter sleep. It is the taking on of surplus nourishment, the building of a reserve of fat. In obedience to a dim behest, the flycatchers now enormously increase their consumption of tree hoppers and crickets, the tanagers hunt crane flies more voraciously than ever, and the dried weed-seeds in man's pastures and gardens are stripped by flocks of finches and sparrows. The birds are insuring that they shall have a reservoir of strength on which to draw, should there be a scarcity of food along their flight-line. If the findings of dissectionists are significant, the tiny brains in these small feathered skulls can hardly be capable of shrewd foresighted reasoning, or indeed of any clear prevision of the journey ahead. The urge which moves them must have another source than mind. No man, yet, can give it any name.

II

In late July the bobolinks vanish. They are among the first to go. The route of their travels has been fully mapped, and it is known that they are on the wing for nearly two months before they reach the small patch of river-watered jungle which for inscrutable reasons they deem the most suitable wintering place. They pass through South Carolina in the latter part of August; at the turn of the month, through Florida; in September they are in Cuba. Sometimes they cover four hundred miles in a single night, and always they press southward . . . down the Andes, across the Amazon, over the great Brazilian plains. When at last they halt, it is in the marshlands on the upper Paraguay River.

The departure of the bobolinks is followed presently, in latter August and throughout September, by the going of the flycatchers, the vireos, the warblers. Our Autumn woods are thronged then with voyaging companies of birds. By October the last of them has passed and disappeared, and by November there have arrived to take their places such Winter visitants as juncos and tree sparrows, crossbills and pine grosbeaks . . . a colorless and relatively songless little band, but hardily equipped for clinging to frozen sumac-stalks in the whipping January wind and foraging in snow-drifted pastures for stray thistle-seeds. They have nested and passed the Summer to the north of us, some of them as far north as Hudson Bay and the Arctic coast, and they will return to those bleak regions before our first hepaticas bloom.

Prodigious as are the travels of the birds — the tiny blackpoll warblers voyaging five thousand miles, the scimitar-winged nighthawks migrating from the Yukon to Argentina — the rate of speed is in most cases not extremely high. The average is usually some thirty or forty miles a day, and on the return-flights in the Spring may be hardly more than twenty. The trek is leisurely and often interrupted, with side-excursions to feeding-grounds en route and sometimes total rests for several days. But sometimes, too, there are flights of five hundred miles without a single pause, as when the ruby-throated hummingbirds cross the Gulf of Mexico to Yucatan, and it is known that the golden plovers which fly from Alaska to Hawaii cover the whole span of two thousand miles without a respite.

Men used to be puzzled by the fact that, although the migrating birds must number many millions, only occasional flocks are seen passing overhead. We know now why it is. We know that only the swiftest travelers — those species that need have no fear of hawks — undertake to fly by day. The rest fly only in the night. On a night in Autumn, when the moon is full, it is possible to watch with field-glasses the endless passing, high above the earth, of feathered legions. It is even possible, if the watcher be in a woods or other quiet place, to hear faintly the remote music of the flight . . . the soft whistle of thrushes, the thin fluting of woodcocks. It is not an experience that the listener readily forgets.

Why do the birds migrate at all? We shall have to be very much wiser than at present before we know. Perhaps it began in the glacial era, when the Arctic ice fields advanced southward; perhaps it is chiefly a physiological problem, subtly allied to periodic changes in the food supply. By what sense, or combination of senses, do thrushes and snipe and meadow larks find their way unerringly along complex thousand-mile routes which no man could possibly follow without directional instruments, and what inner bidding moves the individual members of the flocks to wheel and turn and dip in unbroken unison?

It has been supposed, in answer to the first question, that perhaps the great mountain ranges and watercourses are the guides; and on the second question some ornithologists have theorized that perhaps the birds possess — as almost certainly the ant-world does — some sense that is outside our human ken entirely.

This much only can we say with surety: that every Fall and every Spring the woods and sky present us, for the looking and the listening, with a magic pageantry of beating wings, and with a reminder — not unwelcome in a time as bitterly confused as ours — that the ancient unknowable harmonies of the universe still endure.

APPRECIATION HINTS

1. Mention some mistaken theories once held about how birds pass the winter.
2. In what three ways do birds get ready to migrate?
3. Describe how birds molt.
4. Mention the route taken, and the destination of the migrating bobolink.
5. Tell about the speed at which various birds travel when they migrate.
6. Give some theories put forward to account for the migration of birds.
7. Mention the names of birds which winter in your locality.
8. Tell how you can attract birds by winter feeding.
9. One of the puzzles of ornithologists is how to account for the return journey. Why should birds leave a plenteous food supply in the south to come north? Can you think of any explanation?
10. Write a composition about some experience you have had with birds. Suggestions: Bird Banding, Bird Houses, Canaries, Parrots, Chickens.
11. Write about some phase of " instinct " in animals. Suggestions: The Superior Powers of " Lower " Animals, A Dog's Nose, Horse Sense, How Birds Find the Way, The Wisdom of the Woodchuck.
12. Read in *Phudd Hill*, by Devoe, the essays entitled " A Shack in the Woods," and " The Mole."
13. Read in Chapter Seven of *Nonsuch, Land of Water,* by William Beebe, about the strange migrations of butterflies, birds, and lemmings.

WILLIAM BEEBE 1877– FEW WRITERS of today make as vivid an appeal to youth as does William Beebe, trained scientist, observer, and master of a charming and happy style. Under his guidance science becomes for us a thrilling and moving story. We share his enthusiasms and his zest for living things. We profit from Mr. Beebe's lively and insatiable curiosity as well as from his technical knowledge, and are glad that it has driven him to scientific study, for when he answers the questions he raises, exact science speaks with charm, and the reader is promised hours of pleasure. He has given us knowledge of jungles and of the exotic plant and animal life there. We share with him the sights, smells, and sounds of the woods. Through his pages we catch the witchery of the underworld of water "where great whales come sailing by, sail and sail with unshut eye," and where "seahorses are stabled in great green caves." Poetry and science unite on his pages.

Perhaps the potency of this charm lies in Mr. Beebe's own enthusiasms and in his zest for work. In recent years he has descended in his bathysphere to the greatest depths in the sea ever attained by living man, and the dullest stay-at-home catches a glimpse of his joy in the wonders he describes. "Don't die without having borrowed, stolen, or purchased, or made a helmet, to glimpse for yourself this new world." We are carried away to far lands by the opening sentences of his essays: "Within gun-reach of me trudged my little Akawai Indian hunter." "The edges and rims of things are much more exciting than the things themselves." "On September twelfth I met a Great Blue Shark in the prime of life." "There are three things of the sea which have been delineated by man more than any others — dolphins, mermaids, and seahorses — and there are three things about which we know almost less than any others — seahorses, mermaids, and dolphins."

William Beebe is our foremost authority on tropical birds, and Director of Tropical Research of the New York Zoological Society. A partial list of his books will give some idea of the range of his scientific studies: *Tropical Wild Life*, 1917; *Galapagos, World's End*, 1923; *Jungle Days*, 1925; *The Arcturus Adventure*, 1925; *Pheasant Jungles*, 1927; *Beneath Tropic Seas*, 1928; *Half Mile Down*, 1934.

The Jungle Sluggard

SLOTHS have no right to be living on the earth today; they would be fitting inhabitants of Mars, where a year is over six hundred days long. In fact they would exist more appropriately on a still more distant planet where time — as we know it — creeps and crawls instead of flies from dawn to dusk. Years ago I wrote that sloths reminded me of nothing so much as the wonderful Rath Brother athletes or of a slowed-up moving picture, and I can still think of no better similes.

Sloths live together in trees, but so do monkeys, and the chief difference between them would seem to be that the latter spend their time pushing against gravitation while the sloths pull against it. Botanically the two groups of animals are comparable to the flower which holds its head up to the sun, swaying on its long stem, and, on the other hand, the overripe fruit dangling heavily from its base. We ourselves are physically far removed from sloths — for while we can point with pride to the daily achievement of those ambulatory[1] athletes, floorwalkers and policemen, yet no human being can cling with his hands to a branch for more than a comparatively short time.

Like a rainbow before breakfast, a sloth is a surprise, an unexpected fellow breather of the air of our planet. No one could prophesy a sloth. If you have an imaginative friend who has never

[1] Walking.

seen a sloth and ask him to describe what he thinks it ought to be like, his uncontrolled phrases will fall far short of reality. If there were no sloths, Dunsany would hesitate to put such a creature in the forests of Mluna, Marco Polo would deny having seen one, and Munchausen would whistle as he listened to a friend's description. . . .

It is difficult to find adequate comparisons for a topsy-turvy creature like a sloth, but if I had already had synthetic experience with a Golem,[2] I would take for a formula the general appearance of an English sheep dog, giving it a face with barely distinguishable features and no expression, an inexhaustible appetite for a single kind of coarse leaf, a gamut of emotions well below the animal kingdom, and an enthusiasm for life excelled by a healthy sunflower. Suspend this from a jungle limb by a dozen strong hooks, and — you would still have to see a live sloth to appreciate its appearance.

At rest, curled up into an arboreal [3] ball, a sloth is indistinguishable from a cluster of leaves; in action, the second hand of a watch often covers more distance. At first sight of the shapeless ball of hay, moving with hopeless inadequacy, astonishment shifts to pity, then to impatience, and finally, as we sense a life of years spent thus, we feel almost disgust. At which moment the sloth reaches blindly in our direction, thinking us a barren, leafless, but perhaps climbable tree, and our emotions change again, this time to sheer delight as a tiny infant sloth raises its indescribably funny face from its mother's breast and sends forth the single tone, the high, whistling squeak, which in sloth intercourse is song, shout, converse, whisper, argument, and chant. Separating him from his mother is like plucking a bur from one's hair, but when freed, he contentedly hooks his small self to our clothing and creeps slowly about.

Instead of reviewing all the observations and experiments which I perpetrated upon sloths, I will touch at once the heart of their mysterious psychology, giving in a few words a conception of their strange, uncanny minds. A bird will give up its life in defending its

---

[2] The Talmud tells of the rabbis constructing a shapeless mass called a Golem, and then bringing it to life.

[3] Belonging to the trees.

young; an alligator will not often desert its nest in the face of danger; a male stickleback fish will intrepidly face any intruder that threatens its eggs. In fact, at the time when the young of all animals are at the age of helplessness, he senses of the parents are doubly keen, their activities and weapons are at greatest efficiency for the guarding of the young and the consequent certainty of the continuance of their race.

The resistance made by a mother sloth to the abstraction of its offspring is chiefly the mechanical tangling of the young animal's tiny claws in the long maternal fur. I have taken away a young sloth and hooked it to a branch five feet away. Being hungry it began at once to utter its high, penetrating penny whistle. To no other sound, high or low, with even a half-tone's difference does the sloth pay any heed, but its dim hearing is attuned to just this vibration. Slowly the mother starts off in what she thinks is the direction of the sound. It is the moment of moments in the life of the young animal. Yet I have seen her again and again on different occasions pass within two feet of the little chap, and never look to right or left, but keep straight on, stolidly and unvaryingly to the high jungle, while her baby, a few inches out of her path, called in vain. No kidnaped child hidden in mountain fastness or urban underworld was ever more completely lost to its parent than this infant, in full view and separated by only a sloth's length of space.

A gun fired close to the ear of a sloth will usually arouse not the slightest tremor; no scent of flower or acid or carrion causes any reaction; a sleeping sloth may be shaken violently without awakening; the waving of a scarlet rag, or a climbing serpent a few feet away brings no gleam of curiosity or fear to the dull eyes; an astonishingly long immersion in water produces discomfort but not death. When we think what a constant struggle life is to most creatures, even when they are equipped with the keenest of senses and powerful means of offense, it seems incredible that a sloth can hold its own in this overcrowded tropical jungle.

From birth to death it climbs slowly about the great trees, leisurely feeding, languidly loving, and almost mechanically caring for its young. On the ground a host of enemies await it, but among the

higher branches it fears chiefly occasional great boas, climbing jaguars and, worst of all, the mighty talons of harpy eagles. Its means of
offense is a joke — a slow, ineffective reaching forward with open
jaws, a lethargic stroke of arm and claws which anything but another
sloth can avoid. Yet the race of sloths persists and thrives, and in past
years I have had as many as eighteen under observation at one time.

A sloth makes no nest or shelter; it even disdains the protection
of dense foliage. But for all its apparent helplessness it has a *cheval-
de-frise* [4] of protection which many animals far above it in intelligence
might well envy. Its outer line of defense is invisibility — and there
is none better, for until you have seen your intended prey you can
neither attack nor devour him. No hedgehog or armadillo ever rolled
a more perfect ball of itself than does a sloth, sitting in a lofty, swaying crotch with head and feet and legs all gathered close together inside. This posture, to an onlooker, destroys all thought of a living
animal, but presents a very satisfactory white ants' nest or bunch of
dead leaves. If we look at the hair of a sloth we shall see small, grey
patches along the length of the hairs — at first sight bits of bark and
débris of wood. But these minute, scattered particles are of the utmost aid to this invisibility. They are a peculiar species of alga or
lichen-like growth, which is found only in this peculiar haunt, and
when the rain begins and all the jungle turns a deep, glowing emerald, these tiny plants also react to the welcome moisture and become verdant — thus growing over the sloth a protecting, misty veil
of green.

Even we dull-sensed humans require neither sight nor hearing
to detect the presence of an animal like the skunk; in the absolute
quiet and blackness of midnight we can tell when a porcupine has
crossed our path, or when there are mice in the bureau drawers. But
a dozen sloths may be hanging to the trees near at hand and never
the slightest whiff of odor comes from them. A baby sloth has not even
a baby smell, and all this is part of the cloak of invisibility. The voice,
raised so very seldom, is so ventriloquial, and possesses such a
strange, unanimal-like quality, that it can never be a guide to the
location, much less to the identity of the author. Here we have three

[4] barbed-wire entanglement.

senses — sight, hearing, smell — all operating at a distance, two of them by vibrations, and all leagued together to shelter the sloth from attack.

But in spite of this dramatic guard of invisibility the keen eyes of an eagle, the lapping tongue of a giant boa, and the amazing delicacy of a jaguar's sense of smell break through at times. The jaguar scents sign under the tree of the sloth, climbs eagerly as far as he dares, and finds ready to his paw the ball of animal unconsciousness; a harpy eagle half a mile above the jungle sees a bunch of leaves reach out a sleepy arm and scratch itself — something clumps of leaves should not do. Down spirals the great bird, slowly, majestically, knowing there is no need of haste, and alights close by the mammalian sphere. Still the sloth does not move, apparently waiting for what fate may bring — waiting with that patience and resignation which comes only to those of our fellow creatures who cannot

say, " I am I! " It seems as if Nature had deserted her jungle changeling, stripped now of its protecting cloak.

The sloth, however, has never been given credit for its powers of passive resistance, and now, with its enemy within striking distance, its death or even injury is far from a certainty. The crotch which the sloth chooses for its favorite outdoor sport, sleep, is unusually high up or far out among the lesser branches, where the eight claws of the eagle or the eighteen of a jaguar find but precarious hold. If the victim were a feathery bush turkey or a soft-bodied squirrel, one stroke would be sufficient, but this strange creature is something far different. In the first place, it is only to be plucked from its perch by the exertion of enormous strength. No man can seize a sloth by the long hair of the back and pull it off. So strong are its muscles, so viselike the grip of its dozen talons, that either the crotch must be cut or broken off or the long claws unfastened one by one. Neither of these alternatives is possible to the attacking cat or eagle. They must depend upon crushing or penetrating power of stroke or grasp.

Here is where the sloth's second line of defense becomes operative. First, as I have mentioned, the swaying branch and dizzy height are in his favor, as well as his immovable grip. To begin with the innermost defenses, while his jungle fellows, the ring-tailed and red howling monkeys, have thirteen ribs, the sloth may have as many as twenty; in the latter animal they are, in addition, unusually broad and flat, slats rather than rods. Next comes the skin, which is so thick and tough that many an Indian's arrow falls back without even scratching the hide. The skin of the unborn sloth is as tough and strong as that of a full-grown monkey. Finally we have the fur — two distinct coats, the under one fine, short, and matted, the outer long, harsh, and coarse. Is it any wonder that, teetering on a swaying branch, many a jaguar has had to give up, after frantic attempts to strike his claws through the felted hair, the tough skin, and the bony latticework which protect the vitals of this edentate bur!

Having rescued our sloth from his most immediate peril, let us watch him solve some of the very few problems which life presents to him. Although the Cecropia tree, on the leaves of which he feeds, is scattered far and wide through the jungle, yet sloths are found almost exclusively along river banks, and, most amazingly, they not infrequently take to the water. I have caught a dozen sloths swimming rivers a mile or more in width. Judging from the speed of short distances, a sloth can swim a mile in three hours and twenty minutes. Their thick skin and fur must be a protection against crocodiles, electric eels, and perai [5] fish as well as jaguars. Why they should ever wish to swim across these wide expanses of water is as inexplicable as the migration of butterflies. One side of the river has as many comfortable crotches, as many millions of Cecropia leaves, and as many eligible lady sloths as the other! In this unreasonable desire

---

[5] The blood-fish found in some South American rivers. It attacks and sometimes kills wounded men.

for anything which is out of reach, sloths come very close to a characteristic of human beings.

Even in the jungle, sloths are not always the static creatures which their vegetable-like life would lead us to believe, as I was able to prove many years ago. A young male was brought in by Indians, and after keeping it a few days I shaved off two patches of hair from the center of the back, and labeling it with a metal tag I turned it loose. Forty-eight days later it was captured near a small settlement of Bovianders several miles farther up and across the river. During this time it must have traversed four miles of jungle and one of river.

The principal difference between the male and the female three-toed sloths is the presence on the back of the male of a large, oval spot of orange-colored fur. To any creature of more active mentality such a minor distinction must often be embarrassing. In an approaching sloth, walking upside down as usual, this mark is quite invisible, and hence every meeting of two sloths must contain much of delightful uncertainty, of ignorance whether the encounter presages courtship or merely gossip. But color or markings have no meaning in the dull eyes of these animals. Until they have sniffed and almost touched noses they show no recognition or reaction whatever.

I once invented a sloth island — a large circle of ground surrounded by a deep ditch, where sloths climbed about some saplings and ate, but principally slept, and lived for months at a time. This was within sight of my laboratory table; so I could watch what was taking place by merely raising my head. Some of the occurrences were almost too strange for creatures of this earth. I watched two courtships, each resulting in nothing more serious than my own amusement. A female was asleep in a low crotch, curled up into a perfect ball deep within which was ensconced a month-old baby. Two yards overhead was a male who had slept for nine hours without interruption. Moved by what, to a sloth, must have been a burst of uncontrollable emotion, he slowly unwound himself and clambered downward. When close to the sleeping beauty, he reached out a claw and tentatively touched a shoulder. Even more deliberately she excavated her head and long neck and peered in every direction but the right one. At last she perceived her suitor and looked away as if the sight was too much for her. Again he touched her post-like neck, and now there arose all the flaming fury of a mother at the flirtatious advances of this stranger. With incredible slowness and effort she freed an arm, deliberately drew it back, and then began a slow forward stroke with arm and claws. Meanwhile her gentleman friend had changed his position; so the blow swept or, more correctly, passed, through empty air, the lack of impact almost throwing her out of the crotch. The disdained one left with slowness and dignity — or had he already forgotten why he had descended? — and returned to his perch and slumber, where, I am sure, not even such active things as dreams came to disturb his peace.

The second courtship advanced to the stage where the Gallant actually got his claws tangled in the lady's back hair before she awoke. When she grasped the situation, she left at once and clambered to the highest branch tip followed by the male. Then she turned and climbed down and across her annoyer, leaving him stranded on the lofty branch looking eagerly about and reaching out hopefully toward a big green iguana asleep on the next limb in mistake for his fair companion. For an hour he wandered languidly after her, then gave it up and went to sleep. Throughout these and other emotional crises no sound is ever uttered, no feature altered from its stolid repose. The head moves mechanically and the dull eyes blink slowly, as if striving to pierce the opaque veil which ever hangs between the brain of a sloth and the sights, sounds, and odors of this tropical world. If the orange back-spot was ever of any use in courtship, in arousing any emotion, aesthetic or otherwise, it must have been in ages long past when the ancestors of sloths, contemporaries of their gigantic relatives, the Mylodons, had better eyesight for escaping from saber-toothed tigers than there is need today.

The climax of a sloth's emotion has nothing to do with the opposite sex or with the young, but is exhibited when two females are confined in a cage together. The result is wholly unexpected. After sniffing at one another for a moment, they engage in a slowed-up moving-picture battle. Before any harm is done, one or the other gives utterance to the usual piercing whistle and surrenders. She lies flat on the cage floor and offers no defense while the second female proceeds to claw her, now and then attempting, usually vainly, to bite. It is so unpleasant that I have always separated them at this stage, but there is no doubt that in every case the unnatural affray would go on until the victim was killed. In fact I have heard of several instances where this actually took place.

A far pleasanter sight is the young sloth, one of the most adorable balls of fuzzy fur imaginable. While the sense of play is all but lacking, his trustfulness and helplessness are most infantile. Every person who takes him up is an accepted substitute for his mother, and he will clamber slowly about one's clothing for hours in supreme contentment. One thing I can never explain is that on the ground the baby is even more helpless than his parents. While they can hitch themselves along, body dragging, limbs outspread, until they reach the nearest tree, a young sloth is wholly without power to move. Placed on a flat bit of ground it rolls and tumbles about, occasionally greatly encouraged by seizing hold of its own foot or leg under the impression that at last it has encountered a branch.

Sloths sleep about twice as much as other mammals, and a baby sloth often gets tired of being confined in the heart of its mother's sleeping sphere, and creeping out under her arm will go on an exploring expedition around and around her. When over two weeks old it has strength to rise on its hind legs and sway back and forth like nothing else in the world. Its eyes are only a little keener than those of the parent, and it peers up at the foliage overhead with the most pitiful interest. It is slowly weaned from a milk diet to the leaves of the Cecropia, which the mother at first chews up for her offspring.

I once watched a young sloth about a month old and saw it leave its mother for the first time. As the old one moved slowly back and forth, pulling down Cecropia leaves and feeding on them, the youngster took firm grip on a leaf stem, mumbling at it with no success whatever. When finally it stretched around and found no soft fur within reach it set up a wail which drew the attention of the mother at once. Still clinging to her perch, she reached out a forearm to an unbelievable distance and gently hooked the great claws about the huddled infant, which at once climbed down the long bridge and tumbled headlong in the hollow awaiting it.

When a very young sloth is gently disentangled from its mother and hooked on to a branch something of the greatest interest happens. Instead of walking forward, one foot after the other, and upside down as all adult sloths do, it reaches up and tries to get first one arm then the other *over* the support, and to pull itself into an upright position. This would seem to be a reversion to a time — perhaps millions of years ago — when the ancestors of sloths had not yet begun to hang inverted from the branches. After an interval of clumsy reaching and wriggling about, the baby by accident grasps its own body or limb, and, in this case, convinced that it is at last anchored safely again to its mother, it confidently lets go with all its other claws and tumbles ignominiously to the ground.

The moment a baby sloth dies and slips from its grip on the mother's fur, it ceases to exist for her. If it could call out she would reach down an arm and hook it toward her, but simply dropping silently means no more than if a disentangled bur had fallen from her coat. I have watched such a sloth carefully and have never seen any search of her own body or of the surrounding branches, or a moment's distraction from sleep or food. An imitation of the cry of the dead baby will attract her attention, but if not repeated she forgets it at once.

It is interesting to know of the lives of such beings as this — chronic pacifists, normal morons, the superlative of negative natures, yet holding their own amidst the struggle for existence. Nothing else desires to feed on such coarse fodder, no other creature disputes with it the domain of the under side of branches, hence there is no competition. From our human point of view sloths are degenerate; from another angle they are among the most exquisitely adapted of living beings. If we humans, together with our brains, fitted as well into the possibilities of our own lives we should be infinitely finer and happier — and, besides, I should then be able to interpret more intelligently the life and the philosophy of sloths!

APPRECIATION HINTS

1. Why may the sloth properly be called a sluggard?
2. How did the mother act when her young one was removed?
3. What are the most deadly enemies of the sloth?
4. How is the sloth naturally protected by a " cloak of invisibility "?
5. How is the sloth protected by its structure?
6. Tell about the baby sloth's efforts to climb.
7. In what sense may the sloth be called degenerate?
8. In what sense may it be considered " among the most exquisitely adapted of living beings "?
9. Give other instances of animals which are hard to distinguish from their surroundings.
10. Compare the monkey's adaptation to life in the forest with the sloth's.
11. Write a composition based on the sense of the passing of time. Suggestions: Time Flies — and Time Crawls, Sloth Life versus Commuter Life, Some School Sloths.
12. Write a composition based on protective coloring. Suggestions: Camouflage, Protective Coloring of Birds, Protective Coloring of Insects, The Chameleon, If I Could Make Myself Invisible.
13. Read in *Nonsuch,* by Beebe, Chapter Six, " Flounders are Wonderful," a charming study in adaptation to environment.

In the time of Your Life — Live!   William Saroyan

An alarm clock will wake a man, but he has to get up by himself.

PLINY THE YOUNGER 62–114?

A BOY and his mother, attempting to escape from the tottering buildings of Misenum in ancient Italy, left their carriages stalled on the heaving road, and to avoid being trampled to death in the dark, turned aside and waited in terror through the terrible night of August 25th, 79 A.D. If they had not raised themselves from time to time to shake off the falling ashes we should never have read this vivid account of the last days of Pompeii by an eyewitness.

Pliny the Younger had recently been adopted by his uncle, who was the author of the famous *Natural History*. This account indicates that his uncle's intense curiosity about natural phenomena was in part responsible for his collapse and suffocation on the shore of the bay. The boy was staying with his mother at the villa of his uncle at Misenum on the Bay of Naples when the eruption took place. Misenum is at the western tip of the bay, which sweeps in an arc to the east and south; Vesuvius is about 20 miles away to the east; and Herculaneum, Pompeii, and Stabiae, popular seaside resorts before the eruption, lay close under the volcano. Herculaneum and Pompeii remained buried until 1860. About half of Pompeii has now been unearthed, and if you walk along the narrow streets you can get a clear picture of how people were living 1900 years ago at the moment of the catastrophe.

Pliny's restrained yet dramatic account of this famous catastrophe reads as if it were written by an able reporter on the spot. Pliny was evidently an eager student, and we know from other letters he wrote that his custom was to preserve his impressions in a notebook. It is recorded that he wrote a tragedy in Greek at the age of fourteen, and there is no doubt that he was ambitious to write well. But Pliny was a boy of seventeen or eighteen when the eruption occurred, and this account was written probably not less than twenty-seven years after the event.

The two accounts which follow are pieced together from two of Pliny's letters to Tacitus, the great historian, who had asked Pliny for information about the death of his uncle and his own escape.

The Eruption of Vesuvius

MY UNCLE was at Misenum in supreme command of the fleet. On August 24th, about one o'clock in the afternoon, my mother drew his attention to the appearance of a cloud, unusually large and of a strange shape. He had taken a sun bath followed by a cold bath, and was lying down after lunch, reading. He immediately put on his shoes and climbed to a spot whence he could better see this phenomenon. None of the people who were looking at the cloud from a distance were certain from which mountain it was coming (we found out afterward that it was Vesuvius); it was more like a pine-tree than anything else, for it shot up into a trunk of great height and then spread out into several branches. Sometimes it looked white, sometimes spotted, as though it had drawn up earth or cinders.

To a scholar like my uncle a natural phenomenon of this magnitude seemed worthy of closer study. So he ordered a launch and said I could go with him if I liked. But I said that I would rather go on with my studies, for, as it happened, he had given me some writing to do. Just as he was leaving the house a note came from Rectina, the wife of Bassus, who was terrified at the approaching danger; his villa stood just below ours, and there was no means of escape except by sea; she begged my uncle to save her from this perilous position. So he changed his mind and went out in the guise of a rescuer rather than a scientific observer. Large boats were launched, and he embarked with the intention of carrying help not only to Rectina, but to many others who lived along that shore because it was so pictur-esque. Therefore he hastened in the direction whence fugitives were coming and steered a straight course for the point of danger; so free from fear was he that he dictated and noted down all the motions and shapes of that terrible portent as he went along.

Already ashes were falling on the ships, and the nearer they drew the hotter and thicker grew the showers; then came pumice-stones and other stones, blackened and scorched and cracked by fire, while the sea ebbed suddenly and the shore was blocked by land-slides. The steersman was for turning back, and my uncle hesitated for a moment, and then said to him, "Fortune favors the brave. Try to reach Pomponianus." Pomponianus was at Stabiae, right across the corner of the Bay (for the sea sweeps far into the curving shore just there), where the danger was not yet close at hand; but it was in full view and certain to come nearer as it spread, so he had packed up and gone into a boat, ready to push off directly the contrary wind fell. This wind blew my uncle into Stabiae, and he embraced Pom-ponianus, who was trembling with fright, cheering him up and en-couraging him; in order to calm his friend's fears by showing how safe he felt himself, he ordered a bath, after which he sat down to dinner in high good humor, or at least he managed to assume a mask of good humor, which is equally wonderful.

Meanwhile, broad sheets of flame broke out all over Mount Vesuvius, rising high in the air and lighting up the sky, their bright-ness silhouetted against the darkness of the night. My uncle tried to quiet people's fears by saying that fires had been left burning by terrified peasants when they deserted their houses, which were now in flames and causing this light. Then he went to bed and really slept, for, being a stout man, he breathed heavily and loudly, so that he was heard by the people who were waiting about outside his door. But the courtyard which led to his room was covered to such a depth under a drift of ashes and pumice stones that if he had stayed in bed any longer he would not have been able to get out of the door.

So he was wakened and joined Pomponianus and the others, who had been keeping watch. They consulted together as to whether it would be better to stay under cover or to go wandering about in the open. For the house was beginning to totter under the frequent and violent earthquakes, and it seemed to rock to and fro as though it had been shaken from its foundations. On the other hand, if they went outside they had the falling pumice stones to fear, though, being porous, they were light. After comparing the two risks they chose the latter. They tied pillows on their heads with tablecloths; this was their only protection against the showers of stones and ashes.

Day had now dawned elsewhere, but with them was darkness, blacker and deeper than the deepest night, though here and there it was relieved by torches and other lights. They decided to go down to the shore in order to see from close at hand whether the sea would allow them to get away, but the waves were still high and contrary. There my uncle lay down on a disused sail and again and again called for cold water, which he drank. Then flames, heralded by a strong smell of sulphur, put the others to flight and roused him. Leaning on two slaves he managed to stand up, but instantly fell down again; I think his breathing was blocked by the thick fumes, which choked the narrow passage of his throat; it was never very strong and often got inflamed. When daylight returned — three days after his death — his body was found without any wound or scar, covered with the clothes he had been wearing. He looked more like a man asleep than dead. . . .

After my uncle had gone I spent the rest of the day in study; for I had stayed at home for this purpose. Then I had a bath and supper and went to bed, but I got little sleep and that only in snatches. For several days beforehand we had had earthquakes, which did not alarm us much, as they are common in Campania. But that night the shocks were so violent that the very universe seemed to be uprooted. Mother rushed into my bedroom; I was just getting up, meaning to wake her if she was asleep. We sat down in the courtyard of the house, which separated us by a small space from the sea. I don't know whether I ought to be called brave or foolhardy — I was only seventeen — but I sent for a volume of Livy, the historian, and went on reading it and even copying extracts from it, as though tomorrow would do.

Then in came a friend of my uncle's, who had lately arrived from Spain to visit him; seeing Mother and me sitting there and me actually reading, he spoke sharply to me for being so confident and to her for putting up with it. But I took no notice and remained glued to my book.

It was now six o'clock in the morning, but the light was still faint and tired-looking. The buildings round us were already trembling, and, though we stood on open ground, we should certainly be in danger if they fell. Then we decided to leave the town. When we got beyond the houses we stopped, and there went through an experience which was wonderful but very terrible. The carriages we had ordered to come with us could not keep still, even though they were on level ground and wedged with stones; we saw the sea sucked back to its inmost depths and driven back by the shaking of the earth. On the other side a black, dreadful cloud of fiery vapor yawned open, bursting into weird ribbons of fire, with twisting, forked tongues of flame: they were like flashes of lightning, only larger.

Then the Spanish friend took command and said sharply: " If your brother — your uncle (turning to me) — is still alive, he wants you to be saved; if he is dead he wants you to survive him. Why do you hesitate and linger here? " We said that our own safety was nothing to us if we were uncertain of his. So our friend waited no longer, but rushed away from the danger zone as fast as he could go.

Soon afterward the cloud came down upon the earth and covered the sea; it had encircled and hidden the island of Capri and even blotted out Cape Misenum. Then Mother began to beg and pray and finally to order me to escape as best I could. " You are young," she said, " I am old and good for nothing. I shall die happy, if only I have not caused your death." I said that I would not be saved without her, so I took her by the hand and made her hurry along. Already ashes were falling, but only here and there; I looked behind me and saw dense blackness just at our backs, spreading over the earth like a torrent. " Let us turn aside," I said, " while we can see; then we shan't be knocked down in the road and trampled on by the crowds in the dark."

We had hardly sat down before blackness overtook us, not the blackness of a cloudy or moonless night, but of a room that is shut up with the lamp out. You could hear women shrieking, children screaming, men shouting; some were looking for their parents, others for their children, and others for their wives or husbands, able to recognize them only by their voices; one man would be lamenting his own fate; another the fate of his dear ones; some in terror of death were praying to die. Many were praying to the gods; but most declared that the gods were no more, and that this was the last eternal night of the world.

Gradually it grew light; we did not think it was daylight, but only the sign of approaching fire; however, the fire did not come very near us, and the darkness fell again, and another heavy shower of ashes. All the time we kept on getting up and shaking ourselves; otherwise we should have been buried and crushed under their weight.

At last this darkness melted away into a kind of smoke or cloud and vanished; then followed real daylight, and even the sun came out, though it looked pale as in an eclipse. To our trembling eyes everything appeared different, being covered with deep drifts of ashes. We went back to Misenum, took what rest we could, and passed an anxious night hovering between hope and fear; fear got the upper hand, for the earthquakes were still going on. But even then, after all the dangers we had gone through with the prospect of still worse things ahead of us, we had no idea of leaving the town without news of my uncle.

APPRECIATION HINTS

1. What was the shape of the cloud they saw coming from Vesuvius?
2. What did the elder Pliny do when he saw the cloud?
3. What were the next signs of the eruption on the land and sea, and on Mount Vesuvius?
4. How did Pomponianus and the elder Pliny protect themselves from the falling pumice?
5. Describe the death of the elder Pliny.
6. On what date in August was his body recovered?

7. Why did not Pliny accompany his uncle?
8. What signs of the eruption does Pliny record after he and his mother had escaped beyond the houses?
9. Where did they go when the darkness melted away?
10. What date was it when they returned to Misenum?
11. Trace from these two letters the various stages of the eruption from August 24th.
12. How do you account for the apparent unconcern of the uncle and the nephew?
13. Write a composition based on your own observation of a fire, hurricane, cyclone, flood, blizzard, or thunderstorm.
14. Write a composition in which you explain the scientific causes of eruptions, earthquakes, floods, geysers, or tidal waves.
15. Read *The Last Days of Pompeii*, by Bulwer Lytton.
16. Read in *The Outline of Science*, by J. A. Thomson, vol. 4, page 927, the account of another eruption of Vesuvius described by an eyewitness.

MOPPING UP THE ATLANTIC

In the midst of this sublime and terrible storm, Dame Partington, who lived upon the beach, was seen at the door of her house with mop and pattens, trundling her mop, squeezing out the sea-water, and vigorously pushing away the Atlantic Ocean. The Atlantic was roused; Mrs. Partington's spirit was up. But I need not tell you that the contest was unequal; the Atlantic Ocean beat Mrs. Partington. Sydney Smith

H. J. MULLER 1890– THE vivid symbol employed in the following essay, by which a cord reaching from New Haven to the center of J. P. Morgan's desk in his office in Wall Street is made to represent the elapse of time since life began on the earth, shows that the discovery of America occurred one and a half inches from the end of the cord at the center of Mr. Morgan's desk. You would have to slice off a very thin section of the cord to represent the last twenty-five years. And yet more progress has been made in the solution of evolution's riddles during the past quarter century than in all previous time. In other words during the time represented by the last one-fortieth of an inch of the cord, we have learned more about what has been going on since life began than in all those ages of previous time represented by the distance from Yale to Wall Street.

Whence has come this burst of knowledge? In the words of Professor Conklin of Princeton "organic evolution is no longer a hypothesis. It is an experimental fact; new species *have been built while we look on,* and in some cases we know how they have been built." Some of the most amazing results have come from experiments conducted by H. J. Muller, the author of the following essay, on the *Drosophila,* which is the fancy name for the common fruit fly or the vinegar fly, which breeds in decaying fruit. When the reproductive cells of this fly are stimulated with X rays, the hereditary units can be rearranged, and the results of the rearrangement appear in the next generation. One of the results of this X-ray stimulation that Muller reported was an increase in the proportion of males to females; another was a change in eye color.

It is all too easy to imagine the manifold developments that may be possible after men have learned to make the kind of fruit fly they want. But the real importance of these experiments is that they show us for the first time what mechanisms have been at work in the development of species all along the line — in the making of the dinosaurs crashing about in Harlem, of the monkeys sporting near Forty-second Street, of King Tut standing on Mr. Morgan's desk. And they also suggest, as our author says that we must first seek control of the very small world before we seek to control the very great.

How Has Man Been Made?

OUR IDEAS of what sort of progress is possible or desirable for man must depend in part at least upon our views of his nature, his manner of origination, the methods by which changes have occurred and can occur in him, and the relation which he bears to the rest of nature. . . .

. . . Compared with a living human cell, the mechanism of the most delicate chronometer is perhaps as coarse and simple as is the mechanism of a crowbar when compared with the chronometer itself. And we are composed of many trillions of cells of manifold types, put together in highly special ways. How fine and intricate the organization within an individual cell may be is best realized by thinking of the fact that in development an entire man (or other animal) automatically shapes itself, and grows, from a single cell (the fertilized egg cell), which therefore contains within itself the entire " machinery " to build a man — and that nevertheless the egg cell is itself so tiny that if we could collect together all the human eggs now existing which are going to form the next generation of mankind — two thousands of millions in number — we could pack them into a one-gallon pitcher! And all the fertilizing sperm cells, which equally with the egg cells determine the hereditary traits, would occupy only about half the amount of space of an ordinary aspirin tablet! As a matter of fact, the actual hereditary substance in the eggs would occupy only the same amount of space as the sperm; hence the hereditary substance of both eggs and sperm together would form just one tab-

let of the size of an aspirin tablet. It is hard to realize that in this
amount of physical space there now actually lie all the inheritable
structures for determining and for causing the production of all the
multitudinous characteristics of each individual person of the whole
future world population. Only, of course, this little mass of leaven
today is scattered over the face of the earth in several billion separate bits. Surely, then, this cell-substance is incomparably more intricate, as well as more portentous, than anything else on this earth.

It is thus evident that before we can properly understand the
living things of our world we must first learn to know the structure
of that new world-of-the-small which within the past few decades has
been opened to the mind of man. At first sight the attainment of such
knowledge seems a fantastic dream, but modern genetics [1] is already
beginning to invade the ultra-microscopic land inside the eggs and
sperm cells of the fly *Drosophila* [2] and of some other forms of life;
and to bring back from this survey what we actually call "maps," on
which are shown, within the chromosomes [3] of an individual germ
cell, the locations of hundreds of the separate hereditary particles or
"genes" that help to determine the various visible characters of the
individual growing from that germ cell. After all, the latter — though
tremendously more complicated — is by no means so minute a mechanism as that with which the inorganic chemist works. To gain adequate control over the world of things of our own size, then, we must
first seek knowledge and control of the very small world. The same
conclusion is being reached today, with equally great force, in the
realms of inorganic chemistry and of physics. And surely we cannot
hope to conquer successfully the great masses in the sphere of very
large things until we have control over those of our own size. The
precept therefore follows that, for man, the road to the macrocosm [4]
lies through the microcosm. [5]

Concerning the manner of origin of this staggeringly involved

[1] A study of the origin and development of individuals.
[2] The fruit fly.
[3] Minute bodies in the nucleus of the cell supposed to play an important
part in heredity.
[4] The world at large, exterior to man.
[5] The world of the very small.

fabric of organic nature, all its features bear witness, and countless secondary tokens testify, that it has arisen most gradually through the operation of natural forces no different in kind from those which are working within it today, and which are ultimately referable to the mode of combination of its atoms.

For many millions of years blind chemical forces must have acted and interacted in early times to build up ever different and more complicated organic compounds and systems of compounds; but a turning point was reached when from these shifting combinations those materials which we call " genes " happened to become formed. Genes are self-propagating — that is, growing, multiplying particles within the organic system, which may by their chemical activity affect the characteristics of the system in all sorts of ways: its chemical properties, its shape, its size, its internal and external structure (fine and gross), and its behavior. The genes are themselves subject to occasional internal chemical alterations, or " mutations," which do not deprive them of their power to grow but do change the nature of their action upon the system. From the time of the birth of these mutable genes onward, the different genes (or the little systems of organic matter containing an association of genes) would necessarily enter into a destructive competition for growth and multiplication against each other. Relatively few of all that were produced in the multiplication process would now be able to survive, and to increase still further; indeed this would occur only in the case of those rare ones in which mutations had happened to result in genes whose action was especially favorable for the growth and multiplication of the gene itself and of the organic system (or " protoplasm ") containing it. The other organic corpuscles, containing genes that had not mutated, or that had mutated in ways unfavorable to their growth, were meanwhile weeded out. By the repetition of these events, times without number, a more and more complexly efficient organization became built up within those protoplasmic masses which did manage to persist and multiply. So, step by step, through mutation (the alteration of genes) and heredity (the multiplication of genes) the millions of marvelously fashioned species of animals and plants which now exist were differentiated and integrated.

It should be distinctly realized that, in all of this, there is no evidence of an internal principle in organic nature causing beneficial, adaptive, admirable, or desirable changes to occur, rather than deleterious ones. In fact, the author has found that in the flies the harmful mutations far outnumber the beneficial ones, and this finding is being confirmed in other organisms. Thus, in spite of the great preponderance of detrimental variations, what we call progress ensues in the end, simply because, as Darwin pointed out (and we are not overthrowing Darwin in modern biology, but rather are building ever higher upon the basis that he laid down), the harmful variants perish in the struggle, whereas the accidentally beneficial ones survive. As this happens repeatedly, beneficial characters accumulate in the race. But we can see here that immeasurably more germ plasms finally die than manage to continue, and we owe all our wonderful frame to the cruelty of nature, which from step to step allowed the animals carrying our ancestral genes to multiply only at the cost of a life-and-death struggle in which the others, usually the vast majority, finally perished miserably.

Note, then, that though the evolutionary process may be described as a " progress " in complexity or adaptation, it does not necessarily result in an increase in the well-being or the happiness of the competing individuals, because it provides all survivors with increasingly deadly weapons in a great world war that not only pits species against species, but still more makes the individuals of the same species (in some cases, of different groups of the species) competitors of each other. The latest upstart, man, has been able partly to thwart this tendency only because, along with other advances, he has succeeded to some extent in limiting the growth of his naturally slow-breeding population, and in temporarily and occasionally amplifying his means of subsistence faster than his population has grown. Note also that although the creatures which were allowed to survive in any given age were those which happened, at that time, to fit, this did not by any means imply that they would be found to fit in the long run. Every germ plasm, every species, including man, is still thus on probation; and if — as much more often happens — it does not chance to have (or to acquire by mutation) genes so useful as those of the best competing species, it is eventually snuffed out ruthlessly.

Now this peculiar creature, man, has as yet had only a very short probationary period. Recent findings in radioactive rocks have given testimony that the entire process of organic evolution [6] on the earth has taken something like a thousand million years, at least — possibly even several times as long. Only by comparisons can we grasp such immensities, so let us imagine this period symbolized by a distance along a cord, each yard of which stands for 10,000 years, and which ends, in the present time, at some established point of reference — say the center of the private desk of J. P. Morgan in his office in Wall Street, New York City. To represent the beginning of organic evolution we should have to start the string many miles away — probably at least as far off as New Haven, possibly as far as Boston.

It is of interest to note that, on this scale, a human generation (from one birth to the next) would occupy somewhat less than an eighth of an inch, and that, if our symbolic cord were taken as about three-eighths of an inch wide (a small rope), the portion included within one generation would then be a disk-shaped cross section having the approximate dimensions of an ordinary aspirin tablet. Now this is just equal to the volume of hereditary material which actually is contained in one generation of mankind, and which is to be passed on to the next generation (as was explained on page 78). Hence our cord now acquires a further symbolic significance, in that it may be taken as representing in a certain real physical sense the evolving germ plasm of ourselves and our ancestors — though it would not everywhere be of equal width, as the numbers of the population change. Within this cord the fine fibers represent the chromosomes themselves, which are in fact filamentous bodies that intertwine, separate, and reunite in diverse ways as they pass along from generation to generation in the varying combinations resulting from sexual reproduction. In this cord, then, there would be represented, in one long line of ancestry, all the material which, from the beginning, has continued to make generation after generation of

[6] The evolution of things that have life.

progressing forms. Their bodies (or soma), which constituted a vastly greater volume, may be considered as a series of excrescences about the cord, formed under the influences emanating from the by-products of the cord's chemical activity. The evolutionary changes manifested in their multitudinous characteristics are but reflections of primary changes occurring within the potent particles (genes) composing the tiny filaments of the cord itself. While the cord in question shows our particular line of ancestry, the lines of the millions of other living species would be shown by other, parallel cords — some thin, some thick, some branching as time goes on and as species diverge from one another, and many coming to an early end as species become extinct; but practically all the "higher" forms, at any rate, tracing back their origin to one original cord in the beginning. At any given place there is but a single one, out of all the mass of cords, which has led on so as finally to issue in our branch; this may be distinguished, in our figurative representation, by giving it a red color. It is this red cord which may be regarded as the red "thread of destiny," in a rather literal sense. Its free end is even now being spun further, being transfigured by mutation, being twined and inter-woven, to give a new sort of living world, dependent on its new properties.

   Let us now start at the beginning of the mass of life cords — say at New Haven — and follow along them on their long way towards their present destination in New York City, observing what forms are assumed by their bodily outgrowths (soma) as we travel forward. Except to the trained biologist, it will prove a dreary trip for much the greater part of the distance. For in this whole journey there will be no actual "beasts" as we ordinarily think of them (four-footed land animals) until we are well within the limits of New York City. Not until we are passing through Harlem shall we see any creatures with fur or feathers — i.e., mammals or birds. And note that even at that stage in our journey tremendous reptiles — dinosaurs — are still crashing over the earth; they long remain dominant over the few little warm-blooded pioneers, and they do not disappear until after we cross Forty-second Street. Not far below that point monkeys make their first appearance; but from that point

southward the records show nothing higher than an ape until, having turned the corner of Wall Street, we actually confront our ter-
minal building. There, about 100 feet from the end of the cord, are
found the relics of the famous "missing link" — Pithecanthropus —
not yet a man, but passed beyond the ape. Well within the building,
and only about 15 feet from the desk in question, stands that stoop-
shouldered lowbrow, the Neanderthal man, whom we do not dignify
by classification in our species — the species self-styled *Homo
sapiens,* "man the wise."

Our own *Homo sapiens* leaves his first known remains within the
private office, only seven and a half feet from the desk. The earliest
known "civilization" (not over 14,000 years ago, according to maximum estimates) leaves its crockery a yard and a half from the desk.
On the desk, one foot from the center, stands old King Tut. Five
and a half inches from the center we mark the Fall of Rome and
the beginning of the Dark Ages. Only one and a half inches from the
present end of the cord come the discovery of America and the
promulgation of the Copernican theory — through which man opens
his eyes for the first time to the vastness of the world in which he
lives and to his own relative insignificance. Half an inch from the end
of the cord there start the first faint reverberations of the Industrial
Revolution, which set this desk here and which is now completely
transforming man's mode of existence. A quarter of an inch from the
end Darwin speaks, and man awakes to the transitory character of
his shape and his institutions.

Since we men are, in our present forms, such recent comers upon
the battlefield of the earth, what are the characteristics that have
made us successful in so short a time as all this indicates? The answer
is clear: the combination of intelligence and social behavior — or,
we may say, of cunning and co-operation — who e product is "tradition." Man cannot outrun, outbite, or outclaw the animals; but,
making tools and traps, he can outwit them. His native intelligence,
to be sure, is neither different in kind nor many times greater than
that of some other animals. Individually and untaught, he scarcely
has the wits to fashion the simplest tools. There seems to be needed
a fairly definite critical amount of intelligence (and possibly of the

impulse to imitate) before numerous experiences and customs are
naturally transferred from one animal to another. Man was the first
animal — at the least the first *gregarious* animal — to just overstep
this critical level of intelligence. Accordingly, since he does have the
social impulse to band with others of his kind, one little happy discovery after another, or one slight beneficial modification of usage —
generally hit upon by the most intelligent — has been passed along
from man to man, and from woman to child, in the progress of the
ages, till finally the average individual's cranium carries packed
within it the fruit of the combined experiences of many generations
of the most superior meddlers and tinkerers — engrafted in it not
by heredity at all (since there is no inheritance of acquired characters), but by that usually informal kind of education called " tradition." This process of accumulating tradition we call " social evolution."

Among the important useful traditions that in this way accumulated gradually among early men were language (which was especially important in accumulating more tradition and for which a
special gift was needed), the processes of making and using implements, the customs in regard to fire, food, bodily covering where
necessary, and shelter, and moral codes. And so, in spite of a con-
comitant load of disadvantageous traditions — some of them derived
from useful traditions that became outworn or perverted, others
doubtless based on misconceptions from the start — it has happened
that the not excessive intelligence of man has, after numberless generations (though, geologically speaking, in an extremely short time),
been multiplied to far beyond its native magnitude, thus " artifi-
cially " setting the capabilities of most groups of man at an immeas-
urable distance above those of the cleverest animals and enabling him
to dominate the earth.

APPRECIATION HINTS

1. What does the author mean by a " map " of the chromosomes?
2. What is the purpose of making such maps?
3. What is said about the nature of the genes?
4. There is no evidence that nature prefers changes which benefit us. How then has the race made progress?
5. How long has the evolution of life been going on?
6. What space of time does each yard of the cord represent?
7. What length of the cord will represent one human generation?
8. What do the fine fibers of the cord represent?
9. At what point in the journey from New Haven to J. P. Morgan's desk do mammals appear?
10. At what point does *homo sapiens* appear?
11. At what point do the dinosaurs disappear?
12. What has enabled man to be so successful in so short a time?
13. Can you report on human traits, like color-blindness, which follow certain laws of heredity?
14. Write a composition based on heredity in pets; for example, rabbits, white mice, guinea pigs.
15. Write a composition based on the brief history of *homo sapiens*. Suggestions: Man — the Upstart of the Earth, Can Man Control His Own Destiny?, The Sword of Science, King Tut Faces J. P. Morgan.
16. Read in *Literary Digest* for January 12, 1935, " Unfolding the ' Road-Map ' of Heredity." This article contains an illustration of a giant chromosome.
17. Read " Where Life Begins " in *Harper's* for February, 1937, and report to the class.

UNKNOWN SOLDIERS

Who knows whether the best of men be known? To be nameless in worthy deeds exceeds an infamous history, and who had not rather be the good thief than Pilate?
Sir Thomas Browne

DONALD CULROSS PEATTIE 1898–

DONALD PEATTIE was at work in the Agassiz laboratories at Harvard University extracting chlorophyll from ivy leaves. Chlorophyll is the one link between the sun and life as we know it. When he held the oily extract in his hand and studied its chemical structure, a sudden thought possessed his mind and quickened his pulse. He saw that chlorophyll, which enables us to feed on the sun's energy, and hemoglobin, the essence of our own blood, are closely similar in structure. So that you may, as he remarks, touch the flank of a beech and say, "We are of one blood, brother, thou and I."

In Mr. Peattie's books these fascinating wonders of science are interpreted to us by one who illuminates his thought with stories from his own experience. He is the poet-naturalist, sensitive to all that he observes in the life that lies about him. *A Book of Hours* records the impressions made on such a mind by the passage of time as the clock strikes it off hour by hour. In an essay occurring later in this volume Thoreau asserts that all memorable events happen in the early morning, because that is the only hour when we are really awake. But in the beautiful book from which this essay is taken Mr. Peattie finds an individuality and a character in each of the twenty-four hours as we go round the clock from the stroke of midnight.

Donald Culross Peattie began as a poet, when he won the Witter Bynner poetry prize at Harvard in 1922. Then he studied plants and plant life in many places, particularly in Florida and North Carolina, and more recently made a survey of the flora of the western states. He is a botanist; but don't be afraid that he is going to be dull when he writes as a botanist. He says of his book entitled *Flowering Earth*, 1939, "I have spent twenty years getting ready to write this book, and all the things that would make it thorough and dull I have tried to leave out." *An Almanac for Moderns*, 1935, was awarded the first annual medal of the Limited Editions Club as an American classic. *Singing in the Wilderness*, 1935, is a brilliant narrative of the life of Audubon — a naturalist's hymn to the America which he loves as Audubon loved it.

NOON STANDS overhead, and
from frontier to frontier the whistles salute it. So the cock is supposed
to blow his horn for midnight. But I know of no other animal than
man who makes anything of noon or does it homage. We blast the
zenith air; suddenly, in the cities, the offices empty, and out of them
the noon-flies swarm. White faces by the indistinguishable thousand
show themselves to the sun's yellow face.

Looking down upon the human nest, a naturalist on Venus
might suppose that its members responded simultaneously to the
immense phototropism [1] of high noon — the pull of light. Rather are
they abroad in search of that elusive restaurant where one may fare
better for a few cents less. The bright-winged ones skim the streets
looking for it, the girls clothed in all their salaries, eager with their
inexhaustible appetite for light sweet food and light sweet living.
The men and boys go hunting for it, driven by a hunger that is nerve
hunger; little they eat will go to muscle.

And there are other cravings; the public libraries at noon fill up.
When I was a young twelve-dollar-a-week noon-fly, and no bought
cooking could tempt me, I used sometimes to devour a book instead.
I remember the beautiful girl, of the Galician Jewish type, who came
there every noon and wrestled with the staggering city directory.
Most people, if they cannot find a name in the telephone book, give

[1] The power of light to bend or turn plants.

up their man as lost. Only the lost themselves sometimes learn that every adult among seven millions is listed in the enormous volumes, his name and residence and occupation, if any. The history of all our ephemerid [2] lives is there, and, if you go from volume to volume, you may trace the nomadism of each family, from one of our island wadis [3] to the next, the gradual dispersal of its children, the deceases of the patriarchs, the giving in marriage of the daughters. For whom was this Ruth searching? Father, brother, lover — I never learned, and she never found him, not at least in my city noons.

One o'clock is the executive's hour. There are rich menus in it, and there is leisure. Noon belongs to the people, and the food is such as they can pay for and consume in half an hour. Your noon-fly, presumably, is not of enough importance to need time for more than the endless fight against starvation.

But I wanted to mark the meridian with prayer in some form. I used to see people slipping into the cathedral, and out of envy I followed them. But there was nothing inside except a rose-water twilight. I knelt — I have no hesitancy about kneeling anywhere; it is one of the body's natural attitudes, the way to embrace a standing child or to drink from a spring — but no prayers came.

For a year I had been hiding books on ornithology and plants in my office desk. When spring came I threw up my princely job, at a time when a million returned soldiers were hunting for jobs, and went south. The heaviest part of my baggage was my books, and a hand lens and a pair of field glasses with a scratch in the left eye piece.

As I remember those Blue Ridge weeks they seem to me now to have been all noon. I remember that hour for its sheer sumptuousness, its excess of something good. The setting out and the coming back have faded from my memory. Only the noons are vivid because in them I was, myself, inactive. What I collected then that was green and growing was my thoughts.

The best place for noons is on a high rock, and the best attitude for them is the position that lichens assume. On your back, with your hand flung on your brow, you are in a posture of prayer. On your lips you take the communion of vertical light; it stains, as all wines do.

---

[2] Short.   [3] Watercourses.

So my hand became brown, and I learned a little and did a world of listening and seeing.

There was a valley bell, a very large and old one, that rang news of dinner — golden chicken, and spoon bread, and buttermilk from the springhouse, and soft hill water in the thick tumblers with the horseshoe mark pressed in their bottoms. The noon train, on the other side of the mountain, whistled salute to the zenith hour and from the farm between the brooks came up the sound of cocks blowing.

That was the hour when bushes tucked shade beneath them, like skirts, and nothing escaped the good tyranny of light. You would  have had to be a raccoon with a hollow tree at your command, or a beetle under a rock, to find total shadow at that hour. It was, indeed, the hour of the lizards, who shared the rock with me, of the golden wasp who shared the sweets of my luncheon, fanning the mica dust with the propeller breeze of its wings as it hovered, treading air. It was the hour, too, of the buzzard, who shared space and height with me, performing that feat of birds, a sudden upshooting ascent without a wing-stroke. There is no secret in it, of course; they ride to heaven on the strength of the upward column of air from the sun-baked valley floor. First grow your cambering wings,[4] and you may do the same.

Country noons are prodigal of time and economical of shadow. They invite to the sort of contemplating that is done with the head between the knees, with a good view of a single ant, and in the hearing of a brook.

Contemplation is an art not suddenly to be begun. It takes more time to arrive at it than it does to perform it like a prayer. I am not propounding a literary whimsy; I am talking about the way, it seems to me, that a man may look into himself by staring into the crystal of the world. This is the only safe introspection; the examining of the conscience by night has a great deal too much of the torchlit dungeon

[4] Wings which will take advantage of the wind because of their curvature

and the rack in it. It makes fanatics, and fanatics make life intolerable. Night is a season for music, for love play, for feasting, drinking, dancing, for that blent life of the senses and imagination. These are the ingredients of romance. And night is to lie with. There is no true light in it by which to judge life's colors.

I dare the cynic to try his thoughts out in the noon sunshine that is without shadow. How hard then it is to lock your door, to make a wax image of your fellow man and stick pins in it or melt it! Such stuff is night work. Under noon it is more likely you who will melt, upon your rock, while in the clearing, in the valley below you, man swings his ax — a sun-twinkle and a paddled blow — and man's wife, with the sun on her smooth hair and bare arms, walks out to bring him something: a meal in a pail, a kiss, a bit of news about a sick child or a child coming.

APPRECIATION HINTS

1. What do people do when the noon whistle blows?
2. What was the girl doing in the public library at noon?
3. What was the author's experience in the cathedral?
4. When he went south what did he take with him?
5. What food and drink did the valley bell suggest?
6. What did he see and hear on the high rock at noon?
7. What advantages does he find in daylight meditation?
8. Collect words and phrases which strike you as effective; for example, "noon-fly," "clothed in all their salaries."
9. Write a composition on some topic like the following: Lost Persons, The Old Farm Bell, Noon Whistle, Church Bells, Heat Wave in the City, My Best Time for Meditation.
10. Write a composition based on some other period of the day. Suggestions: Midnight, Daybreak, Twilight, Midafternoon.
11. Read in *A Book of Hours*, by Donald Culross Peattie, the impressions made on him by other hours.
12. Read in Peattie's *Flowering Earth*, the chapters entitled " Chlorophyll — the Sun Trap." " Diatoms — the Grass of the Sea," and " A Transplanting."
13. Read in *Singing in the Wilderness*, by Peattie, Chapter XIII, about Audubon's imprisonment for debt.

GAME OF CHESS

Suppose it were perfectly certain that the life and fortune of every one of us would, one day or other, depend on his winning or losing a game of chess. Don't you think that we should all consider it to be a primary duty to learn at least the names and moves of the pieces; to have a notion of a gambit, and a keen eye for all the means of giving and getting out of check? Do not you think that we should look with a disapprobation amounting to scorn, upon a father who allowed his son, or the state which allowed its members, to grow up without knowing a pawn from a knight?

Yet it is a very plain and elementary truth, that the life, the fortune, and the happiness of every one of us, and, more or less, of those who are connected with us, do depend upon our knowing something of the rules of a game infinitely more difficult and complicated than chess. It is a game which has been played for untold ages, every man and woman of us being one of the two players in a game of his or her own. The chessboard is the world, the pieces are the phenomena of the universe, the rules of the game are what we call the laws of Nature. The player on the other side is hidden from us. We know that his play is always fair, just, and patient. But also we know, to our cost, that he never overlooks a mistake, or makes the smallest allowance for ignorance. To the man who plays well the highest stakes are paid, with that sort of overflowing generosity with which the strong shows delight in strength. And one who plays ill is checkmated — without haste, but without remorse.

Thomas Henry Huxley: *A Liberal Education*

WORDS AND MUSIC

WHY IS it that coal miners strike but artists don't? Whether we buy his pictures or not, the true artist goes on painting, just as Adam and Eve went on working and planting in the first garden and, apparently, enjoyed it. That joy of theirs, writes Charles E. Montague, "goes on to this day wherever a painter, a writer, or any sort of artist is plying his trade to the top of his form."

The essays in this section are by artists plying their trade. They are about art, or the instruments of art, and are the means of bringing to us this joy in creating beautiful things ourselves or appreciating the creations of others. They are pleasant to read and important for two reasons. The United States, so long busy in turning its resources into products for practical use, is rapidly becoming the art center of the world. Its citizens are aware that houses, towns, furniture, rivers and roads ought to be beautiful as well as useful. So we must develop the inner power to discriminate between what is beautiful and what is ugly. Then too these essays help to tell us how leisure may be joyful instead of boring; they help us to answer the question, what may we do in our vacation. We may all share in the joy of the artist; in some art, craft, or hobby we may become creators.

In "Music at Night" Aldous Huxley translates the effect of music into words, and tells us how to listen. David Grayson shows us how the life of a super-salesman may be lighted up, once it feels the beauty of great poetry. All art is a kind of communication, but the supreme instrument of communication is language. Recently people have begun to realize that language can go far to set the world on fire, and that it is high time we knew more about how it works inside and outside of us. S. I. Hayakawa very skilfully explains how much of our language is either snarling or purring; and Hilaire Belloc plays about with one common little word like a cat with a ball of knitting wool.

ALDOUS HUXLEY 1894–   ALMOST without notic-
ing that it came to
pass, we can now listen to music, and often good music, at almost
any time of the day or night. In your grandfather's boyhood people
were, in comparison, without music. To be sure, much of the music
we hear, like that described in the following essay, is mechanically
produced, but the popularity of singing and playing instruments has
been increasing side by side with the widening use of radio and
records. The orchestras and bands and choirs of many high schools
and colleges are magnificent organizations, and their performances
are often of high merit.

But the excellence of these performances depends on audiences
who can appreciate quality in music and can distinguish the good
from the indifferent. So, of course, do the radio programs. We shall
have better music, better plays, better movies, and more beautiful
houses when people want them. People will want them in proportion
as they become sensitive to values in the arts.

The first essay in this section, by an eminent English novelist
and critic, will help to sharpen our perception when we listen to
music. To write adequately about the effect of music demands a delicate sensitiveness to combinations and sequences in sound, and, in
addition, a skill in translating these impressions into fitting words.
Mr. Huxley could hear what the *Benedictus* seemed to " say "; and
then he could find the means of expressing it in language. " Solid clots
of harmonious sounds "; " the blessedness at the heart of things "; such
phrases indicate one who can both hear and then interpret music.
And the essay will also serve to forewarn us against thinking that
when we are given the " plain sense " of a poem or the plot of a play
we know its meaning, or that when we have a picture explained to us
we have received the message of the artist. In " Music at Night " Mr.
Huxley is not content with blurting out what the *Benedictus* " said "
to him, for " the substance of a work of art is inseparable from its
form "; the words that describe a thing of beauty must also reflect a
part of it.

Aldous Leonard Huxley is best known for his novels, *Antic Hay,*
1923; *Point Counter Point,* 1928; and *Brave New World,* 1932.

MOONLESS, this June night is all the more alive with stars. Its darkness is perfumed with faint gusts from the blossoming lime trees, with the smell of wetted earth and the invisible greenness of the vines. There is silence; but a silence that breathes with the soft breathing of the sea and, in the thin shrill noise of a cricket, insistently, incessantly harps on the fact of its own deep perfection. Far away, the passage of a train is like a long caress, moving gently, with an inexorable gentleness, across the warm living body of the night.

Music, you say; it would be a good night for music. But I have music here in a box, shut up, like one of those bottled djinns in the *Arabian Nights,* and ready at a touch to break out of its prison. I make the necessary mechanical magic, and suddenly, by some miraculously appropriate coincidence (for I had selected the record in the dark, without knowing what music the machine would play), suddenly the introduction to the *Benedictus* in Beethoven's *Missa Solemnis* begins to trace its patterns on the moonless sky.

The *Benedictus.* Blessed and blessing, this music is in some sort the equivalent of the night, of the deep and living darkness, into which, now in a single jet, now in a fine interweaving of melodies, now in pulsing and almost solid clots of harmonious sound, it pours itself, stanchlessly pours itself, like time, like the rising and falling, falling trajectories of a life. It is the equivalent of the night in another mode of being, as an essence is the equivalent of the flowers from which it is distilled.

There is, at least there sometimes seems to be, a certain blessedness lying at the heart of things, a mysterious blessedness, of whose existence occasional accidents or providences (for me, this night is one of them) make us obscurely, or it may be intensely, but always fleetingly, alas, always only for a few brief moments aware. In the *Benedictus* Beethoven gives expression to this awareness of blessedness. His music is the equivalent of this Mediterranean night, or rather of the blessedness at the heart of the night, of the blessedness as it would be if it could be sifted clear of irrelevance and accident, refined and separated out into its quintessential purity.

" *Benedictus, benedictus . . .*" One after another the voices take up the theme propounded by the orchestra and lovingly meditated through a long and exquisite solo (for the blessedness reveals itself most often to the solitary spirit) by a single violin. " *Benedictus, benedictus . . .*" And then, suddenly, the music dies; the flying djinn has been rebottled. With a stupid insect-like insistence, a steel point rasps and rasps the silence.

At school, when they taught us what was technically known as English, they used to tell us to " express in our own words " some passage from whatever play of Shakespeare was at the moment being rammed, with all its annotations — particularly the annotations — down our reluctant throats. So there we would sit, a row of inky urchins, laboriously translating " now silken dalliance in the wardrobe lies " into " now smart silk clothes lie in the wardrobe," or " To be or not to be " into " I wonder whether I ought to commit suicide or not." When we had finished, we would hand in our papers, and the presiding pedagogue would give us marks, more or less, according to the accuracy with which " our own words " had " expressed " the meaning of the Bard.

He ought, of course, to have given us naught all round with a hundred lines to himself for ever having set us the silly exercise. Nobody's " own words," except those of Shakespeare himself, can possibly " express " what Shakespeare meant. The substance of a work of art is inseparable from its form; its truth and its beauty are two and yet, mysteriously, one. The verbal expression of even a metaphysic [1] or a system of ethics is very nearly as much of a work of art as a love poem. The philosophy of Plato expressed in the " own words " of Jowett is not the philosophy of Plato; nor in the " own words " of, say, Billy Sunday,[2] is the teaching of St. Paul St. Paul's teaching.

" Our own words " are inadequate even to express the meaning of other words; how much more inadequate, when it is a matter of rendering meanings which have their original expression in terms of music or one of the visual arts! What, for example, does music " say "? You can buy at almost any concert an analytical program that will tell you exactly. Much too exactly; that is the trouble. Every analyst has his own version. Imagine Pharaoh's dream interpreted successively by Joseph, by the Egyptian soothsayers, by Freud, by Rivers, by Adler, by Jung, by Wohlgemuth: [3] it would " say " a great many different things. Not nearly so many, however, as the Fifth Symphony has been made to say in the verbiage of its analysts. Not nearly so many as the Virgin of the Rocks and the Sistine Madonna have no less lyrically said.

Annoyed by the verbiage and this absurd multiplicity of attributed " meanings," some critics have protested that music and painting signify nothing but themselves; that the only things they " say " are things, for example, about modulations and fugues,[4] about colour values and three-dimensional forms. That they say anything about human destiny or the universe at large is a notion which these purists dismiss as merely nonsensical.

If the purists were right, then we should have to regard painters and musicians as monsters. For it is strictly impossible to be a human being and not to have views of some kind about the universe at large, very difficult to be a hu-

[1] A theory of existence or knowledge.
[2] A revivalist preacher.
[3] Five psychologists with somewhat different explanations of dreams.
[4] A musical composition in several harmonizing parts which are independent in melody.

man being and not to express those views, at any rate by implication. Now, it is a matter of observation that painters and musicians are *not* monsters. Therefore . . . The conclusion follows, unescapably.

It is not only in program music and problem pictures that composers and painters express their views about the universe. The purest and most abstract artistic creations can be, in their own peculiar language, as eloquent in this respect as the most deliberately tendentious. . . .

The limits of criticism are very quickly reached. When he has said " in his own words " as much, or rather as little, as " own words " can say, the critic can only refer his readers to the original work of art: let them go and see for themselves. Those who overstep the limit are either rather stupid, vain people, who love their " own words " and imagine that they can say in them more than " own words " are able in the nature of things to express. Or else they are intelligent people who happen to be philosophers or literary artists and who find it convenient to make the criticism of other men's work a jumping-off place for their own creativity.

What is true of painting is equally true of music. Music " says " things about the world, but in specifically musical terms. Any attempts to reproduce these musical statements " in our own words " is necessarily doomed to failure. We cannot isolate the truth contained in a piece of music; for it is a beauty-truth and inseparable from its partner. The best we can do is to indicate in the most general terms the nature of the musical beauty-truth under consideration and to refer curious truth-seekers to the original. Thus, the introduction to the *Benedictus* in the *Missa Solemnis* is a statement about the blessedness that is at the heart of things. But this is about as far as " own words " will take us. If we were to start describing in our " own words " exactly what Beethoven felt about this blessedness, how he conceived it, what he thought its nature to be, we should very soon find ourselves writing lyrical nonsense in the style of the analytical program makers. Only music, and only Beethoven's music, and only this particular music of Beethoven, can tell us with any precision what Beethoven's conception of the blessedness at the heart of things actually was. If we want to know, we must listen — on a still June night, by preference, with the breathing of the invisible sea for background, to the music and the scent of lime trees drifting through the darkness, like some exquisite soft harmony apprehended by another sense.

APPRECIATION HINTS

1. From the first paragraph, where would you guess Huxley was writing?
2. What sense impressions contribute to the picture we get in the first paragraph?
3. What is the central message of the *Benedictus* when he listens to it?
4. Why can't we express a great poem " in our own words "? Explain how its substance and its form are related.
5. How is it that concert programs are sometimes misleading?
6. How was " English " taught to Mr. Huxley?
7. How far is it possible to go in telling what music " says "?
8. How did the other senses help him to comprehend the *Benedictus* as he listened to it?
9. From what plays of Shakespeare are the two quotations taken?
10. Illustrate with examples of poems, pieces of music, pictures, or pieces of sculpture the statement that " the substance of a work of art is inseparable from its form."
11. Illustrate what Huxley says by taking a poem you like, putting it in your own words, and then comparing the two.
12. Write a composition based on a play, movie, concert, piece of music, poem or painting which you like.
13. Write a composition on one of the following topics, or on a topic suggested by them: How Music Affects Me, The Best Place to Listen to Music, Music (or Art) at School, Pictures and Music (Does any music you know suggest definite scenes to you?), Fine Recordings of Music, What Beethoven (or some other composer) Means to Me.

THE QUEST

The indefatigable pursuit of an unattainable Perfection, even though it consist in nothing more than in the pounding of an old piano, is what alone gives a meaning to our life on this unavailing star. Logan Pearsall Smith

HILAIRE BELLOC 1870–

SO MUCH life was poured into Hilaire Belloc that it constantly boiled over. When friends of Christopher Morley called to see Mr. Belloc at his home in England they found him a-straddle on a gigantic wine cask which had just arrived from France, about to bottle the wine with the assistance of a multitude of friends. His life at Oxford was tumultuous; he swam, rode, wrestled, and argued passionately, always on the side of the minority. Exuberant himself, he was the cause of exuberance in all about him. His flashing wit and his infectious laughter made his rooms an informal debating club. These Balliol days were later recalled in the fine poem addressed to his college friends fighting overseas, with the refrain —

> Balliol made me, Balliol fed me,
> Whatever I had, she gave me again;
> And the best of Balliol loved and led me,
> God be with you, Balliol men.

This exuberance of Hilaire Belloc is reflected in the number and variety of his books. One might expect the *Retreat from Moscow* from one who had had four great-uncles fighting as generals under Napoleon. But few historians write such things as *Cautionary Tales* — those terrible tragedies which happen to wilful children who ignore sage advice; children like Maria who would make faces until that last one which she couldn't unmake, or Sarah, who refused to learn to read, and what happened when she walked past the sign " Beware of the very furious bull." Mr. Belloc's sparkling mind is best seen in his many volumes of essays. These are mixed menus — a thousand little inquiries into the nooks and crannies, the odds and ends of his many-sided life and his immense reading. The all-inclusive character of some of these essay volumes is indicated by their titles: *This, That, and the Other; On Everything; On Anything; On Something; On Nothing;* and *On,* (1923), from which this essay is taken. So profoundly did Hilaire Belloc believe that life was meant to be enjoyed, that even when he is most serious the reader must always be prepared for fantasy. Thus his detective stories such as *The Man Who Made Gold* and *Green Overcoat* are likely to develop into burlesques.

Dark eyes adventure bring: the blue, serene,
Do promise Paradise — and yours are green.

THIS little jewel — called " The Lover's Complaint " — is ascribed by some to Herrick. They are wrong. It proceeds from a younger but already faltering pen.

I introduce it only at the head of this to illustrate the singular depth, the weight, the value of the word " and." Even in the English tongue, the noblest vehicle of expression (but in this point weak), the word " and " plays its subtle parts.

We lack the double " and " of antiquity — that subtle repetitive effect in which the classics abound. We have no " *que* " to our " *et* "; we have no τε to our και; we have only our plain " and." But even so, our plain " and " has much diversity about it: a versatile, mercurial word: a knight in the chess play of prose.

" How is this? " you say. " ' And ' would seem to be but a redundant word to express some addition already apparent."

" ' He was drunk, disorderly! ' ' And ' would seem to be stuck in between the two affirmations from a sort of laziness of the mind."

You are wrong. It is a great pleasure to me to tell you that you are wrong.

Even if " and " only pursued this function of letting the mind repose it might be welcomed as a bed; but it does much more. It introduces emphasis, as in the poignant sentence: " Their choice was turbot — and boiled." It also has an elevating effect, hooking up something to the level of the rest; as where it is written:

> Nibbity, bibbity, bobbity bo! —
> *And* the little brown bowl —
> We'll drink to the Barley Mow!

The little brown bowl would have come in absurdly: it would have jolted the mind like a bump in the road, were it not for that precious little " and," which catches it neatly up, putting upon one level that which goes before with that which comes after.

" And " is also indicative. Thus a man whom you meet talks glibly upon one subject after another, rapidly, yet more rapidly, tumbling over himself, desiring to avoid your eye. But he must take breath. You seize your moment and you say, " And what about that five pounds? " The " and " makes all the difference. It makes your remark part of the conversation. A gesture, not a blow.

In the same way you can recall an omitted name. When you have praised Tom, Dick, Harry, you add gently, " And Jack, what about Jack? " It is a pleasant, easy reproach or a reminder. Very much nicer than saying, " Why not a word about Jack? " — which would be brutal.

" And " is also what the older grammarians have called stammerative — that is, it fills a chasm in the public speeches of public men, though here it is not so useful as certain other sounds. I have made a study of the sounds common to politicians in distress. I find that out of one hundred occasions " er — er " will come in eighty times; " I — I — I " eleven times; the less graceful " and . . . , and . . . , and " during periods of embarrassment only accounts for five. Moreover, the repeated " and " is hardly ever used in the absolute; by public speakers it is nearly always used with " er."

" And " also has the value of an affix. It comes before a lot of little phrases, where it acts like glue, sticking that little phrase on to the rest — " and " if, " and " even, " and " though; a humble use, but necessary enough, allowing the mind to work in a soft material.

" And " has various rhetorical uses which are to be admired — you can make long lists with it.

So attractive is " and " to the human mind that it will often expand itself, developing like a lot of soap bubbles — " and so," " and moreover," " and also." But the best of all these phrases — the king of them — is " and also, what is more." It is the most familiar of all phrases in the mouths of politicians. Do violence to yourself, force yourself to listen to a politician making speeches in private conversation as is the politician's way. You will hear that phrase repeated. " And also, what is more." It is native to the tub-thumping fraternity. These things give a sentence the advantage of piling up wordy wealth, as it were, very satisfactory to the fatigued or the empty or the hesitant.

Those great men, our fathers, felt about " and " something reverend or peculiar, so that they hardly thought of it as a word, but as a sort of symbol. They put it at the end of the alphabet, calling it " ampersand." It is one of the worst things about our detestable time that this ancient national thing " ampersand " is forgotten. The old refrain used to be: a, b, c, . . . , x, y, z, *ampersand* — that long word " ampersand," that fine ritual title, referred to the symbol " & " which " and " alone of words possesses. You find it in the old horn books.[1] The children of England knew it by heart for centuries. But the modern flood came: it is gone.

The enemies of " and " will have it that a good style in English is to be obtained by cutting out " and." These are the same people who say that a good style is to be obtained by cutting out adjectives. There are no such short cuts. Also, to be an enemy of " and " is to be an enemy of all good things. It is to fear exuberance, which is the tide of life.

" And " has, again, rhythmical value, as in the ecclesiastical or liturgical line:

And Parson and Clerk and the Devil and all

— with hosts of other lines which dignify the vast storehouse of the English lyric.

Of the modern masterpieces there is one — the best known of all,

[1] The old primers for children, in which the page was covered with transparent horn.

perhaps — where " and " does an enormous amount of work, which is the poem of *Innisfree*. It gives the rhythm as well as the mystery. I should like to see what the fools who are for cutting out " and " would make of that poem.

But the most sublime use of " and," alas! we have not. It is the " and " disjunctive; on which turned one of the great moments of history.

For you must know that when the second Council of Nicea finally condemned the monstrosities of the Iconoclasts, a saintly bishop from Cyprus wrote his opinion in Greek saying, " I revere, I embrace the sacred images, καὶ [2] I give worship to the Life-giving Trinity " — which is as much as to say, that he would be polite enough to an image, *but* his worship he reserved for the only true object of worship.

Now, this pronouncement was carried to a Council of the West, sitting at Frankfort, where there were bishops of the Pyrenees, of

Gaul, of the Rhine Valley, of the Low Countries, of the Burgundian Hills, of the Swiss Mountains — indeed of all parts whatsoever that owed allegiance to Charlemagne.

At that moment Charlemagne was already wishing to be an emperor in the West. Those who served him were only too glad to find the Empire of the East — which claimed to be universal — making a howler. But the swarm of holy and unholy men at Frankfort were abominably ignorant of Greek. They did not understand the disjunctive value of καὶ. They thought it a mere barbaric " and." They translated this famous phrase " I jumble up in one worship God and images." They rushed out with some fury against such a doctrine. They registered their hatred of it. On this point also Gibbon has (as one might expect) abominably falsified history. . . . But no matter.

[2] The Greek word for " and."

The Bishops of Frankfort said what they had to say. In vain did those of Rome, who were acquainted with Greek, tell them that they had taken the sentence exactly upside down — that it meant " I do *not* worship the images. I distinguish the observance I give them from the worship I offer to That which alone is worthy of worship." They still clung to their primitive error. With difficulty were they led back into the right fold. . . .

Now, though it does not concern the little word " and," yet I am reminded (by this mention of the second Council of Nicea) of a certain story which, as you may not previously have heard it, I will now proceed to relate. With that story I shall conclude; nor will your prayers and entreaties, however loud and passionate, move me to continue. I will tell you the story; then I will have done.

The story is this. As the Eastern bishops were traveling to the second Council of Nicea, the more worldly of them (these were the greater part) were very much disgusted to meet one particularly good bishop who had been bred a shepherd. He was poor. His manners were bad. He did not shave regularly. He was badly dressed. He was what they call in Birmingham " no class."

They jeered at him a little, but more than their jeering was their fear lest they should lose caste by entering the Imperial City in such company. So after this saintly man had made himself quite intolerable at dinner, they cast up a plot against him.

He had come with only one deacon, sitting each of them upon a mule, the one a brown mule, the other mottled. The mules were stabled in the great inn of the village where all were assembled. When the saintly, but not smart, bishop had gone to his rest, the smart bishops secretly sent a bravo into the stable to cut off the heads of the two mules. " In this way," said these wicked, worldly bishops, " we shall be spared the humiliating presence of the boor when we enter the imperial town; nor will men ever know that we kept such low company."

Long before it was dawn the poor Bishop's deacon, like a good deacon, a good rustic deacon, shook himself out of sleep. He went down to the stable with a lantern to get ready the beasts against the morning journey. With what horror did he not see there two heads lying upon the ground! The one was of his own mottled mule, the other of his master's brown mule. The mottled head lay severed upon the straw beside the brown head, the headless trunks leaning all collapsed against the stall sides.

The deacon, rushing up to his master, banged at the door, saying, "My Lord! My Lord! Evil men have cut off our mules' heads!" The Right Reverend, only half awake, said, "Sew them on again! When I wake I will attend to it."

The deacon went down to the stable. With many tears he sewed on the two heads of the dead mules. The Bishop, when he had arisen from sleep, said his prayers, came down into the stable, where, he having blessed the two mules, they came to life again in the most natural manner in the world. When he had breakfasted, he rejoined his deacon. Mounting the two beasts, they rode out into the break of the day. But, the light broadening as they approached the city gate, the crowd saw with astonishment a brown mule with a mottled head abreast of a mottled mule with a brown head, for the deacon, confused in the half darkness of the morning, had sewed the wrong heads to the wrong bodies.

Note the effect — as the veracious chronicler gives it. "Thus by that very action whereby these evil men had hoped to bring their companion to shame they did but the rather thrust him into glory; for their cruelty to the dumb beasts did but serve to heighten his holiness, making proof of God's power through him who could bring the dead to life."

Many are the morals of this tale, one of which is that it is silly to take more trouble than is necessary. For if the wicked Bishops had only drugged the mules instead of cutting their heads right off there would have been no miracle, nor glory to their despised colleague. Another is that if a thing is true you must believe it, however astonishing and unlikely it may sound in the ear of the unbeliever. Another is that a bishop has the right to get up rather later than the lower branches of the hierarchy. There are many other morals; but I will end. For if I go on I shall certainly bring " and " into my own sentences, *which up to this point I have managed to avoid.* " And " is not really necessary at all.

APPRECIATION HINTS

1. What double words for " and " did the Latin and Greek languages have?
2. How can " and " be used for emphasis?
3. What does the author mean by the " stammerative " use of " and "?
4. What is the most familiar "and " phrase with politicians?
5. What was the word for the " and " symbol in the alphabet?
6. What example does he use of the " and " disjunctive?
7. Do you notice any places in the essay where " and " has been deliberately left out?
8. The most widely known prose narrative is the first chapter of Genesis. It contains 35 verses. How many of them begin with " and," and how many " and's " are there in the passage? What kind of " and's " are these?
9. Make a brief address to the class without using " and."
10. Think of other verses or jingles where " and " has a rhythmical value.
11. " Innisfree " is a poem by W. B. Yeats, found in many anthologies. Bring it to class and read it; then read it with the " and's " left out.
12. How is the element of surprise used in this essay?
13. Would you *begin* a composition with " and "? Find a collection of poetry and look up " and " in the index of first lines. What are these " and's " doing?
14. Read in Louis Untermeyer's *Yesterday and Today* Belloc's verses on " George, Who Played with a Dangerous Toy " and " Matilda, Who Told Lies and Was Burned to Death." Read Belloc's " Foreword " to Louis Untermeyer's *This Singing World.*
15. Write a composition based on the use of some word. Suggestions: Substitutes for " And," Pet Words of Mine, The Man Who Prefers " But " to " And," Worn-out Words, The Politician in Distress, An " And "-less Anecdote, On " Is."

THE PLAYFUL MOOD

When I'm playful I use the meridians of longitude and parallels of latitude for a seine, and drag the Atlantic for whales. I scratch my head with the lightning and purr myself to sleep with the thunder.

Mark Twain: *Life on the Mississippi*

DAVID GRAYSON 1870– WHEN the electric vacuum cleaner salesman
inches into the sitting room we hardly expect an adventure to blos-
som forth. Yet he is the legitimate descendant of Dixon, the book
agent, who marched so confidently into David Grayson's farmhouse.
But it is in such chance meeting with different kinds of people — a
man with a load of corn, a millionaire, an infidel — that David Grayson found his adventures in contentment. Some of them, like the encounter in this essay, happened at the farm; others on the road, in
the course of leisurely rambles often far from home, wherever this
wholesome and sweet-tempered spirit found a heart that he could
lighten.

But there were intellectual cheats who saw the chance to use
David Grayson for adventures of their own. For this was not the real
name of the writer of this essay. Before the *Adventures in Contentment* began to appear in 1906, the author had been known as one of
the group of writers who were making the *American Magazine* a
crusading organ which stirred the conscience of the country. Now
that he wanted to write something quite different, he adopted the
pseudonym, David Grayson. His essays achieved a sudden popularity. They were republished in book form, and *Adventures in
Friendship* followed in 1910. Still the secret of their authorship was
kept. Then other David Graysons appeared on the scene. On some
nights there would be a dozen men addressing audiences (chiefly in
the west) and all calling themselves David Grayson. It was time to
reveal the fact that David Grayson was really Ray Stannard Baker.
But Grayson is a fairly common name; it had become famous; and
unscrupulous impostors persevered. As late as 1938 Mr. Baker was
receiving hotel bills for the expenses of David Grayson.

Mr. Baker's education began in a little backwoods school in
northern Wisconsin. He began to write for the *Youth's Companion,
McClure's,* and then for the *American Magazine.* He was director of
the American Press Bureau in Paris during the Peace Conference after
the First World War, and there became a close friend of President
Wilson. His *Woodrow Wilson, Life and Letters,* in eight volumes,
completed in 1939, received the Pulitzer Prize in history.

I Entertain an Agent Unawares

WITH THE coming of winter I thought the life of a farmer might lose something of its charm. So much interest lies in the growth not only of crops but of trees, vines, flowers, sentiments and emotions. In the summer the world is busy, concerned with many things and full of gossip: in the winter I anticipated a cessation of many active interests and enthusiasms. I looked forward to having time for my books and for the quiet contemplation of the life around me. Summer indeed is for activity, winter for reflection. But when winter really came every day discovered some new work to do or some new adventure to enjoy. It is surprising how many things happen on a small farm. Examining the book which accounts for that winter, I find the history of part of a forenoon, which will illustrate one of the curious adventures of a farmer's life. It is dated January 5.

I went out this morning with my ax and hammer to mend the fence along the public road. A heavy frost fell last night and the brown grass and the dry ruts of the roads were powdered white. Even the air, which was perfectly still, seemed full of frost crystals, so that when the sun came up one seemed to walk in a magic world. I drew in a long breath and looked out across the wonderful shining country and I said to myself:

"Surely, there is nowhere I would rather be than here." For I could have traveled nowhere to find greater beauty or a better enjoyment of it than I had here at home.

As I worked with my ax and hammer, I heard a light wagon come rattling up the road. Across the valley a man had begun to chop a tree. I could see the ax steel flash brilliantly in the sunshine before i heard the sound of the blow.

The man in the wagon had a round face and a sharp blue eye. I thought he seemed a businesslike young man.

"Say, there," he shouted, drawing up at my gate, "would you mind holding my horse a minute? It's a cold morning and he's restless."

"Certainly not," I said, and I put down my tools and held his horse.

He walked up to my door with a brisk step and a certain jaunty poise of the head.

"He is well contented with himself," I said. "It is a great blessing for any man to be satisfied with what he has got."

I heard Harriet open the door — how every sound rang through the still morning air!

The young man asked some question and I distinctly heard Harriet's answer:

"He's down there."

The young man came back: his hat was tipped up, his quick eye darted over my grounds as though in a single instant he had appraised everything and passed judgment upon the cash value of the inhabitants. He whistled a lively little tune.

"Say," he said, when he reached the gate, not at all disconcerted, "I thought you was the hired man. Your name's Grayson, ain't it? Well, I want to talk with you."

After tying and blanketing his horse and taking a black satchel from his buggy he led me up to my house. I had a pleasurable sense of excitement and adventure. Here was a new character come to my farm. Who knows, I thought, what he may bring with him: who knows what I may send away by him? Here in the country we must set our little ships afloat on small streams, hoping that somehow, some day, they will reach the sea.

It was interesting to see the busy young man sit down so confidently in our best chair. He said his name was Dixon, and he took out from his satchel a book with a fine showy cover. He said it was called *Living Selections from Poet, Sage and Humorist.*

"This," he told me, "is only the first of the series. We publish six volumes full of literchoor. You see what a heavy book this is?"

I tested it in my hand: it was a heavy book.

"The entire set," he said, "weighs over ten pounds. There are 1,162 pages, enough paper if laid down flat, end to end, to reach half a mile."

I cannot quote his exact language: there was too much of it, but he made an impressive showing of the amount of literature that could be had at a very low price per pound. Mr. Dixon was a hypnotist. He fixed me with his glittering eye, and he talked so fast, and his ideas upon the subject were so original that he held me spellbound. At first

I was inclined to be provoked: one does not like to be forcibly hypnotized, but gradually the situation began to amuse me, the more so when Harriet came in.

"Did you ever see a more beautiful binding?" asked the agent, holding his book admiringly at arm's length. "This up here," he said, pointing to the illuminated cover, "is

the Muse of Poetry. She is scattering flowers — poems, you know. Fine idea, ain't it? Coloring fine, too."

He jumped up quickly and laid the book on my table, to the evident distress of Harriet.

"Trims up the room, don't it?" he exclaimed, turning his head a little to one side and observing the effect with an expression of affectionate admiration.

"How much," I asked, "will you sell the covers for without the insides?"

"Without the insides?"

"Yes," I said, "the binding will trim up my table just as well without the insides."

I thought he looked at me a little suspiciously, but he was evidently satisfied by my expression of countenance, for he answered promptly:

"Oh, but you want the insides. That's what the books are for. The bindings are never sold alone."

He then went on to tell me the prices and terms of payment, until it really seemed that it would be cheaper to buy the books than to let him carry them away again. Harriet stood in the doorway behind him frowning and evidently trying to catch my eye. But I kept my face turned aside so that I could not see her signal of distress and my eyes fixed on the young man Dixon. It was as good as a play. Harriet there, serious-minded, thinking I was being befooled, and the agent thinking he was befooling me, and I, thinking I was befooling both of them — and all of us wrong. It was very like life wherever you find it.

Finally, I took the book which he had been urging upon me, at which Harriet coughed meaningly to attract my attention. She knew the danger when I really got my hands on a book. But I made up as innocent as a child. I opened the book almost at random — and it was as though, walking down a strange road, I had come upon an old tried friend not seen before in years. For there on the page before me I read:

> The world is too much with us; late and soon,
> Getting and spending, we lay waste our powers:
> Little we see in Nature that is ours;
> We have given our hearts away, a sordid boon!
> The sea that bares her bosom to the moon;
> The winds that will be howling at all hours,
> But are up-gathered now like sleeping flowers;
> For this, for everything, we are out of tune;

And as I read it came back to me — a scene like a picture — the place, the time, the very feel of the hour when I first saw those lines.

Who shall say that the past does not live! An odor will sometimes set the blood coursing in an old emotion, and a line of poetry is the resurrection and the life. For a moment I forgot Harriet and the agent, I forgot myself, I even forgot the book on my knee — everything but that hour in the past — a view of shimmering hot housetops, the heat and dust and noise of an August evening in the city, the dumb weariness of it all, the loneliness, the longing for green fields; and then these great lines of Wordsworth, read for the first time, flooding in upon me:

> Great God! I'd rather be
> A pagan suckled in a creed outworn:
> So might I, standing on this pleasant lea,
> Have glimpses that would make me less forlorn;
> Have sight of Proteus rising from the sea;
> Or hear old Triton blow his wreathèd horn.

When I had finished I found myself standing in my own room with one arm raised, and, I suspect, a trace of tears in my eyes — there before the agent and Harriet. I saw Harriet lift one hand and drop it hopelessly. She thought I was captured at last. I was past saving. And as I looked at the agent I saw " grim conquest glowing in his eye!" So I sat down not a little embarrassed by my exhibition — when I had intended to be self-poised.

"You like it, don't you?" said Mr. Dixon unctuously.

"I don't see," I said earnestly, "how you can afford to sell such things as this so cheap."

"They *are* cheap," he admitted regretfully. I suppose he wished he had tried me with the half-morocco.

"They are priceless," I said, "absolutely priceless. If you were the only man in the world who had that poem, I think I would deed you my farm for it."

Mr. Dixon proceeded, as though it were all settled, to get out his black order book and open it briskly for business. He drew his fountain pen, capped it, and looked up at me expectantly. My feet actually seemed slipping into some irresistible whirlpool. How well he understood practical psychology! I struggled within myself, fearing engulfment: I was all but lost.

"Shall I deliver the set at once," he said, "or can you wait until the first of February?"

At that critical moment a floating spar of an idea swept my way and I seized upon it as the last hope of the lost.

"I don't understand," I said, as though I had not heard his last question, "how you dare go about with all this treasure upon you. Are you not afraid of being stopped in the road and robbed? Why, I've seen the time when, if I had known you carried such things as these, such cures for sick hearts, I think I should have stopped you myself!"

"Say, you *are* an odd one," said Mr. Dixon.

"Why do you sell such priceless things as these?" I asked, looking at him sharply.

"Why do I sell them?" and he looked still more perplexed. "To make money, of course; same reason you raise corn."

"But here is wealth," I said, pursuing my advantage. "If you have these you have something more valuable than money."

Mr. Dixon politely said nothing. Like a wise angler, having failed to land me at the first rush, he let me have line. Then I thought of Ruskin's words, "Nor can any noble thing be wealth except to a noble person." And that prompted me to say to Mr. Dixon:

"These things are not yours; they are mine. You never owned them; but I will sell them to you."

He looked at me in amazement, and then glanced around — evidently to discover if there were a convenient way of escape.

"You're all straight, are you?" he asked, tapping his forehead; "didn't anybody ever try to take you up?"

"The covers are yours," I continued as though I had not heard him, "the insides are mine and have been for a long time: that is why I proposed buying the covers separately."

I opened his book again. I thought I would see what had been chosen for its pages. And I found there many fine and great things.

"Let me read you this," I said to Mr. Dixon; "it has been mine for a long time. I will not sell it to you. I will give it to you outright. The best things are always given."

Having some gift in imitating the Scotch dialect, I read:

November chill blaws loud wi' angry sugh;
   The short'ning winter day is near a close;
The miry beasts retreating frae the pleugh;
   The black'ning trains o' craws to their repose;
The toil-worn Cotter frae his labor goes,
   This night his weekly moil is at an end,
Collects his spades, his mattocks and his hoes,
   Hoping the morn in ease and rest to spend,
And weary, o'er the moor, his course does hameward bend.

So I read " The Cotter's Saturday Night." I love the poem very much myself, sometimes reading it aloud, not so much for the tenderness of its message, though I prize that, too, as for the wonder of its music.

     Compar'd with these, Italian trills are tame;
      The tickl'd ear no heart-felt raptures raise.

I suppose I showed my feeling in my voice. As I glanced up from time to time I saw the agent's face change, and his look deepen and the lips, usually so energetically tense, loosen with emotion. Surely no poem in all the language conveys so perfectly the simple love of the home, the quiet joys, hopes, pathos of those who live close to the soil. When I had finished — I stopped with the stanza beginning:

     Then homeward all take off their sev'ral way;

the agent turned away his head trying to brave out his emotion. Must of us, Anglo-Saxons, tremble before a tear when we might fearlessly beard a tiger.

I moved up nearer to the agent and put my hand on his knee; then I read two or three of the other things I found in his wonderful book. And once I had him laughing and once again I had the tears in his eyes. Oh, a simple young man, a little crusty without, but soft inside — like the rest of us.

Well, it was amazing, once we began talking not of books but of life, how really eloquent and human he became. From being a distant and uncomfortable person, he became at once like a near neighbor and friend. It was strange to me — as I have thought since — how he conveyed to us in few words the essential emotional note of his life. It was no violin tone, beautifully complex with harmonics, but the clear simple voice of the flute. It spoke of his wife and his baby girl and his home. The very incongruity of detail — he told us how he grew onions in his back yard — added somehow to the homely glamour of the vision which he gave us. The number of his house, the fact that he had a new cottage organ, and that the baby ran away and lost herself in Seventeenth Street — were all, curiously, fabrics of his emotion.

It was beautiful to see commonplace facts grow phosphorescent in the heat of true feeling. How little we may come to know Romance by the cloak she wears and how humble must be he who would surprise the heart of her!

It was, indeed, with an indescribable thrill that I heard him add the details, one by one — the mortgage on his place, now rapidly being paid off, the brother who was a plumber, the mother-in-law who was not a mother-in-law of the comic papers. And finally he showed us the picture of the wife and baby that he had in the cover of his watch; a fat baby with its head resting on its mother's shoulder.

" Mister," he said, " p'r'aps you think it's fun to ride around the country like I do, and be away from home most of the time. But it ain't. When I think of Minnie and the kid — "

He broke off sharply, as if he had suddenly remembered the shame of such confidences.

" Say," he asked, " what page is that poem on? "

I told him.

" One forty-six," he said. " When I get home I'm going to read that to Minnie. She likes poetry and all such things. And where's that other piece that tells how a man feels when he's lonesome? Say, that fellow knew! "

We had a genuinely good time, the agent and I, and when he finally rose to go, I said:

" Well, I've sold you a new book."

" I see now, mister, what you mean."

I went down the path with him and began to unhitch his horse.

" Let me, let me," he said eagerly.

Then he shook hands, paused a moment awkwardly as if about to say something, then sprang into his buggy without saying it.

When he had taken up his reins he remarked:

"Say! but you'd make an agent! You'd hypnotize 'em."

I recognized it as the greatest compliment he could pay me: the craft compliment.

Then he drove off, but pulled up before he had gone five yards. He turned in his seat, one hand on the back of it, his whip raised.

"Say!" he shouted, and when I walked up he looked at me with fine embarrassment.

"Mister, perhaps you'd accept one of these sets from Dixon free gratis, for nothing."

"I understand," I said, "but you know I'm giving the books to you — and I couldn't take them back again."

"Well," he said, "you're a good one, anyhow. Good-by again," and then, suddenly, business naturally coming uppermost, he remarked with great enthusiasm:

"You've given me a new idea. *Say*, I'll sell 'em."

"Carry them carefully, man," I called after him; "they are precious."

So I went back to my work, thinking how many fine people there are in this world — if you scratch 'em deep enough.

APPRECIATION HINTS

1. What three features of *Living Selections* does the agent think are its best selling points?
2. In what respect were Harriet, her brother, and the agent, all "befooled"?
3. What scene in the author's memory did Wordsworth's sonnet recall?
4. What remark of Grayson made the agent suspect that he was insane? What did Grayson mean by this remark?
5. What poem does he read to the agent?
6. What effect does the reading of the poem have on the agent?
7. What does the agent tell Grayson about his home life?
8. What is the great compliment the agent pays Grayson as he is leaving?
9. Explain the full meaning of the title. (Look up Hebrews 13:2.)
10. Name some books you *own* in the sense in which Grayson said he owned *Living Selections*.

11. Tell about an experience of your own in which some one has opened up to you a play, poem, picture, or piece of music.
12. Write a composition based on a new appreciation of something beautiful. Suggestions: Frost Magic, A Moment of Appreciation, The Valley at Sunrise, Effects in Photography.
13. Write a composition based on a personality you have discovered. Suggestions: The Freshman, The Lone Kid, Uncut Diamond, A Personality I Discovered, Queer Characters I Have Met, If You Scratch 'Em Deep Enough.

GOOD BOOKS

As good almost kill a man as kill a good book. Who kills a man kills a reasonable creature, God's image, but he who destroys a good book kills reason itself. Many a man lives a burden to the earth; but a good book is the precious life-blood of a master spirit, embalmed and treasured up on purpose to a life beyond life.

Milton: *Areopagitica*

THE TASK

To be honest, to be kind — to earn a little and to spend a little less, to make upon the whole a family happier for his presence, to renounce, when that shall be necessary, and not to be embittered, to keep a few friends, but these without capitulation — here is a task for all that a man has of fortitude and delicacy.

Stevenson: *A Christmas Sermon*

Teaching is reading Homer at the Rotary Club, so that they forget to take the 3:15 to the Billboard Advertisers' Picnic.

S. I. HAYAKAWA 1906–

SAMUEL HAYAKAWA IS A Canadian citizen who teaches English in an American college. He is a professor at Illinois Institute of Technology in Chicago, and in 1942 did much work for the U. S. government. A few years ago he went to Japan to visit his family who had left their home in Winnipeg ten years earlier to establish an exporting business in Osaka. His sister Grace left Canada at five, speaking English perfectly. Samuel found her in Osaka unable even to make English sounds, and struggling at fifteen to learn English again. " I told her," he writes, " that her English was a disgrace to the city of Winnipeg where she was born, and she told me that my Japanese was a disgrace to the Empire. I would mutter a slangy rejoinder in American which she couldn't understand, and she would reply with some uncomplimentary Japanese slang which I couldn't understand. We got along famously. And Mother was in gales of laughter at us all day long."

Though Mr. Hayakawa can neither read nor write Japanese, it may be that it was this early exposure to two quite different languages that interested him in the study of how language works. For while his father spoke English perfectly, Samuel as a child used to converse with his mother in a home-made language — " an absurd mixture of baby-Japanese, literary English, and American slang." However it happened, the astonishing fact remains that the person who has been most skilful in translating the findings of general semantics (the new science of meanings) into plain English is the Canadian-born son of Japanese parents. In the following essay he is writing about that element in our language which we have in common with cats and dogs — the purr-words and the snarl-words.

Samuel Ichiye Hayakawa was educated in the public schools of Winnipeg, and took a B.A. at the University of Manitoba, and an M.A. at McGill University. He then taught English literature and composition at the University of Wisconsin, where he took his Ph.D. degree. He visited Japan as a child of five, and again at the age of thirty. "Words That Don't Inform " is chapter 5 of Mr. Hayakawa's *Language in Action,* published by Harcourt, Brace and Company, and chosen as the Book of the Month for December, 1941.

Words That Don't Inform

WHAT complicates the problems of interpretation above all is the fact that often words are not used informatively at all. In fact, we have every reason to believe that the ability to use noises as symbols was developed only recently in the course of our evolution. Long before we developed language as we know it, we probably made, like the lower animals, all sorts of animal cries, expressive of such internal conditions as hunger, fear, and triumph. We can recognize a variety of such noises and the conditions they indicate in our domestic animals. Gradually these noises seem to have become more and more differentiated: consciousness expanded. Grunts and gibberings became symbolic language. But, although we developed symbolic language, the habit of making noises *expressing*, rather than *reporting*, our internal conditions has remained. The result is that we use language in *presymbolic* ways: that is, as the equivalent of screams, howls, purrs, and gibbering. These presymbolic uses of language co-exist with our symbolic systems, and we still have constant recourse to them in the talking we do in everyday life.

The presymbolic character of much of our talk is most clearly illustrated in cries expressive of strong emotion of any kind. If, for example, we carelessly step off a curb when a car is coming, it doesn't much matter whether someone yells, " Look out! " or " Kiwotsuke! " or " Hey! " or " Prends garde! " or simply utters a scream, so long as whatever noise is made is uttered loudly enough to alarm us. It is the fear expressed in the *loudness* and the *tone* of the cry that conveys the necessary sensations, and not the words. Similarly, commands given sharply and angrily usually produce quicker results than the same commands uttered tonelessly. The quality of the voice itself, that is to say, has a power of expressing feelings that is almost independent of the symbols used. We can say, " I hope you'll come to see us again," in a way that clearly indicates that we hope they never come back. Or again, if a young lady with whom we are strolling says, " The moon is bright tonight," we are able to tell by the tone whether she is making a meteorological observation or indicating that she wants to be kissed.

The making of noises with the vocal organs is a muscular activity. Many of our muscular activities are involuntary. Many of our speeches — especially exclamations — are likewise involuntary. Our responses to powerful stimuli, such as to something that makes us very angry, are a huge complex of muscular activities — the contracting of fighting muscles, the increasing of blood pressure, the tearing of hair, etc., *and* the making of noises, such as growls and snarls. Human beings, however, probably because they consider it beneath their dignity to express their anger in purely animalistic noises, do not ordinarily growl like dogs, but substitute series of words, such as, " You dirty double-crosser! " " You filthy scum! " Similarly, instead of purring or wagging the tail, the human being again substitutes speeches such as, " She's the sweetest girl in all the world! " " Oh, dear, what a CUTE baby! "

Speeches such as these are, as a rule, merely human equivalents of snarling and purring, and are not symbolic in the same sense that the statement, " Chicago is in the State of Illinois," is symbolic. That is to say, " She's the sweetest girl in all the world " is not a statement about the girl, but a revelation of the speaker's state of mind — a revelation that could be made equally well by movements of the hands and face, purring, etc. Similarly, the ordinary editorial and oratorical denunciations of " Reds," " radicals," " corporate interests," and " Fifth Columnists," are frequently only protracted snarls, growls, and yelps, with, however, the surface appearance of logical and grammatical articulation. These series of "*snarl-words*" and "*purr-words*," as it will be convenient to call them, are not reports describing conditions in the extensional world,[1] but *symptoms of disturbance*, pleasant or unpleasant, in the speaker.

To remember to interpret some uses of language as symptoms rather than as symbols, therefore, is considerable help in the reading of much contemporary debate: newspaper editorials, nominating speeches at political conventions, discussions of "economic principles," etc. Frequently these snarls and purrs are not merely a matter of a few individual words, but of paragraphs, of entire editorials or speeches, and sometimes of entire books. This is not to say that we shouldn't snarl and purr: in the first place, we couldn't stop ourselves if we wanted to; and secondly, there are many occasions that demand good, violent snarls, as well as soft, loving purrs of delight. We must, however, guard ourselves against mistaking these for informative statements.

There are, of course, other presymbolic uses of language. Sometimes we talk simply for the sake of hearing ourselves talk; that is, for the same reason that we play golf or dance: the activity gives us a pleasant sense of being alive. Children prattling, adults singing in the bathtub, are alike enjoying the sound of their voices. Sometimes large groups make noises together, as in group singing, group recitation, or group chanting, for similar presymbolic reasons. In all this, the significance of the words used is almost completely irrelevant: we often, for example, may chant the most lugubrious words about a desire to be carried back to a childhood home in Old Virginia, when in actuality we have never been there and haven't the slightest intention of going.

What we call "social conversation" is again presymbolic in character. When we are at a tea or dinner party, for example, we all have to talk — about anything: the weather, the performance of the Chi-

---

[1] The "extensional world" is the world we know when our language works *outward*, and we check words against the facts to which they refer, as scientists do.

cago White Sox, Thomas Mann's latest book, or Myrna Loy's last picture. It is typical of these conversations that, except among very good friends, few of the remarks made on these subjects are ever important enough to be worth making for their informative value. Nevertheless, it is regarded as " rude " to remain silent. Indeed, in such matters as greetings and farewells: " Good morning," " Lovely day," " And how is your family these days? " " It was a pleasure meeting you," " Do look us up the next time you're in town," etc., it is regarded as a social error not to say these things even if we do not mean them. There are numberless daily situations in which we talk simply because it would be impolite not to. Every social group has its own form of this kind of talking: " the art of conversation," " small talk," or the mutual " kidding " that Americans love so much. From these social practices it is possible to infer, as a general principle, that *the prevention of silence is itself an important function of speech,* and that it is completely impossible for us in society to talk only when we " have something to say."

This presymbolic talk for talk's sake is, like the cries of animals, a form of activity. We talk together about nothing at all and thereby establish friendships. The purpose of the talk is not the communication of information, as the symbols used would seem to imply (" I see the Dodgers are out in the lead again "), but the establishment of communion. Human beings have many ways of establishing communion among themselves: breaking bread together, playing games together, working together. But talking together is the most easily arranged of all these forms of collective activity. The *togetherness* of the talking, then, is the most important element in social conversation; the subject matter is only secondary.

Presymbolic elements in language predominate in all ritual activities. Sermons, political caucuses, conventions, " pep rallies," and all ceremonial gatherings are marked by the abundant use of what might be called *language as ritual.* All groups — religious, patriotic, scientific, political, and occupational — like to gather together at intervals for the purpose of sharing certain accustomed activities, wearing special costumes (vestments in religious organizations, fanciful re-

galia in lodges and fraternal organizations, uniforms in patriotic organizations, etc.), eating together (banquets), displaying the flags,
ribbons, or emblems of their group, and marching in processions.
Among these group activities is always included a number of
speeches, either traditionally worded or specially composed for the
occasion, whose principal function is *not* to give the audience information they did not have before, not to create new ways of feeling,
but to *reaffirm feelings already held.*

We shall return to this subject later, but for now let us look at
what happens at a " pep rally " such as precedes college football
games. The members of " our team " are " introduced " to a crowd
that already knows them. Called upon to make speeches, the players
mutter a few incoherent and often ungrammatical remarks, which are
received with wild applause. The leaders of the rally make fantastic
promises about what the team is going to do the next day. The crowd
utters " cheers " which normally consist of animalistic noises arranged
in extremely primitive rhythms. *No one comes out any wiser or better
informed than he was before he went in.*

To some extent religious ceremonies are equally puzzling at first
glance. The priest or clergyman in charge utters set speeches, *often
in languages incomprehensible to the congregation* (Hebrew in
Jewish synagogues, Latin in the Roman Catholic Church, Sanskrit in
Chinese and Japanese temples, etc.), with the result that, as often as
not, no information whatsoever is communicated to those present.

Only the superficial, however, will dismiss these linguistic events
as " simply showing what fools human beings are." If we approach
these events as students of language trying to understand what is
happening and examine our own reactions when we enter into the
spirit of such occasions, we cannot help observing that, whatever the
words used in ritual utterance may signify, we ordinarily do not think
very much about their signification during the course of the ritual.
Most of us, for example, usually repeat the Lord's Prayer or sing " The
Star-spangled Banner " without thinking about the words. As children we are taught to repeat such sets of words before we can understand them, and many of us continue to say them for the rest of our
lives without bothering about their signification. Yet we cannot re-

gard them as "meaningless," because such utterances have a genuine effect upon us: we often come out of church, for example, with no clear memory of what the sermon was about, but with a sense nevertheless that the service has "done us good."

We may then regard ritualistic utterances, whether made up of words that have symbolic significance at other times, or of words in foreign or obsolete tongues, or of meaningless syllables, as *accustomed sets of noises,* to which certain group feelings are attached. Such utterances rarely make sense to anyone not a member of the group. The Protestant will go to a Catholic church and be amazed that a service conducted in a language that no one in the congregation understands seems to be enjoyed by all present. But, for all that the average Protestant churchgoer ever remembers of the sermons he hears, he might just as well have heard them delivered in Hindustani. The abracadabra [2] of a lodge-meeting is absurd to everyone but a member of the lodge. When language becomes ritual, that is to say, its effect becomes to a considerable extent independent of whatever significations the words possessed.

All of us, of course, use and respond to ritual language. The ritual phrases and speeches to which we respond often reveal our deepest religious, patriotic, social, professional, and political allegiances more accurately than do the citizenship papers or membership cards we may carry in our pockets, or the badges we may wear on our coats. A Catholic or a Buddhist who has changed his religion after reaching adulthood will, on hearing the ritual he was accustomed to hearing in childhood, often feel an urge, however faint, to return to his earlier form of worship.

Presymbolic uses of language have this characteristic in common: their functions can be performed, if necessary, without the use of grammatically and syntactically articulated symbolic words. They can even be performed without recognizable speech at all. Group-feeling may be established, for example, among animals by collective barking or howling, and among human beings by college cheers, community singing, and such collective noise-making activities. Indica-

---

[2] A word supposed to possess a charm.

tions of friendliness such as we give when we say "Good morning" or "Nice day, isn't it?" can be given by smiles, gestures, or, as among animals, by nuzzling or sniffing. Frowning, laughing, smiling, moaning, jumping up and down, can satisfy a large number of our needs for expression, without the use of verbal symbols.

To understand the presymbolic elements that enter into our everyday language is extremely important. The intellectually persnickety are always telling us that we "ought to say what we mean," and "mean what we say," and "talk only when we have something to talk about." These are, of course, impossible prescriptions. We cannot restrict our speaking to the giving and asking of factual information, nor can we ever confine ourselves altogether to statements that are literally true. We should often be unable even to say "Pleased to meet you" when the occasion demanded.

The ignorance of the existence of these presymbolic uses of language is not so common among uneducated people (who often perceive such things intuitively) as it is among those "educated" people who, having a great contempt for the "stupidity" of others, have a correspondingly high opinion of their own perspicacity. Such "enlightened" people listen to the chatter at teas and receptions, and conclude from the triviality of the conversation that all the guests (except themselves) are fools. They may discover that people often come away from church services without any clear memory of what the sermons were about, and conclude that churchgoers are either fools or hypocrites. They may hear the political oratory of the opposition party, wonder "how anybody can believe such rot," and conclude therefrom that people in general are so unintelligent that it would be impossible for democracy to work. (They will overlook the fact, of course, that similar conclusions could be drawn from *their* speeches at their own party conventions.) Almost all such gloomy conclusions about the stupidity or hypocrisy of our friends and neighbors are unjustifiable on such evidence, because they usually come from applying the standards of symbolic language to linguistic events that are either partly or wholly presymbolic in character.

One further illustration may make this clearer. Let us suppose that we are on the roadside, struggling with a flat tire. A not-very-bright-looking but friendly youth comes up and asks, "Got a flat tire?" If we insist upon interpreting his words literally, we will regard this as an extremely silly question and say, "Can't you see I have, you dumb ox?" If we pay no attention to what the words say, however, and understand his meaning, we will return his gesture of friendly interest by showing equal friendliness, and in a short while he may be helping us to change the tire. In a similar way, many situations in life as well as in literature demand that we pay no attention to what the words say, since the meaning may often be a great deal more intelligent and intelligible than the surface *sense* of the words themselves. It is probable that a great deal of our pessimism about the world, about humanity, and about democracy may be due in part to the fact that unconsciously we apply the standards of symbolic language to presymbolic utterances.

APPRECIATION HINTS

1. What is the difference between words that *express* and words that *report*?
2. Give some examples of presymbolic language.
3. What does he mean by snarl-words and purr-words?
4. Explain why much social conversation may properly be called presymbolic?
5. Give examples of occasions when language is used not to inform but to reaffirm feelings already held.
6. Is ritual language meaningless? What does it express?
7. Why is it impossible for us to talk only when we have something to talk about?
8. Give some examples to show that it is sometimes wise to pay no attention to what the words say.
9. Give some examples of historic speeches intended to reaffirm feelings already held.
10. Give some examples of presymbolic language of "lower" animals. (Monkeys are said to have a vocabulary of some seventy words.)
11. Describe some games in which spoken language is forbidden.
12. Write a composition on some topic related to this essay. Suggestions: The Sign Language of My Dog, Bird Language, Indian Sign Language, "Conversation" at the Bridge Club, My Experience of Purr-words (or Snarl-words, Presymbolic Language in the Classroom, Sign

Language of the Catcher (or Coach), The Talking Horse, The Captain's Speech at the Rally.

13. Read "A Japanese American Goes to Japan," in *Asia* for April, 1937; and "My Japanese Father and I," in *Asia* for May, 1937; both by Hayakawa.

14. Read "A Story with a Moral," the introduction to *Language in Action.*

WORDS, WORDS!

For the more languages a man can speak
His talent hath but sprung a larger leak . . .
And he who is but able to express
No sense at all in several languages
Will pass for learneder than he who's known
To speak the deepest wisdom in his own.

Samuel Butler: *Hudibras*

THREE WORDS

Most of all I enjoy the octogenarian poet who joined three words — Go, lovely Rose — so happily together, that he left his name to float down through time on the wings of a phrase and a flower.

Logan Pearsall Smith: *Afterthoughts*

COMMUNICATION

Bruises debt erased afford and erector analysis heard too infectious debt.

This was the form of a telegram delivered in Philadelphia. It came from a farmer's wife in the Pennsylvania-Dutch county of Lancaster. The meaning:

Bruce is dead. He raced a Ford and he wrecked her. And Alice is hurt too. In fact she's dead.

TRUTH

It takes two to speak truth — one to speak and another to hear.   H. D. Thoreau: *Walden*

INNER RESOURCES

THE ESSAYS in this section have to do with the powers possessed by all of us. One test of education is that it makes a man fit company for himself. Steele tells us how Alexander Selkirk, a young half-educated Scotchman, marooned by his fellow-privateers, developed within himself resources which made life so satisfactory on his desert island, that he left it finally after four years with regret.

Two other essayists in this group provide an interesting contrast. Montaigne was fascinated by the mystery he discovered when he examined himself. He turned the microscope inward, and reported with utter frankness whatever he found. Most men are glad enough to keep their secrets; some share them, but only to the closest friends; Montaigne confided his to paper. Mencken loved to cope with life first-hand, and his resources grew with each encounter. He tells with candor about those events of his boyhood which memory after some fifty years preserves. They are recollections of a child's first experiments with his environment; of a fattish infant with "a scow-like beam" eating green cherries and unripe grapes in his mother's garden.

Charles Lamb suffered a more terrible tragedy than being marooned, and yet one would never guess it from the cheerful face he turned to the world. From what inner fountains was he drawing? Can we find them by reading his essays? Emerson spent a lifetime in examining the nature and the source of this inner strength in man, and in exhorting men to trust it and use it. His "Self-Reliance" is his own declaration of independence, and it ought to be the possession of every American boy and girl.

These five writers, each in his own way, illustrate the powers which all of us possess in some degree to think, speak, write and act as individuals. They help us to understand how precious is personal freedom.

H. L. MENCKEN 1880– IN ANOTHER chapter of the merry record of boyhood called *Happy Days* Mr. Mencken tells what started him on his reading. He writes that his discovery of *Huck Finn* was " probably the most stupendous event of my whole life." It set him going on a career of voracious reading which did not begin to let up until he became interested in neckties and the " curiously divergent shapes and dispositions of girls." Mr. Mencken's book has in common with Mark Twain's a keen appreciation of the explosive joys of boyhood. *Happy Days,* the record of these boisterous early years, opens with the following essay and closes with the boy's twelfth birthday. Possibly the unhappy days have dropped from memory after sixty years, for the author writes, " If I had my life to live over again I don't think I'd change it in any particular of the slightest consequence." It was a rollicking family in which the children grew up, " encapsulated in affection, and kept fat, saucy, and contented." Mr. Mencken's latest volume, *Newspaper Days,* 1941, picks up the story of his life a few years later. It begins when he went to work with the Baltimore *Herald,* in 1899, and ends when that paper closed up in 1906. The sprightly account of how a raw kid of eighteen became an editor in seven years should be of great interest to all young journalists and writers.

You might not suspect from this essay that its author is a profound student of English, and especially of the changes and peculiar developments which English has undergone in the United States as the spoken medium of communication. *The American Language* was published first in 1918. But recently Mr. Mencken has issued a revised and enlarged fourth edition of this most readable study of our living language.

Henry Louis Mencken still lives in Baltimore in the house around which these spicy memories of his childhood cling. He holds a unique position among American writers because of his innate and life-long hatred of sham, pretense, and hypocrisy, and his ceaseless and goodtempered ridicule of the American frailties. At twenty-five he was chief editor of the Baltimore *Herald,* for many years a staff member of the Baltimore *Sun,* and editor of *The American Mercury,* 1924–33.

Introduction to the Universe

AT THE instant I first became aware of the cosmos we all infest I was sitting in my mother's lap and blinking at a great burst of lights, some of them red and others green, but most of them only the bright yellow of flaring gas. The time: the evening of Thursday, September 13, 1883, which was the day after my third birthday. The place: a ledge outside the second-story front windows of my father's cigar factory at 368 Baltimore street, Baltimore, Maryland, U. S. A., fenced off from space and disaster by a sign bearing the majestic legend: *Aug. Mencken & Bro.* The occasion: the third and last annual Summer Nights' Carnival of the Order of Orioles, a society that adjourned *sine die,* with a thumping deficit, the very next morning, and has since been forgotten by the whole human race.

At that larval stage of my life, of course, I knew nothing whatever about the Order of Orioles, just as I knew nothing whatever about the United States, though I had been born to their liberties, and was entitled to the protection of their army and navy. All I was aware of, emerging from the unfathomable abyss of nonentity, was the fact that the world I had just burst into seemed to be very brilliant, and that peeping at it over my father's sign was somewhat hard on my still gelatinous bones. So I made signals of distress to my mother and was duly hauled into her lap, where I first dozed and then snored away until the lights went out, and the family buggy wafted me home, still asleep.

The latter details, you will understand, I learned subsequently from historians, but I remember the lights with great clarity, and entirely on my own. They constitute not only the earliest of all my earthly recollections, but also one of my most vivid, and I take no stock in the theories of psychologists who teach that events experienced so early in life are never really recalled, but only reconstructed from family gossip. To be sure, there is a dead line beyond which even the most grasping memory does not reach, but I am sure that in my own case it must have run with my third birthday. Ask me if I recall the occasion, probably before my second, when I was initiated into the game of I-spy by a neighbor boy, and went to hide behind a wire screen, and was astonished when he detected me — ask me about that, and I'll admit freely that I recall nothing of it whatever, but only the ensuing anecdote, which my poor mother was so fond of telling that in the end I hid in the cellar every time she started it. Nor do I remember anything on my own about my baptism (at which ceremonial my father, so I have heard, made efforts to get the rector tight, and was hoist by his own petard),[1] for I was then but a few months old. But not all the psychologists on earth, working in shifts like coal miners, will ever convince me that I don't remember those lights and wholly under my own steam.

They made their flash and then went out, and the fog again closed down. I don't recall moving to the new house in Hollins street that was to be my home for so many years, though we took possession of it only a few weeks later. I don't recall going into pants at about a quarter to four years, though it must have been a colossal experience, full of pride and glory. But gradually, as my consciousness jelled, my days began to be speckled with other events that, for one reason or another, stuck. I recall, though only somewhat vaguely, the deck of an excursion-boat, *circa* 1885, its deafening siren, and the wide, gray waters of Chesapeake Bay. I recall very clearly being taken by my father to a clothing store bright with arc lights, then a novelty in the world, and seeing great piles of elegant Sunday suits, and coming home with one that was tight across the stern. I recall a straw hat

---

[1] Blown up with his own grenade.

with flowing ribbons, a cat named Pinkie, and my brother Charlie, then still a brat in long clothes, howling like a catamount one hot Summer night, while my mother dosed him with the whole phar-macopoeia of the house, and frisked him for outlaw pins. I recall, again, my introduction to the wonderland of science, with an earth-worm (*Lumbricus terrestris*) as my first subject, and the experiment directed toward finding out how long it would take him, laid out in the sun on the backyard walk, to fry to death. And I recall my mother reading to me, on a dark Winter afternoon, out of a book describing the adventures of the Simple Simon who went to a fair, the while she sipped a cup of tea that smelled very cheerful, and I glued my nose to the frosty window pane, watching a lamplighter light the lamps in Union Square across the street and wondering what a fair might be. It was a charming, colorful, Kate Greenaway world that her reading took me into, and to this day I can shut my eyes and still see its little timbered houses, its boys and girls gam-boling on village greens, and its un-clouded skies of pale blue.

I was on the fattish side as an in-fant, with a scow-like beam and notice-able jowls. Dr. C. L. Buddenbohn, who fetched me into sentience at 9 P.M., pre-cisely, of Sunday, September 12, 1880, apparently made a good (though, as I fear, somewhat rough) job of it, despite the fact that his surviving bill, dated October 2, shows that all he charged " to one confinement " was ten dollars. The science of infant feeding, in those days, was as rudi-mentary as bacteriology or social justice, but there can be no doubt that I got plenty of calories and vitamins, and probably even an over-dose. There is a photograph of me at eighteen months which looks like the pictures the milk companies print in the rotogravure sections of the Sunday papers, whooping up the zeal of their cows. If canni-balism had not been abolished in Maryland some years before my birth I'd have butchered beautifully.

My mother used to tell me years afterward that my bulk often attracted public notice, especially when it was set off dramatically against her own lack of it, for she was of slight frame and less than average height, and looked, in her blue-eyed blondness, to be even younger than she actually was. Once, hauling me somewhere by horsecar, she was confronted by an old man who gaped at her and me for a while with senile impertinence, and then burst out: " Good God, girl, is that baby *yours?* " This adiposity passed off as I began to run about, and from the age of six onward I was rather skinny, but toward the end of my twenties my cross section again became a circle, and at thirty I was taking one of the first of the anti-fat cures, and beating it by sly resorts to malt liquor.

My gradually accumulating and clarifying memories of infancy have to do chiefly with the backyard in Hollins street, which had the unusual length, for a yard in a city block, of a hundred feet. Along with my brother Charlie, who followed me into this vale when I was but twenty months old, I spent most of my preschool leisure in it, and found it a strange, wild land of endless discoveries and enchantments. Even in the dead of Winter we were pastured in it almost daily, bundled up in the thick, scratchy coats, overcoats, mittens, leggings, caps, shirts, overshirts and underdrawers that the young then wore. We wallowed in the snow whenever there was any to wallow in, and piled it up into crude houses, forts and snow men, and inscribed it with wavering scrolls and devices by the method followed by infant males since the Würm Glaciation.[2] In Spring we dug worms and watched for robins, in Summer we chased butterflies and stoned sparrows, and in Autumn we made bonfires of the falling leaves. At all times from March to October we made a Dust Bowl of my mother's garden.

The Hollins street neighborhood, in the eighties, was still almost rural, for there were plenty of vacant lots near by, and the open country began only a few blocks away. Across the street from our house was the wide green of Union Square, with a fishpond, a cast-iron Greek temple housing a drinking fountain, and a little brick office and tool house for the square-keeper, looking almost small enough to

[2] One of the glacial stages, named from an Alpine river.

have been designed by Chick Sale. A block to the westward, and well within range of our upstairs windows, was the vast, mysterious compound of the House of the Good Shepherd, with nuns in flapping habits flitting along its paths and alleys, and a high stone wall shutting it in from the world. In our backyard itself there were a peach tree, a cherry tree, a plum tree, and a pear tree. The pear tree survives to this day and is still as lush and vigorous as it was in 1883, beside being thirty feet higher and so large around the waist that its branches bulge into the neighboring yards. My brother and I used to begin on the cherries when they were still only pellets of hard green, and had got through three or four powerful bellyaches before the earliest of them was ripe. The peaches, pears and plums came later in the year, but while we were waiting for them we chewed the gum that oozed from the peach-tree trunk, and practiced spitting the imbedded flies and June bugs at Pinkie the cat.

There was also a grape arbor arching the brick wall, with six vines that flourished amazingly, and produced in the Autumn a huge crop of sweet Concord grapes. My brother and I applied ourselves to them diligently from the moment the first blush of color showed on them, and all the sparrows of West Baltimore helped, but there was always enough in the end to fill a couple of large dishpans, and my mother and the hired girl spent a hot afternoon boiling them down and storing them away in glass tumblers with tin tops. My brother and I, for some reason or other, had no fancy for the grape jelly thus produced with so much travail, but we had to eat it all Winter, for it was supposed, like camomile tea, to be good for us. I don't recall any like embalming of the peaches, plums and pears; in all probability we got them all down before there were any ripe enough to preserve. The grapes escaped simply because some of them hung high, as in the fable of the fox. In later years we collared these high ones by steeple-jacking, and so paid for escape from the jelly with a few additional bellyaches.

But the show-piece of the yard was not the grape arbor, nor even the fruit-trees; it was the Summer-house, a rococo [3] structure ten feet by ten in area, with a high, pointed roof covered with tin, a wooden

[3] Full of ornament.

floor, an ornate railing, and jig-saw spirals wherever two of its members came together. This Summer house had been designed and executed by my mother's father, our Grandfather Abhau, who was a very skillful cabinetmaker and had also made some of the furniture of the house. Everything of his construction was built to last, and when, far on in the Twentieth Century, I hired a gang of house-wreckers to demolish the Summer-house, they sweated half a day with their crowbars and pickaxes. In the eighties it was the throne-room and justice-seat of the household, at least in Summer. There, on fair Sunday mornings, my father and his brother Henry, who lived next door, met to drink beer, try out new combinations of tobacco for their cigar factory, and discuss the credit of customers and the in-famies of labor agitators. And there, on his periodical visitations as head of the family, my Grandfather Mencken sat to determine all the delicate questions within his jurisdiction.

My mother was an active gardener, and during her forty-two years in Hollins street must have pulled at least a million weeds. For this business, as I first recall her, she had a uniform consisting of a long gingham apron and an old-time slat-bonnet — a headdress that went out with the Nineteenth Century. Apron and slat-bonnet hung on nails behind the kitchen door, and on a shelf adjoining were her trowels, shears and other such tools, including always a huge ball of twine. My brother Charlie and I, as we got on toward school age, were drafted to help with the weeding, but neither of us could ever make out any difference between weeds and non-weeds, so we were presently transferred to the front of the house, where every plant that came up between the cobblestones of Hollins street was indubitably verminous. The crop there was always large, and keeping it within bounds was not an easy job. We usually tackled it with broken kitchen knives, and often cut our hands. We disliked it so much that it finally became convict labor. That is to say, it was saved up for use as punishment. I recall only that the maximum penalty was one hour, and that this was reserved for such grave offenses as stealing ginger-snaps, climbing in the pear-tree, hanging up the cat by its hind leg, or telling lies in a gross and obvious manner.

Charlie was somewhat sturdier than I, and a good deal fiercer.

During most of our childhood he could lick me in anything approximating a fair fight, or, at all events, stall me. Civil war was forbidden in Hollins street, but my Grandfather Mencken, who lived in Fayette street, only three blocks away, had no apparent objection to it, save of course when he was taking his afternoon nap. I remember a glorious day when eight or ten head of his grandchildren called on him at once, and began raising hell at once. The affair started as a more or less decorous pillow-fight, but proceeded quickly to much more formidable weapons, including even bed-slats. It ranged all over the house, and must have done a considerable damage to the bric-a-brac, which was all in the Middle Bismarck mode. My grandmother and Aunt Pauline, fixed by my grandfather's pale blue eye, pretended to be amused by it for a while, but when a large china thunder-mug came bouncing down the third-story stairs and a black hair-cloth sofa in the parlor lost a leg they horned in with loud shrieks and lengths of stove-wood, and my grandfather called time.

Charlie and I were very fond of Aunt Pauline, who was immensely hospitable, and the best doughnut cook in all the Baltimores. When the creative urge seized her, which was pretty often, she would make enough doughnuts to fill a large tin wash boiler, and then send word down to Hollins street that there was a surprise waiting in Fayette street. It was uphill all the way, but Charlie and I always took it on the run, holding hands and pretending that we were miraculously dashing car-horses. We returned home an hour or so later much more slowly, and never had any appetite for supper. The immemorial tendency of mankind to concoct rituals showed itself in these feasts. After Charlie had got down his first half dozen doughnuts, and was taking time out to catch his breath and scrape the grease and sugar off his face, Aunt Pauline would always ask "How do they taste?" and he would always answer "They taste like more." Whether this catechism was original with the high contracting parties or had been borrowed from some patent-medicine almanac or other reference-work I don't know, but it never varied and it was never forgotten.

There were no kindergartens, playgrounds or other such Devil's Islands for infants in those innocent days, and my brother and I roved and rampaged at will until we were ready for school. Hollins

street was quite safe for children, for there was little traffic on it, and
that little was slow-moving, and a cart approaching over the cobblestones could be heard a block away. The backyard was enough for us
during our earliest years, with the cellar in reserve for rainy days, but
we gradually worked our way into the street and then across it to
Union Square, and there we picked up all the games then prevailing.
A few years ago, happening to cross the square, I encountered a
ma'am in horn-rimmed spectacles teaching a gang of little girls ring-
around-a-rosy. The sight filled me suddenly with so black an indignation that I was tempted to grab the ma'am and heave her into the
goldfish pond. In the days of my own youth no bossy female on the
public payroll was needed to teach games to little girls. They taught
one another — as they had been doing since the days of Neanderthal
Man.

Nevertheless, there was a constant accretion of novelty, at least
in detail. When we boys chased Indians we were only following the
Sumerian boys who chased Akkadians, but the use of hatchets was
certainly new, and so was the ceremony of scalping; moreover, our
fiends in human forms, Sitting Bull and Rain-in-the-Face, had been
as unknown and unimagined to the Sumerian boys as Henry Ward
Beecher or John L. Sullivan. The group songs we sang were mainly
of English provenance, but they had all degenerated with the years.
Here, precisely, is what we made of " King William " in Hollins street,
circa 1885:

> King William was King James's son;
> Upon a ri' a race he won;
> Upon his breast he wore a star,
> The which was called the life of war.

What a ri' was we never knew and never inquired, nor did we attach any rational concept to *the life of war*. A favorite boys' game,
called " Playing Se*bast*apool " (with a heavy accent on the *bast*),
must have been no older in its outward form than the Crimean War,
for Sebastapool was plainly Sevastopol, but in its essence it no doubt
came down from Roman times. It could be played only when building
or paving was going on in the neighborhood, and a pile of sand lay
conveniently near. We would fashion this sand into circular ramparts

in some friendly gutter, and then bristle the ramparts with gaudy tissue-paper flags, always home-made. Their poles were slivers of firewood, and their tissue-paper came from Newton's toy store at Baltimore and Calhoun streets, which served the boys and girls of West Baltimore for seventy years, and did not shut down at last until the Spring of 1939. The hired girls of the block cooked flour paste to fasten the paper to the poles.

To the garrison of a Sebastapool all the smaller boys contributed tin soldiers, including Indians. These soldiers stood in close and peaceful ranks, for there was never any attempt at attack or defense. They were taken in at night by their owners, but the flags remained until rain washed the Sebastapool away, or the milkman's early morning horse squashed it. There were sometimes two or three in a block. Girls took a hand in making the flags, but they were not allowed to pat the ramparts into shape, or to touch the tin soldiers. Indeed, for a little girl of that era to show any interest in military affairs would have been as indecorous as for her to play leap-frog or chew tobacco. The older boys also kept rather aloof though they stood ready to defend a Sebastapool against raiders. Tin soldiers were only for the very young. The more elderly were beyond such inert and puerile simulacra, which ranked with rag dolls and paper boats. These elders fought in person, and went armed.

In the sacred rubbish of the family there is a specimen of my handwriting dated 1883 — two signatures on a sheet of paper now turned a dismal brown, the one small and rather neat and the other large and ornamented with flourishes. They seem somehow fraudulent, for I was then but three years old, but there they are, and the date, which is in my mother's hand, is very clear. Maybe she guided my stubby fingers. In the same collection there is another specimen dated January 1, 1887. It shows a beginning ease with the pen, though hardly much elegance. My mother also taught me many other humble crafts — for example, how to drive a nail, how to make paper boats, and how to sharpen a lead pencil. She even taught me how to thread a needle, and for a time I hoped to take over darning my own stockings and patching the seats of my own pants, but I never managed to master the use of the thimble, and so I had to give up. Tying knots

was another art that stumped me. To this day I can't tie a bow tie,
though I have taken lessons over and over again from eminent masters, including such wizards as Joe Hergesheimer and Paul Patterson.
When I go to a party some one has to tie my tie for me. Not infrequently I arrive with the ends hanging, and must appeal to my
hostess.

This incapacity for minor dexterities has pursued me all my life,
often to my considerable embarrassment. In school I could never
learn to hold a pen in the orthodox manner: my handwriting satisfied
the professors, but my stance outraged them, and I suffered some
rough handling until they finally resigned me to my own devices. In
later life I learned bricklaying, and also got some fluency in rough
carpentering, but I could never do anything verging upon cabinet-
work. Thus I inherited nothing of the skill of my Grandfather Abhau.
All my genes in that field came from my father, who was probably the
most incompetent man with his hands ever seen on earth. I can't recall him teaching me anything in my infancy, not even marbles. He
would sometimes brag of his youthful virtuosity at all the customary
boys' games, but he always added that he had grown so old (he was
thirty-one when I was six) and suffered so much from dead beats,
noisy children and ungrateful cigarmakers, drummers and bookkeep-
ers that he had lost it. Nor could he match the endless stories that
my mother told me in the years before I could read, or the many
songs. The only song I ever heard him sing was this one:

> Rain forty days,
> Rain forty nights,
> Sauerkraut sticking out the smokestack.

Apparently there were additional words, but if so he never sang
them. The only Märchen [4] in his repertoire had to do with a man who
built a tin bridge. I recall nothing of this tale save the fact that the
bridge was of tin, which astonished my brother and me all over again
every time we heard of it. We tried to figure out how such a thing was
possible, for the mention of tin naturally made us think of tomato-
cans. But we never learned.

4 Story.

APPRECIATION HINTS

1 Exactly what were the first things the author remembers? How old was he?
2. What earlier reported events in his career does he not remember?
3. What memories cluster about 1885, when he was five years old?
4. What was his appearance as an infant?
5. How did the two small boys spend their time in the backyard in Hollins Street? Tell about their study of earthworms.
6. What fruit grew in the backyard, and what became of it?
7. What help did the boys give to their mother in the garden?
8. Describe the affair at Grandfather Mencken's.
9. Tell about Aunt Pauline's in Fayette Street, and her doughnuts.
10. Explain the boys' game Sebastapool.
11. What minor dexterities did Mencken learn, and fail to learn?
12. What is it that gives us the impression that this is a frank, unvarnished account of the author's childhood?
13. Tell about your recollections of memorable cooks and dainties of your childhood.
14. Tell of your own experiences in the family garden.
15. Write a composition based on memories of your childhood. Suggestions: The Earliest Thing I Remember, The Games We Used to Play, Stories My Mother Tells About Me, Chores of My Childhood, Early Feuds in the Family, Forbidden Fruit, Cupboard Love.
16. *Happy Days* is really a series of essays, some of which first appeared in the *New Yorker*. You may enjoy reading " Larval Stage of a Bookworm," " Cops and Their Ways," " From the Records of an Athlete," " First Steps in Divinity."

Experience is the name everyone gives to his mistakes.   Oscar Wilde: *Lady Windermere's Fan*

MICHEL DE MONTAIGNE
1533–1592

" I HAVE never seen a greater monster or miracle in the world than myself." From these words of his and from the account of himself and his writings given in the following extracts from his essays one might be led to think of Montaigne as a weakling in body and mind. In this respect the picture is false.

Michel Eyquem de Montaigne was lawyer, courtier, politician, traveler, above all philosopher and observer of life. Born at Château Montaigne, he was educated at home under his father's guidance; he spoke Latin before he learned French. He studied law, went to court and became the friend of two kings of France, traveled in Germany, Switzerland, and Italy, and became Mayor of Bordeaux.

But the picture is true in that it shows Montaigne's purpose and incentive in writing; to examine himself, his thoughts, his nature, and the reason for his actions, which he details with amazing frankness. " I speak with the paper," he says, " as with the first man I meet." He is inclined to doubt; he examines everything in a spirit of scepticism; " I do not understand; I pause; I examine." No single whole essay of Montaigne will portray him clearly. His essays, as he confesses, are discursive; in some of them the title-topic merely pops out at you now and then. The essays are given unity only by the writer's endeavor to discover and explain himself.

Though it is often said that Montaigne invented the essay, he himself disclaims any such pretension, and acknowledges his predecessors. Among these were Cicero, Plutarch, and Plato. Plutarch's famous forty-six parallel lives of Greeks and Romans go beyond biography into reflections on men and events, and the dialogues of Plato contain many essay-like passages. Montaigne invented not the form, but a name for it. He called his compositions *essais;* that is, attempts, incomplete endeavors. He found the material for immortal literature, quite unconsciously, by examining and reporting himself. His essays are the record of the inmost thoughts and experiences of a modest, tolerant, and truth-speaking man. They appeared in 1580 and were translated into English in 1601 by the Italian Florio. These extracts are from the translation of William C. Hazlitt, the grandson of William Hazlitt (see page 227).

About Himself and His Essays

HOW INCONSIDERABLE soever these essays of mine may be, I will ingenuously confess I never intended to conceal them, any more than my old, bald, grizzled portrait before them, where the painter has presented you not with a perfect face, but with a resemblance of mine. For these are my own particular opinions and fancies, and I deliver them for no other but only what I myself believe, and not what others are to believe, neither have I any other end in this writing but only to discover myself, who shall, peradventure, be another thing tomorrow, if I chance to meet any book or friend to convince me in the mean time. I have no authority to be believed, neither do I desire it, being too conscious of my own inerudition to be able to instruct others. . . .

(ON THE EDUCATION OF CHILDREN)

His Mind and Body

IT WERE very difficult, methinks, that any other should have a meaner opinion of himself, nay, that any other should have a meaner opinion of me, than I have of myself. I look upon myself as one of the common sort, saving in this, that I have no better opinion of myself; guilty of the meanest and most popular defects, but not disowned or excused, and do not value myself upon any other account than because I know my own value.

If there be any glory in the case, 'tis superficially infused into me by the treachery of my complexion, and has no body that my judgment can discern; I am sprinkled, but not dyed; for in truth, as to the effects of the mind, there is nothing ever went from me, be it what it will, with which I am satisfied; and the approbation of others makes me not think the better of myself. My judgment is tender and difficult, especially in things that concern myself; I disown myself continually, and feel myself float and waver by reason of my weakness; I have nothing of my own that satisfies my judgment. My sight is clear and regular enough, but in working it is apt to dazzle: as I most manifestly find in poetry; I love it infinitely, and am able to give a tolerable judgment of other men's works; but in truth, when I apply myself to it, I play the child, and am not able to endure myself. . . .

I am, as to the rest, strong and well knit; my face is not puffed, but full; my complexion betwixt jovial and melancholic, moderately sanguine and hot, my health vigorous and sprightly, even to a well advanced age, and rarely troubled with sickness. Such I was; for I do not make any reckoning of myself now that I am engaged in the avenues of old age, being already past forty; what I shall be from this time forward will be but half being, and no more me; I every day escape and steal away from myself:

> Singula de nobis anni praedantur euntes,
> "I find I am grown old, and every year,
> Steals something from me."

Agility and address I never had, and yet am the son of a very active and sprightly father, and that continued to be so to an extreme old age. I have seldom known any man of his condition his equal in bodily exercises; as I have seldom met with any who have not excelled me, except in running, at which I was pretty good. In music, in singing, for which I have a very unfit voice, or in playing on any sort of instrument, they could never teach me anything. I could never arrive to more than an ordinary pitch; in swimming, fencing, vaulting, and leaping, to none at all. My hands are so clumsy that I cannot so much as write, so as to read it myself, so that I had rather do what I have scribbled over again than to take upon me the trouble to make it out;

and do not read much better than I write, at least to please my hearers. I cannot handsomely fold up a letter, nor could ever make a pen, or carve at table worth a pin, nor saddle a horse, nor carry a hawk and fly her, nor hunt the dogs, nor lure a hawk, nor speak to a horse. In fine my bodily qualities are very well suited to those of my soul; there is nothing sprightly, only a full and warm vigor; I am patient enough of labor and pain, but it is only when I go voluntarily to the work, and only so long as my own desire prompts me to it; otherwise, if I am not allured with some pleasure, or have other guide than my own pure and free inclination, I am there good for nothing; for I am of a humor that, life and health excepted, there is nothing for which I would bite my nails, or that I would purchase at the price of annoyance of mind and constraint. Extremely idle, extremely given up to my own inclination, both by nature and art, I would as willingly lend a man my blood as my pains. I have a soul free and utterly its own, and accustomed to guide itself after its own fashion; having hitherto never had either master or governor imposed upon me, I have walked as far as I would, and the pace that best pleased myself; this it is that has rendered me of no use to any one but myself. (OF PRESUMPTION)

His Memory

THERE IS not a man living whom it would so little become to speak of memory as myself, for I have scarcely any at all; and do not think that the world has again another so marvelously treacherous as mine. My other faculties are all very ordinary and mean; but in this I think myself so singular, and to have the defect to such a degree of excellence, that I deserve, methinks, to be famous for it, and to have more than a common reputation. Besides the natural inconveniences which I experience from this cause, (for, in truth, the use of memory considered, Plato had reason when he called it a great and powerful Goddess;) in my country, when they would describe a man that has no sense, they say, such an one has no memory; and when I complain of mine, they seem not to

believe I am in earnest, and presently reprove me, as though I ac-
cused myself for a fool, not discerning the difference betwixt memory
and understanding; wherein they are very wide of my intention, and
do me wrong, experience rather daily showing us, on the contrary,
that a strong memory is commonly coupled with infirm judgment.
And they do me, moreover, who am so perfect in nothing as in friendship, a greater wrong in this, that they make the same words which
accuse my infirmity, represent me for an ungrateful person; bringing
my affection into question upon the account of my memory, and from
a natural imperfection, unjustly derive a defect of conscience. " He
has forgot," says one, " this request, or that promise; he no longer remembers his friends, he has forgot to say or do, or to conceal, such
and such a thing for my sake." And truly, I am apt enough to forget
many things, but to neglect anything my friend has given me in
charge, I never do it. And it should be enough, methinks, that I feel
malice, a vice so contrary to my nature.   (ON LIARS)

His Attitude towards Lying

                                        I HAVE a good fellow for my
tailor who, yet, I never knew guilty of one truth; no, not even when
it had been to his advantage. If falsehood had, like truth, but one face
only, we should be upon better terms; for we should then take the
contrary to what the liar says for certain truth; but the reverse of truth
has a hundred thousand shapes, and a field indefinite, without bound
or limit. The Pythagoreans [1] make *good* to be certain and finite; evil,
infinite and uncertain; there are a thousand ways to miss the white,
there is only one to hit it. For my own part, I have this vice in so great
horror, that I am not sure I could prevail with my conscience to secure myself from the most manifest and extreme danger by an impu-
dent and solemn lie. An ancient father says that a dog we know is
better company than a man whose language we do not understand.
And how much less sociable is false speaking than silence!

                                                          (ON LIARS)

[1] Those believing in the philosophy of Pythagorus, a Greek of Samos.

His Virtues and Vices

I HAVE sometimes known my friends call that prudence in me which was merely fortune, and repute that courage and patience which was judgment and opinion; and to attribute to me one title for another, sometimes to my advantage and sometimes otherwise. As to the rest, I am so far from being arrived at the first and most perfect degree of excellence, that even of the second I have made no great trial. I have not been very solicitous to curb the desires by which I have been importuned. My virtue is a virtue, or rather an innocence, casual and incidental. If I had been born of a more irregular complexion, I am afraid I should have made scurvy work on't; for I never observed any great stability in my soul to resist passions, if they were never so little vehement. . . .

I have naturally a horror for most vices. The answer of Antisthenes [2] to him who asked him which was the best apprenticeship: " To unlearn evil," seems to point at this. I have them in horror, I say, with a detestation so natural and so much my own that the same instinct and impression I brought with me from my nurse I yet retain, no temptation whatever having had the power to make me alter it; not so much as my own discourses, which, in some things, dashing out of the common road, might easily license me to actions that my natural inclination makes me hate. I will say a prodigious thing, but I will say it however; I find myself, in many things, more curbed and retained by my manners than my opinion, and my concupiscence [3] is less debauched than by reason.   (OF CRUELTY)

His Digressions

THIS MEDLEY is a little from my subject; I go out of my way, but 'tis rather by license than oversight; my fancies follow one another, but sometimes at a great distance, and

[2] A Greek philosopher, a pupil of Socrates and founder of the school of the cynics.

[3] Strong desire for that which is agreeable.

look towards one another, but 'tis with an oblique glance. I have read a dialogue of Plato, of such a motley and fantastic composition; the beginning about love and all the rest about rhetoric: they stick not at these variations, and have a marvellous grace in letting themselves be carried away at the pleasure of the winds, or at least to seem as if they were.

The titles of my chapters do not always comprehend the whole matter; they often denote it by some mark only. I love a poetic march, by leaps and skips; 'tis an art, as Plato says, light, nimble, and a little demoniacal. There are pieces in Plutarch where he forgets his theme; where the proposition of his argument is only incidental, and stuffed throughout with foreign matter; do but observe his meanders in the *Demon of Socrates.* Good God! how beautiful are his variations and digressions; and then, most of all, when they seem to be fortuitous, and introduced for want of heed. 'Tis the indiligent reader that loses my subject, not I; there will always be found some words or other in a corner that are to the purpose, though it lie very close. I ramble about, indiscreetly and tumultuously; my style and my wit wander at the same rate. A little folly is desirable in him that will not be guilty of stupidity.   (OF VANITY)

APPRECIATION HINTS

1. What is the only reason Montaigne has for valuing himself?
2. What does Montaigne tell us of his physical appearance?
3. What does he tell us about his accomplishments?
4. What does he say about his methods of work?
5. What does Montaigne say about his memory?
6. Describe the lying tailor, and Montaigne's attitude toward lying.
7. What is the "prodigious thing" which Montaigne says in speaking of his vices?
8. How does he explain the digressions he makes from the topics of his essays?
9. In spite of what Montaigne says about himself, would you not like him for a friend? Is there anything he says in these extracts which indicates that he would be a good friend?

10. Compare these extracts with the titles of the essays in which they appear. Do you find any connection?
11. Explain "to miss the white"; "I am sprinkled but not dyed."
12. Write a composition on some such topic as the following: Knowing Your Own Value, True Revelations, Sociable Silence, When They Thought Me Better Than I Was, Unlearning Evil, A Little Folly Is Desirable.

Nothing prevents our being natural so much as the desire to appear so.

When we resist temptation it is usually because temptation is weak, not because we are strong.

Our true qualities never make us as ridiculous as those we affect.

Duc de la Rochefoucauld: *Maxims*

OCEAN OF TRUTH

I do not know what I may appear to the world; but to myself I seem like a boy playing on the seashore, and diverting myself in now and then finding a smoother pebble or a prettier shell than ordinary, whilst the great ocean of truth lay all undiscovered before us.

Sir Isaac Newton: *Brewster's Memoirs*

THE IVORY TOWER

I cannot praise a fugitive and cloistered virtue, unexercised and unbreathed, that never sallies out and seeks her adversary, but slinks out of the race where that immortal garland is to be run for, not without dust and heat.

Milton: *Areopagitica*

RICHARD STEELE 1672–1729 AN ADVENTURER with the strange

experiences of Alexander Selkirk, coming to the London of 1709, would have news value for any journalist, but especially for Richard Steele, who was always on the lookout for "all matters of what kind soever." In his essays he showed the "town" that they were a parcel of fools, fops, and coquettes, and did it so good-naturedly that they liked it. In a flippant and vicious age he wanted to show "much shorter methods to be happy than those men ordinarily practice," and that appears to be one object of this essay on Alexander Selkirk.

Richard Steele was a perfect example of the kind of person who makes good resolutions and breaks them. "I see and approve the better way," he says of himself, "but I follow the worse." Always honest, he was always in debt; always preaching sobriety, he was frequently overtaken in his cups; he wrote vigorously against fighting duels, and fought one; but throughout his life he was a warm-hearted, courteous, and good-humored gentleman. Steele is best known as the founder of the *Tatler* in 1709 and the *Spectator* in 1711, and as the collaborator with his old schoolmate Addison. When the *Spectator* ended in 1712, several other short-lived publications followed. Among these was the *Englishman,* of which this essay is number 26.

When Alexander Selkirk was still a boy, he ran away from his Scotch home to join a privateering expedition to the South Seas under the pirate, William Dampier. Dampier had been as wild a buccaneer as can be imagined. At one time, according to the diary which he kept, he and his captain would have been killed and eaten by a starving and mutinous crew had they not sighted and landed at Guam in the Ladrones. Selkirk was sailing-master on the Cinque Ports (Captain Stradling), which put in to Juan Fernandez in September 1704 to take off two stranded sailors. It was with Captain Stradling that Selkirk had the quarrel mentioned by Steele, which resulted in his being marooned on the island. Dampier touched again at Juan Fernandez on January 31, 1709, and took Selkirk off. On reaching London he made the acquaintance of Steele, but before long was off to sea again and died on board ship. Selkirk met Daniel Defoe at Bristol and related his adventures; *Robinson Crusoe* appeared in 1719.

Alexander Selkirk

Talia monstrabat, relegens errata retrorsum [1]

Virgil, *Aeneid*, III, 690

Under the title of this paper, I do not think it foreign to my design to speak of a man born in her Majesty's dominions, and relate an
adventure in his life so uncommon that it is doubtful whether the like
has happened to any of the human race. The person I speak of is
Alexander Selkirk, whose name is familiar to men of curiosity from
the fame of his having lived four years and four months alone in the
island of Juan Fernandez. I had the pleasure frequently to converse
with the man soon after his arrival in England in the year 1711. It was
matter of great curiosity to hear him, as he is a man of good sense,
give an account of the different revolutions in his own mind in the
long solitude. When we consider how painful absence from company
for the space of but one evening is to the generality of mankind, we
may have a sense how painful this necessary and constant solitude
was to a man bred a sailor, and ever accustomed to enjoy and suffer,
eat, drink, and sleep, in fellowship and company. He was put ashore
from a leaky vessel, with the captain of which he had had an irrecon-
cilable difference; and he chose rather to take his fate in this place
than in a crazy vessel, under a disagreeable commander. His portion
was a sea-chest, his wearing clothes and bedding, a firelock, a pound
of gunpowder, a large quantity of bullets, a flint and steel, a few

---

[1] Such things he showed as he retraced the track of his past wanderings.

pounds of tobacco, an hatchet, a knife, a kettle, a Bible, and other books of devotion, together with pieces that concerned navigation, and his mathematical instruments. Resentment against his officer, who had ill-used him, made him look forward on this change of life as the more eligible one, till the instant in which he saw the vessel put off; at which moment his heart yearned within him, and melted at the parting with his comrades and all human society at once. He had in provisions for the sustenance of life but the quantity of two meals, the island abounding only in wild goats, cats, and rats. He judged it most probable that he should find more immediate and easy relief by finding shellfish on the shore than seeking game with his gun. He accordingly found great quantities of turtles, whose flesh is extremely delicious, and of which he frequently ate very plentifully on his first arrival, till it grew disagreeable to his stomach, except in jellies. The necessities of hunger and thirst were his greatest diversions from the reflection on his lonely condition. When those appetites were satisfied, the desire of society was as strong a call upon him, and he appeared to himself least necessitous when he wanted everything; for the supports of his body were easily attained, but the eager longings for seeing again the face of man during the interval of craving bodily appetites were hardly supportable. He grew dejected, languid, and melancholy, scarce able to refrain from doing himself violence, till by degrees, by the force of reason, and frequent reading of the Scriptures, and turning his thoughts upon the study of navigation, after the space of eighteen months he grew thoroughly reconciled to his condition. When he had made this conquest, the vigour of his health, disengagement from the world, a constant, cheerful, serene sky, and a temperate air made his life one continual feast, and his being much more joyful than it had before been irksome. He, now taking delight in everything, made the hut in which he lay, by ornaments which he cut down from a spacious wood, on the side of which it was situated, the most delicious bower, fanned with continual breezes and gentle aspirations of wind, that made his repose after the chase equal to the most sensual pleasures.

I forgot to observe that, during the time of his dissatisfaction, monsters of the deep, which frequently lay on the shore, added to the horrors of his solitude; the dreadful howlings and voices seemed too terrible to be made for the human ears; but upon the recovery of his temper, he could with pleasure not only hear their voices, but approach the monsters themselves with great intrepidity. He speaks of sea-lions, whose jaws and tails were capable of seizing or breaking the limbs of a man, if he approached them; but at that time his spirits and life were so high, and he could act so regularly and unconcerned, that merely from being unruffled in himself he killed them with the greatest ease imaginable; for observing that, though their jaws and tails were so terrible, yet the animals being mighty slow in working themselves round, he had nothing to do but place himself exactly opposite to their middle, and as close to them as possible, he dispatched them with his hatchet at will.

The precaution which he took against want, in case of sickness, was to lame kids when very young, so as that they might recover their health, but never be capable of speed. These he had in great numbers about his hut; and when he was himself in full vigour, he could take at full speed the swiftest goat running up a promontory, and never failed of catching them but on descent.

His habitation was extremely pestered with rats, which gnawed his clothes and feet when sleeping. To defend him against them, he fed and tamed numbers of young kitlings, who lay about his bed and preserved him from the enemy. When his clothes were worn out, he dried and tacked together the skins of goats, with which he clothed himself, and was inured to pass through woods, bushes, and brambles with as much carelessness and precipitance as any other animal. It happened once to him that, running on the summit of a hill, he made a stretch to seize a goat, with which under him he fell down a precipice, and lay helpless for the space of three days, the length of which time he measured by the moon's growth since his last observation. This manner of life grew so exquisitely pleasant that he never had a moment heavy on his hands; his nights were untroubled, and his days joyous, from the practice of temperance and exercise. It was his manner to use stated hours and places for exercises of devotion, which he performed aloud, in order to keep up the faculties of speech, and to utter himself with greater energy.

When I first saw him, I thought, if I had not been let into his character and story, I could have discerned that he had been much separated from company, from his aspect and gesture; there was a strong but cheerful seriousness in his look, and a certain disregard to the ordinary things about him, as if he had been sunk in thought. When the ship which brought him off the island came in, he received them with the greatest indifference, with relation to the prospect of going off with them, but with great satisfaction in an opportunity to refresh and help them. The man frequently bewailed his return to the world, which could not, he said, with all its enjoyments, restore him to the tranquillity of his solitude. Though I had frequently conversed with him, after a few months' absence he met me in the street, and though he spoke to me, I could not recollect that I had seen him; familiar converse in this town had taken off the loneliness of his aspect, and quite altered the air of his face.

This plain man's story is a memorable example that he is happiest who confines his wants to natural necessities; and he that goes further in his desires increases his wants in proportion to his acquisitions; or to use his own expression, " I am now worth eight hundred pounds, but shall never be so happy as when I was not worth a farthing."

(NO. 26 OF THE ENGLISHMAN, DECEMBER 3, 1713)

APPRECIATION HINTS

1. What articles was Selkirk allowed to take ashore with him?
2. What food was there on the island?
3. What was it that caused him to think of committing suicide, and what occupations brought back mental health?
4. How did he now find that he could cope with the " monsters of the deep "?
5. How did he provide against lack of food?

6. Tell about his mishap in goat-hunting.
7. What was there strange about Selkirk when Steele first met him? what change did life in London make in him?
8. What general conclusion does Steele draw from the example of Selkirk?
9. Gather information about Juan Fernandez: its climate, animal life, mountains, etc.
10. Write a composition on some experience of solitude. Suggestions: All Alone at Night, My Natural Necessities, Short Rations, " I Am Monarch of All I Survey," " There Is Society Where None Intrudes."
11. Read Cowper's poem " supposed to be written by Alexander Selkirk."
12. Read some of the essays in the *Tatler* or *Spectator*. Suggestions: " The Trumpet Club," " Recollections of Childhood," " The Fine Lady's journal," " Sir Roger de Coverley Hare-Hunting."
13. Read " What I Lived For," in Thoreau's *Walden*, and then report to the class, comparing Selkirk's life on the island with Thoreau's at Walden Pond.

COURAGE

The greatest glory that has ever come to me was to be swallowed up in London, not knowing a soul, with no means of subsistence, and the fun of working till the stars went out. To have known any one would have spoilt it.
J. M. Barrie: *Rectorial Address at St. Andrews*

Grief can take care of itself; but to get the full value of joy you must have somebody to divide it with.
Mark Twain

CHARLES LAMB 1775–1834

NO ENGLISH essays hold so firm a place in the affection of readers as the *Essays of Elia*. They are part of the heritage of English literature that all should claim; and the purpose of representing Lamb by a series of extracts from five essays is to induce you to read them and to make this heritage yours.

Charles Lamb was a poor boy who went to a Charity school. At fourteen he was perched on a clerk's stool in the City of London. Three years later he entered the accountant's office of the East India House, where he remained until, thirty-three years later, he was pensioned off, a "superannuated man." There was a taint of insanity in the family, and in 1796, when Charles was twenty-one, his sister suddenly stabbed their mother to death. Charles obtained her release from the asylum on the condition that he himself would look after her. This he did for all the rest of his life, for she survived him nearly thirteen years. When recurrent attacks of insanity occurred, he led her to the asylum and back again home when they had ceased. Wedded to affliction, he had to abandon any plans he may have had for his own marriage.

That is the dark side of Lamb's life, and he revealed it only to his closest friends. To the rest of the world and to the readers of Elia he appeared as a man of delicate humor, a lover of innocent vanities, jests, candle light, and the cheerful glass — a fellow of infinite jest who delighted to juggle fact and fiction. He said that once, on his way to the East India House, he met Coleridge, who began a discourse on fate and freewill, meanwhile holding on to the top button of Lamb's coat. He listened for some time, and then cut the button off with his penknife and continued on his way. On his return some hours later, says Elia, he found Coleridge still holding the button and holding forth to his imagined auditor. This union of pathos and humor, of the heroic and the whimsical has endeared Lamb to generations of readers of the *Essays of Elia*. And while he lived no man was ever more loved by a wide circle of friends.

It was in 1820 that "The South-Sea House," the first of *The Essays of Elia* appeared in the *London Magazine*. They were collected and published in 1823.

His Father

I KNEW this Lovel. He was a man of an incorrigible and losing honesty. . . . In the cause of the oppressed he never considered inequalities, or calculated the number of his opponents. He once wrested a sword out of the hand of a man of quality that had drawn upon him, and pommelled him severely with the hilt of it. The swordsman had offered insult to a female — an occasion upon which no odds against him could have prevented the interference of Lovel. . . . L. was the liveliest little fellow breathing, had a face as gay as Garrick's, whom he was said greatly to resemble (I have a portrait of him which confirms it), possessed a fine turn for humorous poetry — next to Swift and Prior — molded heads in clay or plaster of Paris to admiration, by the dint of natural genius merely; turned cribbage-boards, and such small cabinet toys, to perfection; took a hand at quadrille or bowls with equal facility; made punch better than any man of his degree in England; had the merriest quips and conceits; and was altogether as brimful of rogueries and inventions as you could desire. He was a brother of the angle, moreover, and just such a free, hearty, honest companion as Mr. Izaak Walton would have chosen to go a fishing with. I saw him in his old age and the decay of his faculties, palsy-smitten, in the last sad stage of human weakness — " a remnant most forlorn of what he was," — yet even then his eye would light up upon the mention of his favourite Garrick. . . . At intervals, too, he would speak of his former life, and how he came up a little boy from Lincoln to go to service, and how his mother cried at parting with him, and how he returned, after some few years absence, in his smart new livery to see her, and she blest herself at the change, and could hardly be brought to believe that it was " her own bairn." And then, the excitement subsiding, he would weep, till I have wished that sad second-childhood might have a mother still to lay its head upon her lap. But the common mother of us all in no long time after received him gently into hers. . . .

A Colleague at the South-Sea House

THE CASHIER at that time was one Evans, a Cambro-Briton. He had something of the choleric complexion of his countrymen stamped on his visage, but was a worthy, sensible man at bottom. He wore his hair, to the last, powdered and frizzed out, in the fashion which I remember to have seen in caricatures of what were termed, in my young days, *Maccaronies*.[1] He was the last of that race of beaux. Melancholy as a gib-cat over his counter all the forenoon, I think I see him making up his cash (as they call it) with tremulous fingers, as if he feared every one about him was a defaulter; in his hypochondry, ready to imagine himself one; haunted, at least, with the idea of the possibility of his becoming one: his tristful visage clearing up a little over his roast neck of veal at Anderton's at two (where his picture still hangs, taken a little before his death by desire of the master of the coffee-house which he had frequented for the last five and twenty years), but not attaining the meridian of its animation till evening brought on the hour of tea and visiting. The simultaneous sound of his well-known rap at the door with the stroke of the clock announcing six, was a topic of never-failing mirth in the families which this dear old bachelor gladdened with his presence. Then was his *forte*, his glorified hour! How would he chirp and expand over a muffin! How would he dilate into secret history!   (THE SOUTH-SEA HOUSE)

---

[1] Fops; dandies.

Ralph Bigod Esq., Borrower

THE HUMAN species, according
to the best theory I can form of it, is composed of two distinct races,
the men who borrow, and *the men who lend.* To these two original
diversities may be reduced all those impertinent classifications of
Gothic and Celtic tribes, white men, black men, red men. All the
dwellers upon earth, " Parthians, and Medes, and Elamites," flock
hither, and do naturally fall in with one or other of these primary
distinctions. The infinite superiority of the former, which I choose to
designate as the *great race,* is discernible in their figure, port, and a
certain instinctive sovereignty. The latter are born degraded. " He
shall serve his brethren." There is something in the air of one of this
cast, lean and suspicious; contrasting with the open, trusting, generous manners of the other. . . .

Reflections like the foregoing were forced upon my mind by the
death of my old friend, Ralph Bigod, Esq.,[2] who parted this life on
Wednesday evening; dying, as he had lived, without much trouble.
He boasted himself a descendant from mighty ancestors of that name,
who heretofore held ducal dignities in this realm. In his actions and
sentiments he belied not the stock to which he pretended. Early in
life he found himself invested with ample revenues; which, with that
noble disinterestedness which I have noticed as inherent in men of
the *great race,* he took almost immediate measures entirely to dissi-
pate and bring to nothing: for there is something revolting in the idea
of a king holding a private purse; and the thoughts of Bigod were all
regal. Thus furnished, by the very act of disfurnishment; getting rid
of the cumbersome luggage of riches, more apt (as one sings)

> To slacken virtue, and abate her edge,
> Than prompt her to do aught may merit praise,

he set forth, like some Alexander, upon his great enterprise, " bor-
rowing and to borrow! "

[2] In 1803 Lamb had tried journalism, and he knew Ralph Bigod at
that time.

In his periegesis, or triumphant progress throughout this island, it has been calculated that he laid a tithe part of the inhabitants under contribution. I reject this estimate as greatly exaggerated: — but having had the honor of accompanying my friend, divers times, in his perambulations about this vast city, I own I was greatly struck at first with the prodigious number of faces we met, who claimed a sort of respectful acquaintance with us. He was one day so obliging as to explain the phenomenon. It seems, these were his tributaries; feeders of his exchequer; gentlemen, his good friends (as he was pleased to express himself), to whom he had occasionally been beholden for a loan. Their multitudes did no way disconcert him. He rather took a pride in numbering them; and, with Comus, seemed pleased to be "stocked with so fair a herd."

With such sources, it was a wonder how he contrived to keep his treasury always empty. He did it by force of an aphorism, which he had often in his mouth, that "money kept longer than three days stinks." So he made use of it while it was fresh. . . .

When I think of this man; his fiery glow of heart; his swell of feeling; how magnificent, how *ideal* he was; how great at the midnight hour; and when I compare with him the companions with whom I have associated since, I grudge the saving of a few idle ducats, and think that I am fallen into the society of *lenders,* and *little* men.   (THE TWO RACES OF MEN)

Elia Himself

IF I KNOW aught of myself, no one whose mind is introspective — and mine is painfully so — can have a less respect for his present identity, than I have for the man Elia. I know him to be light, and vain, and humoursome; a notorious . . . ; addicted to . . . ; averse from counsel, neither taking it, nor offering it; — . . . besides; a stammering buffoon; what you will; lay it on, and spare not; I subscribe to it all, and much more, than thou canst be willing to lay at his door — but for the child Elia — that "other me," there, in the background — I must take leave to cherish the remembrance of that young master — with as little reference, I protest, to his

stupid changeling of five and forty, as if it had been a child of some
other house, and not of my parents. I can cry over its patient small-
pox at five, and rougher medicaments. I can lay its poor fevered head
upon the sick pillow at Christ's, and wake with it in surprise at the
gentle posture of maternal tenderness hanging over it, that unknown
had watched its sleep. I know how it shrank from any the least
color of falsehood. — God help thee, Elia, how art thou changed! —
Thou art sophisticated. — I know how honest, how courageous (for a
weakling) it was — how religious, how imaginative, how hopeful!
From what have I not fallen, if the child I remember was indeed myself, — and not some dissembling guardian, presenting a false identity, to give the rule to my unpracticed steps, and regulate the tone
of my moral being!

    That I am fond of indulging, beyond a hope of sympathy, in such
retrospection, may be the symptom of some sickly idiosyncrasy. Or is
it owing to another cause: simply, that being without wife or family,
I have not learned to project myself enough out of myself; and having
no offspring of my own to dally with, I turn back upon memory, and
adopt my own early idea, as my heir and favorite? If these speculations seem fantastical to thee, Reader — (a busy man, perchance), if
I tread out of the way of thy sympathy, and am singularly conceited
only, I retire, impenetrable to ridicule, under the phantom cloud of
Elia.

    . . . Not childhood alone, but the young man till thirty, never
feels practically that he is mortal. He knows it indeed, and, if need
were, he could preach a homily on the fragility of life; but he brings
it not home to himself, any more than in a hot June we can appropriate to our imagination the freezing days of December. But now,
shall I confess a truth? — I feel these audits [3] but too powerfully. I
begin to count the probabilities of my duration, and to grudge at the
expenditure of moments and shortest periods, like misers' farthings.
In proportion as the years both lessen and shorten, I set more count
upon their periods, and would fain lay my ineffectual finger upon the
spoke of the great wheel. I am not content to pass away " like a weav-
er's shuttle." Those metaphors solace me not, nor sweeten the un-

<hr>

         [3] Reckonings.

palatable draught of mortality. I care not to be carried with the tide, that smoothly bears human life to eternity; and reluct [4] at the inevitable course of destiny. I am in love with this green earth; the face of town and country; the unspeakable rural solitudes, and the sweet security of streets. I would set up my tabernacle here. I am content to stand still at the age to which I am arrived; I, and my friends: to be no younger, no richer, no handsomer. I do not want to be weaned by age; or drop, like mellow fruit, as they say, into the grave. — Any alteration, on this earth of mine, in diet or in lodging, puzzles and discomposes me. My household gods plant a terrible fixed foot, and are not rooted up without blood. They do not willingly seek Lavinian shores.[5] A new state of being staggers me.

Sun, and sky, and breeze, and solitary walks, and summer holidays, and the greenness of fields, and the delicious juices of meats and fishes, and society, and the cheerful glass, and candlelight, and fireside conversations, and innocent vanities, and jests, and *irony itself* — do these things go out with life?

Can a ghost laugh, or shake his gaunt sides, when you are pleasant with him?   (NEW YEAR'S EVE)

Alice and John, His Children That Might Have Been

CHILDREN love to listen to stories about their elders, when *they* were children; to stretch their imagination to the conception of a traditionary great-uncle, or grandame, whom they never saw. It was in this spirit that my little ones crept about me the other evening to hear about their great-grandmother Field, who lived in a great house in Norfolk (a hundred times bigger than that in which they and papa lived) which had been the scene — so at least it was generally believed in that part of the country — of the tragic incidents which they had lately become familiar with from the ballad of the Children in the Wood. Certain it is that the whole story of the children and their cruel uncle was to be seen fairly carved out in wood upon the chimney-piece of the great hall,

---

⁴ Hold back.   ⁵ Like Æneas after the sack of Troy.

the whole story down to the Robin Redbreasts; till a foolish rich person pulled it down to set up a marble one of modern invention in its stead, with no story upon it. Here Alice put out one of her dear mother's looks, too tender to be called upbraiding. Then I went on to say, how religious and how good their great-grandmother Field was, how beloved and respected by everybody, though she was not indeed the mistress of this great house, but had only the charge of it; but still she lived in it in a manner as if it had been her own, and kept up the dignity of the great house in a sort while she lived, which afterwards came to decay, and was nearly pulled down, and all its old ornaments stripped and carried away to the owner's other house, where they were set up, and looked as awkward as if someone were to carry away the old tombs they had seen lately at the Abbey, and stick them up in Lady C.'s tawdry gilt drawing room. Here John smiled, as much as to say, "that would be foolish indeed." And then I told how, when she came to die, her funeral was attended by a concourse of all the poor, and some of the gentry too, of the neighborhood for many miles round, to show their respect for her memory, because she had been such a good and religious woman; so good indeed that she knew all the Psaltery by heart, ay, and a great part of the Testament besides. Here little Alice spread her hands. Then I told what a tall, upright, graceful person their great-grandmother Field once was; and how in her youth she was esteemed the best dancer — here Alice's little right foot played an involuntary movement, till, upon my looking grave, it desisted — the best dancer, I was saying, in the county, till a cruel disease called a cancer, came, and bowed her down with pain; but it could never bend her good spirits, or make them stoop, but they were still upright, because she was so good and religious.

Then I told how good she was to all her grandchildren, having us to the great house in the holy-days, where I in particular used to spend many hours by myself, sometimes in the spacious old-fashioned gardens, which I had almost to myself, unless when now and then a solitary gardening man would cross me — and how the nectarines and peaches hung upon the walls, without my ever offering to pluck them, because they were forbidden fruit, unless now and then, — and be-

cause I had more pleasure in strolling about among the old melan-
choly-looking yew trees, or the firs, and picking up the red berries,
and the fir-apples, which were good for nothing but to look at — or
in lying about upon the fresh grass, with all the fine garden smells
around me — or basking in the orangery, till I could almost fancy
myself ripening too along with the oranges and the limes in that
grateful warmth — or in watching the dace that darted to and fro in
the fishpond, at the bottom of the garden, with here and there a great
sulky pike hanging midway down the water in silent state, as if it
mocked at their impertinent friskings, — I had more pleasure in these
busy-idle diversions than in all the sweet flavors of peaches, nectarines, oranges, and such-like common baits for children. Here John
slyly deposited back upon the plate a bunch of grapes, which, not
unobserved by Alice, he had meditated dividing with her, and both
seemed willing to relinquish them for the present as irrelevant. Then,
in somewhat a more heightened tone, I told how, though their great-
grandmother Field loved all her grandchildren, yet in an especial
manner she might be said to love their uncle, John L——,[6] because he
was so handsome and spirited a youth, and a king to the rest of us;
. . . and how when he died, though he had not been dead an hour, it
seemed as if he had died a great while ago, such a distance there is
betwixt life and death; and how I bore his death as I thought pretty
well at first, but afterwards it haunted and haunted me; and though I
did not cry or take it to heart as some do, and as I think he would have
done if I had died, yet I missed him all day long, and knew not till

then how much I had loved
him. I missed his kindness,
and I missed his crossness, and
wished him to be alive again,
to be quarreling with him
(for we quarreled sometimes),
rather than not have him
again, and was as uneasy without him, as he, their poor
uncle, must have been when

[6] John Lamb, the brother of Charles.

the doctor took off his limb. Here the children fell a crying, and asked if their little mourning which they had on was not for uncle John, and they looked up, and prayed me not to go on about their uncle, but to tell them some stories about their pretty dead mother. Then I told how for seven long years, in hope sometimes, sometimes in despair, yet persisting ever, I courted the fair Alice W——n; [7] and, as much as children could understand, I explained to them what coyness, and difficulty, and denial, meant in maidens — when suddenly turning to Alice, the soul of the first Alice looked out at her eyes with such a reality of re-presentment, that I became in doubt which of them stood there before me, or whose that bright hair was; and while I stood gazing, both the children gradually grew fainter to my view, receding, and still receding, till nothing at last but two mournful features were seen in the uttermost distance, which, without speech, strangely impressed upon me the effects of speech: " We are not of Alice, nor of thee, nor are we children at all. The children of Alice call Bartrum father. We are nothing; less than nothing, and dreams. We are only what might have been, and must wait upon the tedious shores of Lethe millions of ages before we have existence, and a name "—— and immediately awaking, I found myself quietly seated in my bachelor armchair, where I had fallen asleep, with the faithful Bridget unchanged by my side — but John L. (or James Elia) was gone forever.

(DREAM CHILDREN: A REVERIE)

APPRECIATION HINTS

A few facts will help you. Charles's father John Lamb (Lovel) died in 1796, soon after the family tragedy. John Lamb, Jr., the brother of Charles, died in 1821; Charles had really no cause to love or respect him because he shirked his family responsibilities. Lamb drew up, for one of his friends in the East India House, a " key " to his veiled references to persons, and in it Alice W—— appears as Alice Winterton. But this is mere mystification; Lamb's sweetheart was Ann Simmons, who married a wealthy London pawnbroker called Bartrum. Charles met Ann at the great house in Norfolk.

[7] Ann Simmons, Lamb's early love.

1. What were the accomplishments of Lamb's father? What seems to you to have been his most admirable qualities?
2. By what hour of the day had Evans recovered his cheerfulness? What had occasioned the recovery?
3. Where did Ralph Bigod get his money, and how did he spend it?
4. For what reasons does Lamb wish to hold back the passage of time?
5. Pick out some long sentences from " Dream-Children." Do you think such long sentences are appropriate in this essay? Why?
6. Would you guess that Lamb was more inclined to borrow than to lend? In reality he was constantly lending, and once gave a friend in need one hundred pounds which he needed himself. How do you account for this admiration of the borrower?
7. Contrast Lamb's portrait of himself as a boy with Mencken's. Which had the happier childhood?
8. Lamb's style is characterized by memorable phrases; for example, his father was a man " of incorrigible and losing honesty." Make a list of the phrases which seem to you most effective.
9. What similarities did you notice between Montaigne and Lamb when they write about their own personal qualities?
10. It is said that in Lamb smiles and tears are sometimes close together. Can you find examples?
11. Write a composition on one of the following topics or, better, on a topic of your own suggested by your reading in Lamb: The Child is Father of the Man, Memories of Childhood, An Early School Friend, Sun, Sky and Breeze, The Sweet Security of Streets, Chirping Over a Muffin, Oh . . . How Art Thou Changed!
12. Read in the Essays of Elia, " A Dissertation upon Roast Pig," " Christ's Hospital Five-and-Thirty Years Ago," " A Quakers' Meeting."

The greatest pleasure I know is to do a good action by stealth — and to have it found out by accident.

Charles Lamb

RALPH WALDO EMERSON
1803–1882

THOUSANDS of American students have for the first time in their lives been startled into thinking by reading Emerson. He had the habit of packing a provocative thought into a brief statement, and flinging it out like a challenge; just as a famous football coach had the habit of drawing the diagram of a new offensive play, planking it down before one of his assistants, and saying, " There! What's your reply to that? " " Whoso would be a man," says Emerson in this essay, " must be a nonconformist " . . . " consistency is the hobgoblin of little minds." Such affirmations as these — bald and stripped of saving clauses — have been self-starters to many minds. One of the most provocative and challenging of Emerson's essays is " Self-Reliance," part of which is here reprinted.

In 1833 Emerson had been in England, visiting kindred spirits. In his diary written during his voyage home there is a passage which strikingly resembles what is said in the following essay. " A man contains all that is needful to his government within himself. . . . All real good or evil that can befall a man must be from himself." Emerson wrote this eight or nine years before this essay took shape, and his method of composition is interesting to anyone who wants to write well. In his notebooks he used to jot down his observations, stray thoughts, reflections and any striking phrases which occurred to him, and these he used in the lectures by which he earned a living and which won his first fame. A subject for a lecture would, as he thought it over, gather ideas and attract phrases and illustrations from his notebooks. His essays are revised and rearranged lectures and, like the essays of Montaigne, will sometimes seem to lack structural progression, unless the reader keeps in mind the central idea which the lecturer was illustrating.

Ralph Waldo Emerson was born in Boston and educated at Harvard. He taught for a while, studied theology, became for a short time a minister, but resigned his pulpit in 1832 because of his doubts concerning certain Christian doctrines. After a trip abroad he went to live at Concord, and began his long career as a successful lecturer. Collections of essays appeared in 1841 and 1844, and *English Traits,* in 1856.

I READ the other day some verses written by an eminent painter which were original and not conventional. The soul always hears an admonition in such lines, let the subject be what it may. The sentiment they instill is of more value than any thought they may contain. To believe your own thought, to believe that what is true for you in your private heart is true for all men, — that is genius. Speak your latent conviction, and it shall be the universal sense; for the inmost in due time becomes the outmost, and our first thought is rendered back to us by the trumpets of the Last Judgment. Familiar as the voice of the mind is to each, the highest merit we ascribe to Moses, Plato, and Milton is that they set at naught books and traditions, and spoke not what men, but what *they* thought. A man should learn to detect and watch that gleam of light which flashes across his mind from within, more than the luster of the firmament of bards and sages. Yet he dismisses without notice his thought, because it is his. In every work of genius we recognize our own rejected thoughts; they come back to us with a certain alienated majesty. Great works of art have no more affecting lesson for us than this. They teach us to abide by our spontaneous impression with good-humored inflexibility, then most when the whole cry of voices is on the other side. Else tomorrow a stranger will say with masterly good sense precisely what we have thought and felt all the time, and we shall be forced to take with shame our own opinion from another. . . .

Trust thyself: every heart vibrates to that iron string. Accept the place the divine providence has found for you, the society of your contemporaries, the connection of events. Great men have always done so, and confided themselves childlike to the genius of their age, betraying their perception that the absolutely trustworthy was seated at their heart, working through their hands, predominating in all their being. And we are now men, and must accept in the highest mind the same transcendent destiny; and not minors and invalids in a protected corner, not cowards fleeing before a revolution, but guides, redeemers and benefactors, obeying the Almighty effort and advancing on Chaos and the Dark.

What pretty oracles nature yields us on this text in the face and behavior of children, babes, and even brutes! That divided and rebel mind, that distrust of a sentiment because our arithmetic has computed the strength and means opposed to our purpose, these have not. Their mind being whole, their eye is as yet unconquered, and when we look in their faces we are disconcerted. Infancy conforms to nobody; all conform to it; so that one babe commonly makes four or five out of the adults who prattle and play to it. So God has armed youth and puberty and manhood no less with its own piquancy and charm, and made it enviable and gracious and its claims not to be put by, if it will stand by itself. Do not think the youth has no force, because he cannot speak to you and me. Hark! in the next room his voice is sufficiently clear and emphatic. It seems he knows how to speak to his contemporaries. Bashful or bold then, he will know how to make us seniors very unnecessary.

The nonchalance of boys who are sure of a dinner, and would disdain as much as a lord to do or say aught to conciliate one, is the healthy attitude of human nature. A boy is in the parlor what the pit is in the playhouse; independent, irresponsible, looking out from his corner on such people and facts as pass by, he tries and sentences them on their merits, in the swift, summary way of boys, as good, bad, interesting, silly, eloquent, troublesome. He cumbers himself never about consequences, about interests; he gives an independent, genuine verdict. You must court him; he does not court you. But the man is as it were clapped into jail by his consciousness. As soon as he has once acted or spoken with *éclat* he is a committed person, watched by the sympathy or the hatred of hundreds, whose affections must now enter into his account. There is no Lethe [1] for this. Ah, that he could pass again into his neutrality! Who can thus avoid all pledges and, having observed, observe again from the same unaffected, unbiased, unbribable, unaffrighted innocence, — must always be formidable. He would utter opinions on all passing affairs, which being seen to be not private but necessary, would sink like darts into the ear of men and put them in fear.

These are the voices which we hear in solitude, but they grow faint and inaudible as we enter into the world. Society everywhere is in conspiracy against the manhood of every one of its members. Society is a joint-stock company, in which the members agree, for the better securing of his bread to each shareholder, to surrender the liberty and culture of the eater. The virtue in most request is conformity. Self-reliance is its aversion. It loves not realities and creators, but names and customs.

Whoso would be a man, must be a nonconformist. He who would gather immortal palms must not be hindered by the name of goodness, but must explore if it be goodness. Nothing is at last sacred but the integrity of your own mind. Absolve you to yourself, and you shall have the suffrage of the world. I remember an answer which when quite young I was prompted to make to a valued adviser who was wont to importune me with the dear old doctrines of the church. On my saying, "What have I to do with the sacredness of traditions, if I live wholly from within?" my friend suggested, — "But these impulses may be from below, not from above." I replied, "They do not seem to me to be such; but if I am the Devil's child, I will live then from the Devil." No law can be sacred to me but that of my nature. Good and bad are but names very readily transferable to that or this; the only right is what is after my constitution; the only wrong what is against it. A man is to carry himself in the presence of all opposition as if everything were titular [2] and ephemeral but he. I am ashamed to think how easily we capitulate to badges and names, to large societies and dead institutions. Every decent and well-spoken

---

[1] Forgetfulness.   [2] Mere names.

individual affects and sways me more than is right. I ought to go up-right and vital, and speak the rude truth in all ways. If malice and vanity wear the coat of philanthropy, shall that pass? If an angry bigot assumes this bountiful cause of Abolition, and comes to me with his last news from Barbados, why should I not say to him, " Go love thy infant; love thy wood-chopper; be good-natured and modest; have that grace; and never varnish your hard, uncharitable ambition with this incredible tenderness for black folk a thousand miles off. Thy love afar is spite at home." Rough and graceless would be such greeting, but truth is handsomer than the affectation of love. Your goodness must have some edge to it, — else it is none. The doc-trine of hatred must be preached, as the counteraction of the doctrine of love, when that pules and whines. I shun father and mother and wife and brother when my genius calls me. I would write on the lin-tels of the door-post, *Whim*. I hope it is somewhat better than whim at last, but we cannot spend the day in explanation. Expect me not to show cause why I seek or why I exclude company. Then again, do not tell me, as a good man did today, of my obligation to put all poor men in good situations. Are they *my* poor? I tell thee thou foolish philanthropist that I grudge the dollar, the dime, the cent I give to such men as do not belong to me and to whom I do not belong. There is a class of persons to whom by all spiritual affinity I am bought and sold; for them I will go to prison if need be; but your miscellaneous popular charities; the education at college of fools; the building of meetinghouses to the vain end to which many now stand; alms to sots, and the thousandfold Relief Societies; — though I confess with shame I sometimes succumb and give the dollar, it is a wicked dollar, which by and by I shall have the manhood to withhold. . . .

What I must do is all that concerns me, not what the people think. This rule, equally arduous in actual and in intellectual life, may serve for the whole distinction between greatness and meanness. It is the harder because you will always find those who think they know what is your duty better than you know it. It is easy in the world to live after the world's opinion; it is easy in solitude to live after our own; but the great man is he who in the midst of the crowd keeps with perfect sweetness the independence of solitude. . . .

For nonconformity the world whips you with its displeasure. And therefore a man must know how to estimate a sour face. The by-standers look askance on him in the public street or in the friend's parlor. If this aversation [3] had its origin in contempt and resistance like his own he might well go home with a sad countenance; but the sour faces of the multitude, like their sweet faces, have no deep cause, but are put on and off as the wind blows and a newspaper directs. Yet is the discontent of the multitude more formidable than that of the senate and the college. It is easy enough for a firm man who knows the world to brook the rage of the cultivated classes. Their rage is decorous and prudent, for they are timid, as being very vulnerable themselves. But when to their feminine rage the indignation of the people is added, when the ignorant and the poor are aroused, when the unintelligent brute force that lies at the bottom of society is made to growl and mow,[4] it needs the habit of magnanimity and religion to treat it godlike as a trifle of no concernment.

The other terror that scares us from self-trust is our consistency; a reverence for our past act or word because the eyes of others have no other data for computing our orbit than our past acts, and we are loath to disappoint them.

A foolish consistency is the hobgoblin of little minds, adored by little statesmen and philosophers and divines. With consistency a great soul has simply nothing to do. He may as well concern himself with his shadow on the wall. Speak what you think now in hard words and tomorrow speak what tomorrow thinks in hard words again, though it contradict everything you said today.— " Ah, so you shall be sure to be misunderstood." — Is it so bad then to be misunderstood? Pythagoras was misunderstood, and Socrates, and Jesus, and Luther, and Copernicus, and Galileo, and Newton, and every pure and wise spirit that ever took flesh. To be great is to be misunderstood. . . .

I hope in these days we have heard the last of conformity and consistency. Let the words be gazetted [5] and ridiculous hencefor-ward. Instead of the gong for dinner, let us hear a whistle from the Spartan fife. Let us never bow and apologize more. A great man is

---

[3] Turning away.   [4] Make faces.   [5] Declared bankrupt.

coming to eat at my house. I do not wish to please him; I wish that he should wish to please me. I will stand here for humanity, and though I would make it kind, I would make it true. Let us affront and reprimand the smooth mediocrity and squalid contentment of the times, and hurl in the face of custom and trade and office, the fact which is the upshot of all history, that there is a great responsible Thinker and Actor working wherever a man works; that a true man belongs to no other time or place, but is the center of things. Where he is, there is nature. He measures you and all men and all events. Ordinarily, everybody in society reminds us of somewhat else, or of some other person. Character, reality, reminds you of nothing else; it takes place of the whole creation. The man must be so much that he must make all circumstances indifferent. Every true man is a cause, a country, and an age; requires infinite spaces and numbers and time fully to accomplish his design; — and posterity seems to follow his steps as a train of clients. A man Caesar is born, and for ages after we have a Roman Empire. Christ is born, and millions of minds so grow and cleave to his genius that he is confounded with virtue and the possible of man. An institution is the lengthened shadow of one man; as, Monachism,[6] of the Hermit Antony; the Reformation, of Luther; Quakerism, of Fox; Methodism, of Wesley; Abolition, of Clarkson. Scipio, Milton called " the height of Rome "; and all history resolves itself very easily into the biography of a few stout and earnest persons.

Truly it demands something godlike in him who has cast off the common motives of humanity and has ventured to trust himself for a taskmaster. High be his heart, faithful his will, clear his sight, that he may in good earnest be doctrine, society, law, to himself, that a simple purpose may be to him as strong as iron necessity is to others!

Insist on yourself; never imitate. Your own gift you can present every moment with the cumulative force of a whole life's cultivation; but of the adopted talent of another you have only an extemporaneous [7] half possession. That which each can do best, none but his Maker can teach him. No man yet knows what it is, nor can, till that person has exhibited it. Where is the master who could have taught Shakespeare? Where is the master who could have instructed Frank-

---

[6] The institution of monasteries.   [7] For the time only.

lin, or Washington, cr Bacon, or Newton? Every great man is a
unique. The Scipionism of Scipio is precisely that part he could not
borrow. Shakespeare will never be made by the study of Shakespeare.
Do that which is assigned you, and you cannot hope too much or dare
too much. There is at this moment for you an utterance brave and
grand as that of the colossal chisel of Phidias, or trowel of the Egyp-
tians, or the pen of Moses or Dante, but different from all these. Not
possibly will the soul, all rich, all eloquent, thousand-cloven tongue,
deign to repeat itself; but if you can hear what these patriarchs say,
surely you can reply to them in the same pitch of voice; for the ear
and the tongue are two organs of one nature. Abide in the simple and
noble regions of thy life, obey thy heart and thou shalt reproduce the
Foreworld again.

APPRECIATION HINTS

1. What does Emerson say is the highest merit of Moses,
   Plato, and Milton?
2. In what does he find the strength of the babe and the
   child?
3. Emerson considers the boy *freer* than the man. For
   what reason?
4. What does Emerson mean by saying that the boy is in
the parlor what the pit is in the playhouse?
5. What influences make the boy less independent as he becomes a member of adult society?
6. What was Emerson's reply to the religious adviser?
7. On what grounds did Emerson denounce the abolitionist?
8. Why does he begrudge the money he gives to miscellaneous popular
charities?
9. What are the two chief influences which prevent a man from relying
on himself?
10. What is it that Emerson compares with a man's shadow on the wall?
11. What, according to Emerson, are the benefits of solitude?
12. What is Emerson's conception of history?
13. On what grounds does he think that we ought not to fear being in-
consistent?
14. "The doctrine of hatred must be preached." It was preached during
the First World War, when a German wrote a Hymn of Hate. Would
this have had Emerson's approval? Give reasons for your opinion.

15. Emerson mentions Moses, Plato, and others as examples of men who became great and good men because they trusted in themselves. Make a list of other great figures in history who also trusted in themselves, but whose influence on the world was evil.

16. Hitler trusted himself; he was a nonconformist; he did not fear inconsistency; he " insisted on himself "; he resorted to solitude for his intuitions. Why, then, is Hitler not a perfect example of the virtue that Emerson is writing about?

17. According to Emerson how may each man find out what for him is right or wrong?

18. Can you find out from this essay what, according to Emerson, is the source of " that gleam of light which flashes across a man's mind from within "?

19. Give examples from your own knowledge of the statement " infancy conforms to nobody, all conform to it."

20. Discuss Emerson's statement about history. Can you mention other forces in history besides those of individual men?

21. Discuss the statement, " Whoso would be a man must be a nonconformist."

22. Give some examples of people you know who might be called nonconformists.

23. Make a list of men and women in the past who were nonconformists. Would Washington and Lincoln be on the list?

24. There are in this book good examples of self-reliant men, women, boys, and girls. Make a list of these as you read.

25. Write a composition on a topic drawn from your reading of this essay. Suggestions: My Own Rejected Thoughts, When I Was a Nonconformist, How Society Limits Our Freedom, Foolish Consistencies I Have Observed, How Emerson Set Me Thinking, How Men Make History.

26. Suggestions for further reading in Emerson: " The American Scholar," his address before the Phi Beta Kappa Society of Cambridge in 1837; his essay entitled " Compensation."

HOW TO BE COMPETENT

Could the young but realize how soon they will become mere walking bundles of habits, they would give more heed to their conduct while in the plastic stage. We are spinning our own fates, good or evil, and never to be

*undone. Every smallest stroke of virtue or of vice leaves
its never so little scar. The drunken Rip Van Winkle, in
Jefferson's play, excuses himself from every fresh derelic-
tion by saying " I won't count this time! " Well! he may not
count it, and a kind Heaven may not count it; but it is
being counted none the less. Down among his nerve-cells
and fibers the molecules are counting it, registering and
storing it up to be used against him when the next temptation comes. Nothing we ever do is, in strict scientific lit-
eralness, wiped out. Of course, this has its good side as
well as its bad one. As we become permanent drunkards
by so many separate drinks, so we become saints in the
moral, and authorities and experts in the practical and
scientific spheres, by so many separate acts and hours of
work. Let no youth have any anxiety about the upshot of
his education, whatever the line of it may be. If he keep
faithfully busy each hour of the working day, he may
safely leave the final result to itself. He can with perfect
certainty count on waking up some fine morning, to find
himself one of the competent ones of his generation, in
whatsoever pursuit he may have singled out. Silently, between all the details of his business, the power of judging
in all that class of matter will have built itself up within
him as a possession that will never pass away. Young
people should know this truth in advance. The ignorance
of it has probably engendered more discouragement and
faint-heartedness in youths embarking on arduous careers
than all other causes put together.*

William James: *Principles of Psychology*

PERSON TO PERSON

THE ESSAYS in the preceding section had to do with the resources we have within us; the essays in this section deal with our relations with others. In Cicero's famous statement about friendship, it is interesting to compare the words of Laelius as he speaks of his friend Scipio, with the words of Christopher Morley two thousand years later, as he pours his heart out in protestations of his affection for Bill — and continues unanswering Bill's letter. The beautiful little essay of Mary Coleridge probes deep into our customary exchanging of gifts, and gives us a new insight into what makes a gift a perfect symbol of these person-to-person relationships. Most of the essays of the Warners deal with relationships intimately personal, usually between members of the same family. The family reappears as the background for "To Horse!", but to justify the inclusion of this essay here we must count the horse as a person. That is exactly what he is. He has more personality than any other animal in the parade.

Geoffrey, however, had not known his mount until the parade was forming. There could be none of that complete understanding between a boy or a girl and an animal which is often just as strong as the ties which exist between human beings. Everyone who has ever raised and cared for a pet will appreciate Lincoln Steffens' sincere and charming essay. As a man of sixty he looks back on his education, and puts his finger on certain influences which were of the utmost importance in his development. One of these was the influence of the little wild horse. The title "I Get a Colt to Break In" might just as well be "A Colt Gets a Boy to Break In." It was a colt at one end of the log and a boy at the other.

When Geoffrey and Lennie came home from riding they would be ordered to wipe the mud off before coming into the house. Winifred Kirkland tells all men and boys that they are just a big nuisance to the womenfolk — but she does it with a twinkle in her eye, which really spells "Welcome home!"

CHRISTOPHER MORLEY
1 8 9 0 –

THIS AUTHOR often warns us against taking his numerous essays too much in earnest. "Only a mind 'debauched by learning' (in Doctor Johnson's phrase) will scrutinize them too seriously," he writes; and among the instructions he furnishes to the reader of *Mince Pie* are the following: "This book is intended to be read in bed. . . . Do not read a borrowed copy, but buy one. If the bed is a double bed, buy two." Veteran readers of Morley need not be cautioned about taking him too seriously.

Among the multitude of essays he has written, some of the best are in his earlier volumes. One of these, in lighter vein, is the following essay from *Mince Pie*. To be sure Christopher is not on oath to tell the whole truth about his correspondence with Bill, but nonetheless all who have neglected attending to their correspondence will appreciate in this essay that subtle rationalizing which soothes our minds with promises that we are going to answer that letter come next Sunday.

Many of Mr. Morley's essays were first written in his routine work as a journalist in Philadelphia and New York. His love of England is reflected in the titles of his collected essays, which are catchy and descriptive of the contents: *Shandygaff,* 1918; *Mince Pie,* 1919; *Plum Pudding,* 1921. It is a fact that plum pudding is heavier than mince pie, and not so sparkling as shandygaff.

One of three gifted sons of gifted parents, Kit Morley studied at Haverford College, Pennsylvania, where his father was professor of mathematics. The three sons won successive Rhodes scholarships at Oxford, and the book of verses called *Parson's Pleasure* records impressions of the pleasant life at New College. On his return from abroad Christopher Morley went into journalism, and in 1920 began conducting the column known as *The Bowling Green* in the New York *Evening Post.*

Among his novels may be mentioned *Parnassus on Wheels,* 1917; *The Haunted Bookshop,* 1919, and *Thunder on the Left,* 1925. His most successful novel, *Kitty Foyle,* 1940, is reminiscent of Morley's life in and around Philadelphia. It was followed in 1943 by *Thorofare.*

THERE ARE a great many people who really believe in answering letters the day they are received, just as there are people who go to the movies at nine o'clock in the morning; but these people are stunted and queer.

It is a great mistake. Such crass and breathless promptness takes away a great deal of the pleasure of correspondence.

The psychological didoes involved in receiving letters and making up one's mind to answer them are very complex. If the tangled process could be clearly analyzed and its component involutions isolated for inspection we might reach a clearer comprehension of that curious bag of tricks, the efficient Masculine Mind.

Take Bill F., for instance, a man so delightful that even to contemplate his existence puts us in good humor and makes us think well of a world that can exhibit an individual equally comely in mind, body and estate. Every now and then we get a letter from Bill, and immediately we pass into a kind of trance, in which our mind rapidly enunciates the ideas, thoughts, surmises and contradictions that we would like to write to him in reply. We think what fun it would be to sit right down and churn the inkwell, spreading speculation and cynicism over a number of sheets of foolscap to be wafted Billward.

Sternly we repress the impulse for we know that the shock to Bill of getting so immediate a retort would surely unhinge the well-fitted panels of his intellect.

We add his letter to the large delta of unanswered mail on our desk, taking occasion to turn the mass over once or twice and run through it in a brisk, smiling mood, thinking of all the jolly letters we shall write some day.

After Bill's letter has lain on the pile for a fortnight or so it has been gently silted over by about twenty other pleasantly postponed manuscripts. Coming upon it by chance, we reflect that any specific problems raised by Bill in that manifesto will by this time have settled themselves. And his random speculations upon household management and human destiny will probably have taken a new slant by now, so that to answer his letter in its own tune will not be congruent with his present fevers. We had better bide a wee until we really have something of circumstance to impart.

We wait a week.

By this time a certain sense of shame has begun to invade the privacy of our brain. We feel that to answer that letter now would be an indelicacy. Better to pretend that we never got it. By and by Bill will write again and then we will answer promptly. We put the letter back in the middle of the heap and think what a fine chap Bill is. But he knows we love him, so it doesn't really matter whether we write or not.

Another week passes by, and no further communication from Bill. We wonder whether he does love us as much as we thought. Still — we are too proud to write and ask.

A few days later a new thought strikes us. Perhaps Bill thinks we have died and he is annoyed because he wasn't invited to the funeral. Ought we to wire him? No, because after all we are not dead, and even if he thinks we are, his subsequent relief at hearing the good news of our survival will outweigh his bitterness during the interval. One of these days we will write him a letter that will really express our heart, filled with all the grindings and gear-work of our mind, rich in affection and fallacy. But we had better let it ripen and mellow for a while. Letters, like wines, accumulate bright fumes and bubblings if kept under cork.

Presently we turn over that pile of letters again. We find in the lees of the heap two or three that have gone for six months and can

12. What do you think that Cicero understood by " Nature "?
13. " To make the interest of society and the individual one and the same." Do you know of any government that is founded on this principle?
14. What reason is there for thinking that Cicero would have approved of a League of Nations?
15. By giving examples illustrate the statement that " the more noble a man's character, the more he prefers a life of service to a life of pleasure."
16. Hints for essays of your own: Honor Among Thieves, Friends I Have Kept, A Friend Made Too Hastily, Rivals but Friends, A Life-Long Friendship, Ants and Bees as Citizens, Parental Advice, Competition Vs. Co-operation.

LOYALTY

For loyalty is still the same
Whether it win or lose the game;
True as a dial to the sun
Although it be not shined upon.
            Samuel Butler: *Hudibras*

Heraclitus saith well in one of his enigmas, Dry light is ever the best. *And certain it is that the light that a man receiveth by counsel from another is drier and purer than that which cometh from his own understanding and judgment; which is ever infused and drenched in his affections and customs. So as there is as much difference between the counsel that a friend giveth, and that a man giveth himself, as there is between the counsel of a friend and of a flatterer. For there is no such flatterer as is a man's self; and there is no such remedy against flattery of a man's self as the liberty of a friend.*
            Francis Bacon: *Of Friendship*

WINIFRED KIRKLAND 1872– time that Winifred Kirkland was writing some of her sparkling, mock-serious essays about the superiority of women to men, the House of Representatives was killing the Equal Suffrage Amendment by a vote of 174 to 204. It will help us to appreciate this essay if we think of it as the product of one of the irregulars, the guerrillas, in the army of women in the long struggle for their " rights." She fought with a delicate satire and wit — the natural weapon of a merry heart.

The Joys of Being a Woman, the collection from which the following essay is taken, appeared halfway between the defeat of the Nineteenth Amendment in 1915 and its adoption in 1920, after ratification by thirty-six states. " It is accepted as axiomatic," Miss Kirkland writes in the essay which gives its title to the book, " that every woman would be a man if she could, while no man would be a woman if he could help it." She is concerned to disprove this axiom, and she goes about it in downright fashion. It is a strong argument, she says, for the superiority of woman " that there is nothing which frightens a man so much as a woman's threatening to be like him, . . . and to confess the truth there is nothing that frightens a woman so much as becoming like a man." In the essay that follows, in like manner, she puts the opposite sex in its place by showing men what nuisances they are about the house.

The First World War made a profound impression on Winifred Kirkland. She tried to shed gleams of light on the depressed and despairing minds of postwar youth in such books as *Where the Star Still Shines,* 1924. In one of her latest books, the collection of essays called *The View Vertical,* 1920, is a call for courage, with " feet to the sturdy earth, head to the jocund sun." But to Miss Kirkland the essay properly is " sheer chuckle," and to find that in her writing one has to go back to the years before 1914.

Winifred Margaretta Kirkland graduated at Vassar College in 1897, and for ten years taught English in two girls schools in Bryn Mawr, Pennsylvania. Her best-known collections of essays are *The Joys of Being a Woman,* 1918, and *The View Vertical,* 1920. Her latest book is entitled *Star in the East.*

A Man in the House

THERE PERSISTS much of the harem in every well-regulated home. In every house arranged to make a real man happy, that man remains always a visitor, welcomed, honored, but perpetually a guest. He steps in from the great outside for rest and refreshment, but he never belongs. For him the click and hum of the harem machinery stops, giving way to love and laughter, but there is always feminine relief when the master departs and the household hum goes on again. The anomaly lies in the fact that in theory all the machinery exists but for the master's comfort; but in practice, it is much easier to arrange for his comfort when he is not there. A house without a man is savorless, yet a man in a house is incarnate interruption. No matter how closely he incarcerates himself, or how silently, a woman always feels him there. He may hide beyond five doors and two flights of stairs, but his presence somehow leaks through, and unconsciously dominates every domestic detail. He does not mean to; the woman does not mean him to; it is merely the nature of him. Keep a man at home during the working hours of the day, and there is a blight on that house, not obvious, but subtle, touching the mood and the manner of the maidservant and manservant, cat, dog, and mistress, and affecting even the behavior of inanimate objects, so that there is a constraint about the sewing machine, a palsy on the vacuum cleaner, and a *gaucherie* [1] in the stove

[1] Awkwardness.

lids. Over the whole household spreads a feeling of the unnatural, and a resulting sense of ineffectuality. Let the man go out, and with the closing of the front door, the wheels grow brisk again, and smooth. To enjoy a home worth enjoying, a man should be in it as briefly as possible.

By nature man belongs to the hunt in the open, and woman to the fire indoors, and just here lies one of the best reasons for being a woman rather than a man, because a woman can get along without a man's out-of-doors much better than a man can get along without a woman's indoors, which proves woman of the two the better bachelor, as being more self-contained and self-contented. Every real man when abroad on the hunt is always dreaming of a hearth and a hob and a wife, whereas no real woman, if she has the hearth and the hob, is longing for man's hunting spear or quarry. If she is indeed a real woman she is very likely longing to give a man the comfort of the fire, provided he will not stay too long at a stretch, but get out long enough to give her time to brush up his hearth and rinse his teapot satisfactorily to herself.

A man's homecoming is not an end in itself, its objective is the woman; but a woman's homemaking exists both for the man and for itself. A woman needs to be alone with her house because she talks to it, and in a tongue really more natural than her talk with her husband, which is always better for having a little the company flavor, as in the seraglio.[2] The most devoted wives are often those frankest in their abhorrence of a man in the house. It is because they do not like to keep their hearts working at high pressure too long at a time; they prefer the healthy relief of a glorious day of sorting or shopping between the master's breakfast and his dinner.

It is a rare *ménage* [3] that is not incommoded by having its males lunch at home. It is much better when a woman may watch their dear coattails round the corner for the day, with an equal exaltation in their freedom for the fray and her own. A woman whose males have their places of business neither on the great waters nor in the great streets, but in their own house, is of all women the most perpetually pitied by other women, and the most pathetically patient. She never

2 Harem.   3 Household.

looks quite like other women, this doctor's, minister's, professor's, writer's wife. Her eyes have a harassed patience, and her lips a protesting sweetness, for she does not belong to her house, and so she does not belong to herself. When a man's business-making and a woman's homemaking live under the same roof, they never go along in parallel independence: always the man's overlaps, invades. Kitchen and nursery are hushed before the needs of office and study, and the professional telephone call postpones the orders to the butcher. The home suffers, but the husband suffers more, for he is no longer a guest in his own house, with all a guest's prerogatives; he now belongs there, and must take the consequences.

Fortunately the professional men-about-the-house are in small minority, and so are their housekeepers, but all women have sometimes to experience the upheaval incident on a man's vacation at home; whether father's, or husband's, or college brother's, or son's, the effect is always the same: the house stands on its head, and for two days it kicks up its heels and enjoys it, but after two weeks, two months, that is, on the removal of the exciting stimulus, it sinks to coma for the rest of the season. The different professions differ in their treatment of a holiday, except that all men at home on a vacation act like fish on land or cats in water, and expect their womenfolk either to help them pant, or help them swim. They seem to go out a great deal, — at least they are always clamoring to have their garments prepared for sorties, social or piscatorial, — and yet they always seem to be under heel. Some men on a home holiday tinker all day long, others bring with them a great many books which they never read, and the result in both cases is that housekeeping becomes a prolonged picking up. All men at home on a vacation eat a great deal more than other men, or than at other times; but with the sole exception of the anomalous academic, who is always concerned for his gastronomy, they will eat anything and enjoy it, — and say so. A man at home for his

holidays is always vociferously appreciative. His happiness is almost enough to repay a woman for the noise he makes, and the mess; yet statistics would show that during any man's home vacation the women of the house lose just about as many pounds as the man gains. But what are women for, or homes?

After all, you can have a house without a man in it if you are quite sure you want to, but you cannot have a home without one. You cannot make a home out of women alone, or men alone; you have to mix them. Still every woman must admit, and every man with as much sense as a woman, that it's very hard to make a home for any man if he is always in it. Every honest front door must confess that it is glad to see its master go forth in the morning; but this is only because it is so much gladder to see him come back at night.

APPRECIATION HINTS

1. What are the author's reasons for saying a man is " perpetually a guest " in the house?
2. What is " one of the best reasons for being a woman rather than a man "?
3. What does she mean by saying that a woman " talks to her house "?
4. What troubles result when a man's place of business is his house?
5. Why do vacations make the house " stand on its head "?
6. What distinction does she make between a house and a home?
7. Collect some of the neat phrases in this essay; for example, " a man is an incarnate interruption."
8. Where do you notice glimpses of humor and playful exaggeration?
9. Think of some incidents resulting from reversed conditions — the woman invading the domain of the man.
10. Describe the duties of the wife of a doctor whose office is his house.
11. Write a composition suggested by this essay. Possible titles: The Man in the House at Spring Cleaning Time, The Husband Breaks in on the Bridge Club, Our House in Vacation Time, When the Wife Comes to the Office, The Fishermen Arrive (from the woman's point of view), The Golfer's Return, The Advantages of Being a Man, On Leave at Home.
12. Read the title essay and " The Farm Feminine " from *Joys of Being a Woman,* and " Faces from Fiction " from *The View Vertical.*

WISDOM IN LIVING

WE OUGHT to get a variety of opinion about the elements which make for wisdom in living from the authors represented in this section. They include a Catholic layman, a Russian-born New York journalist, a Chinese who has become a scholar in English, a friend of Coleridge and Lamb, and an English Viscount and lawyer who was fined £40,000 for accepting bribes. On the theory that he who drives fat oxen should himself be fat, we might be inclined to suspect the value of any comment on wisdom in living which comes from a person who has not lived wisely himself. And it is indeed interesting to notice what Bacon wrote about riches before the chances of taking a bribe came along. But we have only to look at ourselves to appreciate the difference between principles and performance, and to look at the lives of great men to see that immortal works can come from very imperfect beings. It happens that the man in this group who made the greatest disaster of his life is the very one who is pre-eminent in the civil and moral counsel of his penetrating essays. Further we may expect inconsistencies and even contradictions between the views expressed, especially when the ideals of wise living of a culture so different from ours as the Chinese are included in the picture. How to reconcile the American ideal of work with the Chinese ideal of leisure? Bacon would tell us not to let the golden moments slip; Lin Yutang would tell us that to let them slip is the only way to make them golden. Perhaps John Wesley's pathetic attempt in " Romance " to snatch a few golden moments on the northbound subway is an indication that the Chinese have something to teach us.

G. K. CHESTERTON
1874–1936

ONCE Chesterton was in Edinburgh at a dinner conference of people interested in education. He winced at the pink lemonade masquerading as something stronger, and then, in a brief and witty speech, presented himself, huge, ruddy and smiling, as the perfect example of the uneducable Englishman. Such a figure running after his silk hat in Hyde Park would have been a sight for the gods. His girth prompted his friend and fellow wit Bernard Shaw, when he had just produced *Fanny's First Play*, to describe Chesterton's maiden dramatic effort, *Magic*, as *Fatty's First Play*.

He *was* uneducable in so far as education implies unthinking conformity to customary opinion and action. But if it implies intelligent and fresh appraisal of accepted doctrine, he was among the best educated men of his time. Like Einstein, he was always challenging axioms. And he was great also in character. A man of deep religious convictions, yet of nimble wit in speech and writing, he was a stanch defender of faith and ideals — after his own fashion. No one ever defended conventionality in so unconventional a manner. For example, most people defend the family because it is supposed to be the focus of love and happiness; Chesterton defended it because of its tendency to be exactly the opposite — because it is the hardest place in the world in which to get on with other people. " The best way that a man could test his readiness to encounter the common variety of mankind," he writes, "would be to climb down the chimney into any house at random, and get on as well as possible with the people inside. And that is essentially what each of us did on the day he was born."

Gilbert Keith Chesterton was born in London, and educated at St. Paul's School. He studied art, but almost immediately began writing book reviews for magazines. Collections of his various essays and articles began to appear early in the century. *Heretics*, 1905, begins with " introductory remarks on the importance of orthodoxy "; *Orthodoxy*, 1908, begins with "Introduction in Defense of Everything Else." You would enjoy as examples of his fiction *The Man Who Was Thursday — A Nightmare*, and as examples of his poetry, *Lepanto*, 1911, and *The Ballad of the White Horse*, 1911.

On Running after One's Hat

I FEEL an almost savage envy on hearing that London has been flooded in my absence, while I am in the mere country. My own Battersea has been, I understand, particularly favored as a meeting of the waters. Battersea was already, as I need hardly say, the most beautiful of human localities. Now that it has the additional splendor of great sheets of water, there must be something quite incomparable in the landscape (or waterscape) of my romantic town. Battersea must be a vision of Venice. The boat that brought the meat from the butcher's must have shot along those lanes of rippling silver with the strange smoothness of the gondola. The greengrocer who brought cabbages to the corner of the Latchmere Road must have leant upon the oar with the unearthly grace of the gondolier. There is nothing so perfectly poetical as an island; and when a district is flooded it becomes an archipelago.

Some consider such romantic views of flood or fire slightly lacking in reality. But really this romantic view of such inconveniences is quite as practical as the other. The true optimist who sees in such things an opportunity for enjoyment is quite as logical and much more sensible than the ordinary " indignant Ratepayer " who sees in them an opportunity for grumbling. Real pain, as in the case of being burnt at Smithfield or having a toothache, is a positive thing; it can be supported, but scarcely enjoyed. But, after all, our toothaches are the exception, and as for being burnt at Smithfield, it only happens to us at the very longest intervals. And most of the inconveniences that make men swear or women cry are really sentimental or imaginative inconveniences — things altogether of the mind. For instance, we often hear grown-up people complaining of having to hang about a railway station and wait for a train. Did you ever hear a small boy complain of having to hang about a railway station and wait for a train? No; for to him to be inside a railway station is to be inside a cavern of wonder and a palace of poetical pleasures. Because to him the red light and the green light on the signal are like a new sun and a new moon. Because to him when the wooden arm of the signal falls down suddenly, it is as if a great king had thrown down his staff as a signal and started a shrieking tournament of trains. I myself am of little boys' habit in this matter. They also serve who only stand and wait for the two-fifteen. Their meditations may be full of rich and fruitful things. Many of the most purple hours of my life have been passed at Clapham Junction, which is now, I suppose, under water. I have been there in many moods so fixed and mystical that the water might well have come up to my waist before I noticed it particularly. But, in the case of all such annoyances, as I have said, everything depends upon the emotional point of view. You can safely apply the test to almost every one of the things that are currently talked of as the typical nuisances of daily life.

For instance, there is a current impression that it is unpleasant to have to run after one's hat. Why should it be unpleasant to the well-ordered and pious mind? Not merely because it is running, and running exhausts one. The same people run much faster in games and sports. The same people run much more eagerly after an uninteresting little leather ball than they will after a nice silk hat. There is an idea that it is humiliating to run after one's hat, and when people say it is humiliating they mean that it is comic. It certainly is comic; but man is a very comic creature, and most of the things he does are comic — eating, for instance. And the most comic things of all are exactly the things that are most worth doing — such as making love. A man running after a hat is not half so ridiculous as a man running after a wife.

Now a man could, if he felt rightly in the matter, run after his hat with the manliest ardor and the most sacred joy. He might re-gard himself as a jolly huntsman pursuing a wild animal, for cer-tainly no animal could be wilder. In fact, I am inclined to believe that hat hunting on windy days will be the sport of the upper classes in the future. There will be a meet of ladies and gentlemen on some high ground on a gusty morning. They will be told that the profes-sional attendants have started a hat in such-and-such a thicket, or whatever be the technical term. Notice that this employment will in the fullest degree combine sport with humanitarianism. The hunters would feel that they were not inflicting pain. Nay, they would feel that they were inflicting pleasure, rich, almost riotous pleasure, upon the people who were looking on. When last I saw an old gentleman running after his hat in Hyde Park, I told him that a heart so benevo-lent as his ought to be filled with peace and thanks at the thought of how much unaffected pleasure his every gesture and bodily atti-tude were at that moment giving to the crowd.

The same principle can be applied to every other typical do-mestic worry. A gentleman trying to get a fly out of the milk or a piece of cork out of his glass of wine often imagines himself to be irritated. Let him think for a moment of the patience of anglers sitting by dark pools, and let his soul be immediately irradiated with gratifi-cation and repose. Again, I have known some people of very modern views driven by their distress to the use of theological terms to which they attached no doctrinal significance, merely because a drawer was jammed tight and they could not pull it out. A friend of mine was particularly afflicted in this way. Every day his drawer was jammed, and every day in consequence it was something else that rhymes to

it. But I pointed out to him that this sense of wrong was really subjective and relative; it rested entirely upon the assumption that the
drawer could, should, and would come out easily. " But if," I said,
" you picture to yourself that you are pulling against some powerful
and oppressive enemy, the struggle will become merely exciting and
not exasperating. Imagine that you are roping up a fellow creature
out of an Alpine crevasse. Imagine even that you are a boy again and
engaged in a tug of war between French and English." Shortly after
saying this I left him; but I have no doubt at all that my words bore
the best possible fruit. I have no doubt that every day of his life he
hangs on to the handle of that drawer with a flushed face and eyes
bright with battle, uttering encouraging shouts to himself, and seeming to hear all round him that roar of an applauding ring.

So I do not think it altogether fanciful or incredible to suppose
that even the floods in London may be accepted and enjoyed poet-
ically. Nothing beyond inconvenience seems really to have been
caused by them; and inconvenience, as I have said, is only one aspect,
and that the most unimaginative and accidental aspect of a really
romantic situation. An adventure is only an inconvenience rightly
considered. An inconvenience is only an adventure wrongly considered. The water that girdled the houses and shops of London must,
if anything, have only increased their previous witchery and wonder.
For as the Roman Catholic priest in the story said: " Wine is good
with everything except water," and on a similar principle, water is
good with everything except wine.

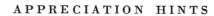

APPRECIATION HINTS

1. On what grounds does Chesterton justify taking a romantic view of the Battersea flood?
2. How does he brush away the objection that it is comic
   to run after one's hat?
3. How does he describe the sport of hat hunting on a
   windy day?
4. What is his advice to his friend with the jammed door?
5. With what thoughts should the man with a fly in his milk quiet his
   spirit?

6. Tell about the "romantic" side of a big snowstorm.

7. "I myself am of little boys' habit in this matter." Mention other writers represented in this collection who have preserved the fancy of childhood.

8. Mention some of our conventions which, considered logically, might appear comical; for example, men's evening clothes, women's furs in summer.

9. Illustrate Chesterton's statement that most of our inconveniences are imaginary, by thinking of examples.

10. Recall some exciting events like a flood in your town while you were away. Suggest introductory sentences for an essay on such an experience.

11. Recall some inconvenience in your life which grew into an adventure.

12. What example is there in *Who's Catching?* (p. 10) of overcoming emotional worry by thinking of something else?

13. Write a composition suggested by this essay. Examples of possible titles: Romance in a Railway Station, If My Town Were Flooded, On Bureau Drawers, The Wind and the Umbrella, When I Was Unintentionally Funny, A "Purple Hour" of My Life, Mental Attitude in Athletics, During the Hurricane, Typical Nuisances.

14. Read "The Romantic in the Rain" from *All Things Considered;* "Omar and the Sacred Vine" from *Heretics;* "On Lying in Bed" from *Tremendous Trifles;* "On Broadcasting" from *Generally Speaking;* "On Certain Modern Writers and the Institution of the Family" from *Heretics.*

You cannot prevent the birds of sorrow from flying over your head, but you can prevent them from building nests in your hair.   Chinese proverb

DEFINITIONS

What is a cynic? A man who knows the price of everything, and the value of nothing.
                              Oscar Wilde: *Lady Windermere's Fan*

What is an optimist? An optimist is a man who makes glasses for your eyes, and a pessimist is a man who takes corns from your feet.   Classroom Wisdom

WILLIAM HAZLITT
1778–1830

GENE TUNNEY has stated that in his opinion one reason for the rejection of so high a percentage of candidates for the army is that our legs are deteriorating from disuse, and many old football and track coaches would support him. The work of the heart, the heel, and the toe has been taken over by the internal combustion engine, air, and rubber. And unless we bridge the gap between travel now and travel one hundred and twenty years ago, when Hazlitt wrote this memorable essay, we cannot appreciate even its first sentence, "One of the pleasantest things in the world is going a journey."

The word *journey* suggests at once to us the full gas tank, or else the ticket for train, bus, plane, or steamer, and the hotel reservations at the other end. To Hazlitt a journey meant putting on the oiled boots, taking down the mackintosh (then recently invented), picking up the ash walking stick, and putting the green turf under his feet. There was no railroad in England until eight years after this essay was written. There were, of course, stagecoaches, and De Quincey, in a later essay in this book, tells us how that kind of travel tyrannized over the dreams of one who mounted a coach after a dose of laudanum. But Hazlitt mentions the post chaise and the Tilbury only to reject them. It was heel and toe for him and a three hours' march to dinner. When the long twilight ended there would be the lights of an English inn, the fire in the private room, and the basking before it to dry off from that last shower while the supper he had ordered was cooking. But what this essay preserves for all time is a supreme expression of the joys which all may have who travel with alert and sensitive minds.

As a person and as an essayist Hazlitt was intensely subjective. In this respect he resembles Montaigne, even though the personality revealed to us is by no means so pleasing. This preoccupation with himself perhaps contributed to the unhappiness of Hazlitt's life, and the frequent breaking of his friendships.

William Hazlitt spent three years of his childhood in the United States; his father at the time was preaching and lecturing in Philadelphia. Returning to England, he began writing for magazines. This essay first appeared in the *New Monthly Magazine* in January, 1822.

On Going a Journey

ONE OF the pleasantest things
in the world is going a journey; but I like to go by myself. I can enjoy
society in a room; but out of doors, nature is company enough for me.
I am then never less alone than when alone.

The fields his study, nature was his book.

I cannot see the wit of walking and talking at the same time.
When I am in the country, I wish to vegetate like the country. I am
not for criticizing hedgerows and black cattle. I go out of town in
order to forget the town and all that is in it. There are those who for
this purpose go to watering places, and carry the metropolis with
them. I like more elbowroom, and fewer incumbrances. I like solitude, when I give myself up to it, for the sake of solitude; nor do I
ask for

> . . . a friend in my retreat,
> Whom I may whisper solitude is sweet.

The soul of a journey is liberty, perfect liberty, to think, feel, do just
as one pleases. We go a journey chiefly to be free of all impediments
and of all inconveniences; to leave ourselves behind, much more to
get rid of others. It is because I want a little breathing space to muse
on indifferent matters, where Contemplation

May plume her feathers and let grow her wings,
That in the various bustle of resort
Were all to-ruffled, and sometimes impair'd,[1]

that I absent myself from the town for a while, without feeling at a loss the moment I am left by myself. Instead of a friend in a post chaise or in a Tilbury,[2] to exchange good things with, and vary the same stale topics over again, for once let me have a truce with impertinence. Give me the clear blue sky over my head, and the green turf beneath my feet, a winding road before me, and a three hours' march to dinner — and then to thinking! It is hard if I cannot start some game on these long heaths. I laugh, I run, I leap, I sing for joy. From the point of yonder rolling cloud, I plunge into my past being, and revel there, as the sun-burnt Indian plunges headlong into the wave that wafts him to his native shore. Then long-forgotten things, like " sunken wrack and sumless treasuries," burst upon my eager sight, and I begin to feel, think, and be myself again. Instead of an awkward silence, broken by attempts at wit or dull commonplaces, mine is that undisturbed silence of the heart which alone is perfect eloquence. No one likes puns, alliterations, antitheses, argument, and analysis better than I do; but I sometimes had rather be without them. "Leave, oh, leave me to my repose!" I have just now other business in hand, which would seem idle to you, but is with me " very stuff of the conscience." Is not this wild rose sweet without a comment? Does not this daisy leap to my heart set in its coat of emerald? Yet if I were to explain to you the circumstance that has so endeared it to me, you would only smile. Had I not better then keep it to myself, and let it serve me to brood over, from here to yonder craggy point, and from thence onward to the far-distant horizon? I should be but bad company all that way, and therefore prefer being alone. I have heard it said that you may, when the moody fit comes on, walk or ride on by yourself, and indulge your reveries. But this looks like a breach of manners, a neglect of others, and you are thinking all the time that you ought to rejoin your party. " Out upon such half-faced fellowship," say I. I like to be either entirely to myself, or entirely at the disposal of others; to talk or be silent, to walk or sit still, to

---

[1] This is from Milton's *Comus.*   [2] A two-wheeled carriage.

be sociable or solitary I was pleased with an observation of Mr. Cobbett's,[3] that "he thought it a bad French custom to drink our wine with our meals, and that an Englishman ought to do only one thing at a time." So I cannot talk and think, or indulge in melancholy musing and lively conversation by fits and starts. "Let me have a companion of my way," says Sterne, "were it but to remark how the shadows lengthen as the sun declines." It is beautifully said: but in my opinion, this continual comparing of notes interferes with the involuntary impression of things upon the mind, and hurts the sentiment. If you only hint what you feel in a kind of dumb show, it is insipid: if you have to explain it, it is making a toil of a pleasure. You cannot read the book of nature, without being perpetually put to the trouble of translating it for the benefit of others.

I am for the synthetical method on a journey, in preference to the analytical. I am content to lay in a stock of ideas then, and to examine and anatomize them afterward. I want to see my vague notions float like the down of the thistle before the breeze, and not to have them entangled in the briers and thorns of controversy. For once, I like to have it all my own way; and this is impossible unless you are alone, or in such company as I do not covet. I have no objection to argue a point with anyone for twenty miles of measured road, but not for pleasure. If you remark the scent of a bean field crossing the road, perhaps your fellow traveler has no smell. If you point to a distant object, perhaps he is shortsighted, and has to take out his glass to look at it. There is a feeling in the air, a tone in the color of a cloud which hits your fancy, but the effect of which you are unable to account for. There is then no sympathy, but an uneasy craving after it, and a dissatisfaction which pursues you on the way, and in the end probably produces ill humor. Now I never quarrel with myself, and take all my own conclusions for granted till I find it necessary to defend them against objections. It is not merely that you may not be of accord on the objects and circumstances that present themselves before you — these may recall a number of objects, and lead to associations too delicate and refined to be possibly communicated to

[3] William Cobbett, author of *Rural Rides.* In 1799 he was publishing a Federalist paper in Philadelphia.

others. Yet these I love to cherish, and sometimes still fondly clutch
them, when I can escape from the throng to do so. To give way to our
feelings before company, seems extravagance or affectation; and on
the other hand, to have to unravel this mystery of our being at every
turn, and to make others take an equal interest in it (otherwise the
end is not answered) is a task to which few are competent. We must
"give it an understanding, but no tongue." My old friend C——,[4] however, could do both. He could go on in the most delightful explana-
tory way over hill and dale, a summer's day, and convert a landscape
into a didactic poem or a Pindaric ode. "He talked far above singing." If I could so clothe my ideas in sounding and flowing words, I
might perhaps wish to have someone with me to admire the swelling
theme; or I could be more content, were it possible for me still to hear
his echoing voice in the woods of Alfoxden. . . .

In general, a good thing spoils out-of-door prospects: it should
be reserved for Table-talk. L—— [5] is for this reason, I take it, the worst
company in the world out of doors; because he is the best within.
I grant, there is one subject on which it is pleasant to talk on a journey; and that is, what one shall have for supper when we get to our
inn at night. The open air improves this sort of conversation or
friendly altercation, by setting a keener edge on appetite. Every mile
of the road heightens the flavor of the viands we expect at the end
of it. How fine it is to enter some old town, walled and turreted just
at the approach of nightfall, or to come to some straggling village,
with the lights streaming through the surrounding gloom; and then
after inquiring for the best entertainment that the place affords, to
"take one's ease at one's inn"! These eventful moments in our lives'
history are too precious, too full of solid, heartfelt happiness to be
frittered and dribbled away in imperfect sympathy. I would have
them all to myself, and drain them to the last drop: they will do to
talk of or to write about afterward. What a delicate speculation it is,
after drinking whole goblets of tea,

The cups that cheer, but not inebriate,

---

[4] Samuel Taylor Coleridge, who had a lasting influence on Hazlitt.
[5] Charles Lamb, one of Hazlitt's best friends.

and letting the fumes ascend into the brain, to sit considering what we shall have for supper — eggs and a rasher, a rabbit smothered in onions, or an excellent veal cutlet! Sancho [6] in such a situation once fixed upon cowheel; and his choice, though he could not help it, is not to be disparaged. Then in the intervals of pictured scenery and Shandean contemplation, to catch the preparation and the stir in the kitchen — *Procul, O procul este profani!* [7] These hours are sacred to silence and to musing, to be treasured up in the memory, and to feed the source of smiling thoughts hereafter. I would not waste them in idle talk; or if I must have the integrity of fancy broken in upon, I would rather it were by a stranger than a friend. A stranger takes his hue and character from the time and place; he is a part of the furniture and costume of an inn. If he is a Quaker, or from the West Riding of Yorkshire, so much the better. I do not even try to sympathize with him, and he breaks no squares. I associate nothing with my traveling companion but present objects and passing events. In his ignorance of me and my affairs, I in a manner forget myself. But a friend reminds one of other things, rips up old grievances, and destroys the abstraction of the scene. He comes in ungraciously between us and our imaginary character. Something is dropped in the course of conversation that gives a hint of your profession and pursuits; or from having someone with you that knows the less sublime portions of your history, it seems that other people do. You are no longer a citizen of the world: but your " unhoused free condition is put into circumscription and confine."

The *incognito* of an inn is one of its striking privileges — " lord of one's-self, uncumber'd with a name." Oh! it is great to shake off the trammels of the world and of public opinion — to lose our importunate, tormenting, everlasting personal identity in the elements of nature, and become the creature of the moment, clear of all ties — to hold to the universe only by a dish of sweetbreads, and to owe nothing but the score of the evening — and no longer seeking for applause and meeting with contempt, to be known by no other title than *the Gentleman in the Parlor!* One may take one's choice of all

[6] Sancho Panza, the squire of Don Quixote.
[7] Stand far off. O profane souls!

characters in this romantic state of uncertainty as to one's real pre-
tensions, and become indefinitely respectable and negatively right-
worshipful. We baffle prejudice and disappoint conjecture; and from
being so to others, begin to be objects of curiosity and wonder even
to ourselves. We are no more those hackneyed commonplaces that
we appear in the world: an inn restores us to the level of nature, and
quits scores with society! I have certainly spent some enviable hours
at inns — sometimes when I have been left entirely to myself, and
have tried to solve some metaphysical problem, as once at Withman-
common, where I found out the proof that likeness is not a case
of the association of ideas — at other times, when there have been
pictures in the room, as at St. Neot's (I think it was), where I first
met with Gribelin's engravings of the Cartoons,[8] into which I entered at once and at a little inn on the borders of Wales, where there
happened to be hanging some of Westall's drawings, which I compared triumphantly (for a theory that I had, not for the admired
artist) with the figure of a girl who had ferried me over the Severn,
standing up in the boat between me and the twilight — at other times
I might mention luxuriating in books, with a peculiar interest in this
way, as I remember sitting up half the night to read *Paul and Virginia*,[9] which I picked up at an inn at Bridgewater, after being
drenched in the rain all day; and at the same place I got through
two volumes of Madame D'Arblay's *Camilla*. It was on the tenth of
April, 1798, that I sat down to a volume of the *New Eloise*,[10] at the
inn at Llangollen, over a bottle of sherry and a cold chicken. The
letter I chose was that in which St. Preux describes his feelings as he
first caught a glimpse from the heights of the Jura of the Pays de
Vaud, which I had brought with me as a *bon bouche* [11] to crown the
evening with. It was my birthday, and I had for the first time come
from a place in the neighborhood to visit this delightful spot. The
road to Llangollen turns off between Chirk and Wrexham; and on
passing a certain point, you come all at once upon the valley, which

---

[8] The designs and drawings of Raphael.
[9] St. Pierre's beautiful novel, published in 1788.
[10] A novel by Rousseau.
[11] A tidbit.

opens like an amphitheater, broad, barren hills rising in majestic state on either side, with " green upland swells that echo to the bleat of flocks " below, and the river Dee babbling over its stony bed in the midst of them. The valley at this time " glittered green with sunny showers," and a budding ash tree dipped its tender branches in the chiding stream. How proud, how glad I was to walk along the high road that overlooks the delicious prospect, repeating lines from Mr. Coleridge's poems! But besides the prospect which opened beneath my feet, another also opened to my inward sight, a heavenly vision, on which were written, in letters large as Hope could make them, these four words, LIBERTY, GENIUS, LOVE, VIRTUE; which have since faded into the light of common day, or mock my idle gaze.

> The beautiful is vanished, and returns not.

Still I would return some time or other to this enchanted spot; but I would return to it alone. What other self could I find to share that influx of thoughts, of regret, and delight, the fragments of which I could hardly conjure up to myself, so much have they been broken and defaced! I could stand on some tall rock, and overlook the precipice of years that separates me from what I then was. I was at that time going shortly to visit the poet whom I have above named. Where is he now? Not only I myself have changed; the world, which was then new to me, has become old and incorrigible. Yet will I turn to thee in thought, O sylvan Dee, in joy, in youth and gladness as thou then wert; and thou shalt always be to me the river of Paradise, where I will drink of the waters of life freely! . . .

APPRECIATION HINTS

1. What is Hazlitt's opinion about the object of going a journey?
2. Why does he prefer to go alone?
3. What are the positive disadvantages of having a companion?
4. If he had a companion, what would be the best thing to talk about?

5. What is it he liked about an inn? Name some of his experiences.
6. Hazlitt had studied art. What evidence is there in this essay that he looked at things with the eye of the artist?
7. Is Hazlitt right or is Cicero, who says that every pleasure is doubled when we have a friend to share it?
8. Hazlitt is recognized as one of the great masters of English prose. What passages in this essay might deserve this appraisal?
9. Write a composition based on travel. Suggestions: Joys of the Open Road, An Argument That Spoiled the Hike, That Supper at the End, A Night at an Inn, A Scene Remembered from Childhood, The Lake (House or Village) Revisited, Pros and Cons of the Automobile.
10. Describe as vividly as you can a scene on one of your journeys which stands out in your memory like the Valley of the Dee in Hazlitt's.
11. If you like Hazlitt read " On a Sundial," " On the Feeling of Immortality in Youth," " The Indian Jugglers," " On Going to a Prize Fight."

We should cultivate the power of seeing plain things in a kind of sunlight of surprise; the power of jumping at the sight of a bird as if at a winged bullet; the power of being brought to a standstill by a tree as by the gesture of some gigantic hand.

I know of no better exercise in this art of wonder, which is the beginning of the praise of God, than to travel in a train through a tunnel. At last, after a long stretch of darkness, the wall will suddenly break in two, and give a glimpse of the land of the living. It may be a chasm of daylight showing a bright and busy street. It may be a flash of light on a lonely road, with a solitary figure plodding across the vast countryside. Sometimes the darkness is broken by the lighted windows of a house, and for an instant we look deep into chamber within chamber of a glowing human home.

That is the way in which objects ought to be seen: separate, illuminated, and above all, contrasted against blank night or bare walls; as indeed these living creations do stand eternally contrasted with the colorless chaos out of which they came.

G. K. Chesterton, *The Colored Lands* (Sheed and Ward)

SIMEON STRUNSKY 1879–

HOWEVER light and amusing an essay by Simeon Strunsky may be, it is never merely fooling — it always contains something worth saying. Often, as in this one, the reader must do his part to find out what that something is. When we have read the last sentence — "After dinner Wesley went out to look at the lawn" — we are likely to turn back and check the title, and then, with last night's movie still glowing in our minds, we say to ourselves, "And that's what this guy calls *romance*."

If we only will go on from there, that state of mind is precisely what Strunsky intended. A story which heralded the so-called romantic movement, written more than one hundred years before this essay, has essentially the same plot. It is in verse written by Coleridge. The ancient mariner, drifting homeward and recognizing his native village exclaims,

Is this the hill? Is this the kirk?
Is this mine own countree?

John Wesley, back again home to his wife, exclaims, "It's good to see you again." The old sailor has been to the ends of the earth; John Wesley has "done a Corrigan," and gone to 125th Street on the subway. But the emotion of the two is identical. Romance?

Simeon Strunsky's essays remind one of O. Henry's stories. Both writers had the journalist's eye for the significance of trifles, of moments or incidents in our lives that seem to others quite unworthy of notice. This fresh observation of the journalist, so noticeable in "Romance," is combined in Strunsky's writings with the subtle flavor and humor of the older essayists.

Simeon Strunsky was born in Russia, and educated at Horace Mann High School and Columbia University. He did six years' hard labor as one of the editors of the *New International Encyclopaedia,* joined the staff of the New York *Evening Post,* and later of the New York *Times.* Some of his best known collections of essays are *Belshazzar Court,* 1914, *Post-Impressions,* 1914, from which this essay is taken, *Sinbad and His Friends,* 1921, and *The Rediscovery of Jones,* 1931.

AT 5:15 IN THE afternoon of an exceptionally sultry day in August, John P. Wesley, forty-seven years old, in business at No. 634 East Twenty-sixth Street as a jobber in tools and hardware, was descending the stairs to the downtown platform of the Subway at Twenty-eighth Street, when it occurred to him suddenly how odd it was that he should be going home. His grip tightened on the handrail and he stopped short in his tracks, his eyes fixed on the ground in pained perplexity. The crowd behind him, thrown back upon itself by this abrupt action, halted only for a moment and flowed on. Cheerful office boys looked back at him and asked what was the answer. Stout citizens elbowed him aside without apology. But Wesley did not mind. He was asking himself why it was that the end of the day's work should invariably find him descending the stairs to the downtown platform of the Subway. Was there any reason for doing that, other than habit? He wondered why it would not be just as reasonable to cross the avenue and take an uptown train instead.

Wesley had been taking the downtown train at Twenty-eighth Street at 5:15 in the afternoon ever since there was a Subway. At Brooklyn Bridge he changed to an express and went to the end of the line. At the end of the line there was a boat which took him across the harbor. At the end of the boat ride there was a trolley car which wound its way up the hill and through streets lined with yellow-bricked, easy-payment, two-family houses, out into the open country, where it dropped him at a crossroad. At the end of a ten minutes' walk there was a new house of stucco and timber, standing away from the road, its angular lines revealing mingled aspirations toward the Californian bungalow and the English Tudor. In the house lived a tall, slender, gray-haired woman who was Wesley's wife, and two young girls who were his daughters. They always came to the door when his footsteps grated on the garden path, and kissed him welcome. After dinner he went out and watered the lawn, which, after his wife and the girls, he loved most. He plied the hose deliberately, his eye alert for bald patches. Of late the lawn had not been coming on well, because of a scorching sun and the lack of rain. A quiet chat with his wife on matters of domestic economy ushered in the end of a busy day. At the end of the day there was another day just like it.

And now, motionless in the crowd, Wesley was asking whether right to the end of life this succession of days would continue. Why always the southbound train? He was aware that there were good reasons why. One was the tall gray-haired woman and the two girls at home who were in the habit of waiting for the sound of his footsteps on the garden path. They were his life. But apparently, too, there must be life along the uptown route of the Interborough. He wanted to run amuck, to board a northbound train without any destination in mind, and to keep on as far as his heart desired, to the very end perhaps, to Van Cortlandt Park, where they played polo, or the Bronx, where there was a botanical museum and a zoo. Even if he went only as far as Grand Central Station, it would be an act of magnificent daring.

Wesley climbed to the street, crossed Fourth Avenue, descended to the uptown platform, and entered a train without stopping to see whether it was Broadway or Lenox Avenue. Already he was thinking of the three women at home in a remote, objective mood. They would be waiting for him, no doubt, and he was sorry, but what else could he do? He was not his own master. Under the circumstances it was a comfort to know that all three of them were women of poise, not given to making the worst of things, and with enough work on their hands to keep them from worrying over-much.

Having broken the great habit of his life by taking an uptown train at 5:15, Wesley found it quite natural that his minor habits should fall from him automatically. He did not relax into his seat and lose himself in the evening paper after his usual fashion. He did not look at his paper at all, but at the people about him. He had never seen such men and women before, so fresh-tinted, so outstanding, so electric. He seemed to have opened his eyes on a mass of vivid colors and sharp contours. It was the same sensation he experienced when he used to break his gold-rimmed spectacles, and after he had groped for a day in the mists of myopia, a new, bright world would leap out at him through the new lenses.

Wesley did not make friends easily. In a crowd he was peculiarly shy. Now he grew garrulous. At first his innate timidity rose up and choked him, but he fought it down. He turned to his neighbor on the right, a thickset, clean-shaven youth who was painfully studying the comic pictures in his evening newspaper, and remarked, in a style utterly strange to him:

" Looks very much like the Giants had the rag cinched? "

The thickset young man, whom Wesley imagined to be a butcher's assistant or something of the sort, looked up from his paper and

said, " It certainly does seem as if the New York team had established its title to the championship."

Wesley cleared his throat again.

" When it comes to slugging the ball you've got to hand it to them," he said.

" Assuredly," said the young man, folding up his paper with the evident design of continuing the conversation.

Wesley was pleased and frightened. He had tasted another new sensation. He had broken through the frosty reserve of twenty years and had spoken to a stranger after the free and easy manner of men who make friends in Pullman cars and at lunch counters. And the stranger, instead of repulsing him, had admitted him, at the very first attempt, into the fraternity of ordinary people. It was pleasant to be one of the great democracy of the crowd, something which Wesley had never had time to be. But on the other hand, he found the strain of conversation telling upon him. He did not know how to go on.

The stranger went out, but Wesley did not care. He was lost in a delicious reverie, conscious of being carried forward on free-beating wings into a wonderful, unknown land. The grinding of wheels and brakes as the train halted at a station and pulled out again made a languorous, soothing music. The train clattered out of the tunnel into the open air, and Wesley was but dimly aware of the change from dark to twilight. The way now ran through a region of vague apartment houses. There were trees, stretches of green field waiting for the builder, and here or there a colonial manor house with sheltered windows, resigned to its fate. Then came cottages with gardens. And in one of these Wesley, shocked into acute consciousness, saw a man with a rubber hose watering a lawn. Wesley leaped to his feet.

The train was at a standstill when he awoke to the extraordinary fact that he was twelve miles away from South Ferry and going in the wrong direction. The imperative need of getting home as soon as he could overwhelmed him. He dashed for the door, but it slid shut in his face and the train pulled out. His fellow passengers grinned. One of the most amusing things in the world is a tardy passenger who tries to fling himself through a car door and flattens his nose against the glass. It is hard to say why the thing is amusing, but it is. Wesley did not know he was being laughed at. He merely knew that he must go home. He got out at the next station, and when he was seated in a corner of the southbound train, he sighed with unutterable relief. He was once more in a normal world where trains ran to South Ferry instead of away from it. He dropped off at his road crossing, just two hours late, and found his wife waiting.

They walked on side by side without speaking, but once or

twice she turned and caught him staring at her with a peculiar mixture of wonder and unaccustomed tenderness.

Finally he broke out.

"It's good to see you again!"

She laughed and was happy. His voice stirred in her memories of long ago.

"It's good to have you back, dear," she said.

"But you really look remarkably well," he insisted.

"I rested this afternoon."

"That's what you should do every day," he said. "Look at that old maple tree! It hasn't changed a bit!"

"No," she said, and began to wonder.

"And the girls are well?"

"Oh, yes."

"I can hardly wait till I see them," he said; and then, to save himself, "I guess I am getting old, Alice."

"You are younger tonight than you have been for a long time," she said.

Jennie and her sister were waiting for them on the porch. They wondered why father's kiss fell so warmly on their cheeks. He kissed them twice, which was very unusual; but being discreet young women they asked no questions. After dinner Wesley went out to look at the lawn.

APPRECIATION HINTS

1. What was Wesley's customary route home?
2. What was his routine on arriving at home?
3. Tell about his efforts at conversation on the northbound subway train.
4. What was it that roused Wesley from his reverie?
5. Describe the meeting with the family at the end of his adventure.
6. Explain the title. Where did the romance come in? Was it in the excursion or the home-coming?
7. Try to put the central theme of Strunsky's little essay in four or five words.
8. Compare John P. Wesley with Winifred Kirkland's man in the house.

9. What is your idea of the routine of Mrs. Wesley and of the two girls?
10. Compare the truancy of Aram in *The Circus*, by Saroyan, to the truancy of Wesley. What has produced the difference?
11. Recount the occasion of some sudden impulse to break the routine of the day in your own experience.
12. Construct a similar adventure in "romance" on the part of Mrs. Wesley or the daughters.
13. Write a composition on some topic suggested by the essay. Possible titles: Subway Conversation, Taking the Wrong Train, Shut Out of the Subway, That Sudden Impulse, Routine — Bore or Blessing?, Cafeteria Acquaintances, My Daily Chores.
14. Read "On the Floor of the Library" (about detective stories) from *Sinbad and His Friends;* "On Calling White Black" and "The Commuter" from *The Patient Observer;* "The Street" and "Night Life" from *Belshazzar Court;* "Nocturne" from *Post-Impressions.*

What is an adventure? Not necessarily a thrilling escape from death, a holdup on a dark road at midnight. There are others.

The newsboy, for instance, who runs after you when you have overpaid him a penny; the lark by the roadside of a spring morning; the hilltop where life seems suddenly fresh and worth while again; the fireside and a good friend when the blizzard howls without; the limping dog, the sobbing child, the merry quip, the chance acquaintance. These and a thousand other bits of living are all adventures, and those who meet them with the adventurer's heart will catch the extra pungency of their flavor till the day of their death.   G. K. Chesterton

LIN YUTANG 1895 – SOME YEARS ago there appeared, in an American edition, a little book first published in England entitled *Letters from a Chinese Official,* and presumably written by a Chinese living in England. William Jennings Bryan, assuming the letters were genuine, wrote a similar little book in reply. The letters were really written by an Englishman, but so completely did they reflect the Chinese mind that Mr. Bryan had good reason to take them as genuine. In the first letter there is a sort of epitome of Lin Yutang's theme in *The Importance of Living.* "We measure the degree of civilization," writes the "Chinese official," not by the accumulation of the means of living, but by the character and value of the life lived. . . . You, as always, are thinking of the means of living; we of the quality of the life lived." In the following essay a native Chinese, who has made himself a master of English, draws a whimsical comparison between the merits of being busy and of merely being. Everyone knows that the Chinese working on his own land is industrious to an extent hardly known elsewhere; the kind of loafing which the author has in mind is explained in his first paragraph.

China today is engaged in stanchly defending its own culture and its own way of life. This essay helps us to understand one attitude toward living which goes to make that culture which the Chinese intend to preserve. We are all of us trained to worship efficiency in production; we need to see life whole, and to appreciate that it has other and greater values.

Lin Yutang was born in China and educated in Shanghai, Harvard, and Germany. He was in the foreign ministry of the Hankow Government, and has been active in the creation of the new China. In the United States his reputation as critic, essayist and novelist has been established by such books as *My Country and My People,* 1935, an admirable interpretation of East to West; *The Importance of Living,* 1937, an examination of the deeper philosophic differences of the two cultures; *Essays about Nothing,* 1936; and *Moment in Peking,* 1940, a novel dealing with contemporary Chinese life.

The Importance of Loafing

CULTURE, as I understand it, is essentially a product of leisure. The art of culture is therefore essentially the art of loafing. From the Chinese point of view, the man who is wisely idle is the most cultured man. For there seems to be a philosophic contradiction between being busy and being wise. Those who are wise won't be busy, and those who are too busy can't be wise. The wisest man is therefore he who loafs most gracefully. Here I shall try to explain, not the technique and varieties of loafing as practiced in China, but rather the philosophy which nourishes this divine desire for loafing in China and gives rise to that carefree, idle, happy-go-lucky — and often poetic — temperament in the Chinese scholars, and to a lesser extent, in the Chinese people in general. How did that Chinese temperament — that distrust of achievement and success and that intense love of living as such — arise?

In the first place, the Chinese theory of leisure, as expressed by a comparatively unknown author of the eighteenth century, Shu Paihsiang, who happily achieved oblivion, is as follows: time is useful because it is not being used. "Leisure in time is like unoccupied floor space in a room." Every working girl who rents a small room where every inch of space is fully utilized feels highly uncomfortable because she has no room to move about, and the moment she gets a raise in salary, she moves into a bigger room where there is a little more unused floor space, besides those strictly useful spaces occupied by her single bed, her dressing table and her two-burner gas range. It is that unoccupied space which makes a room habitable, as it is our leisure hours which make life endurable. I understand there is a rich woman living on Park Avenue, who bought up a neighboring lot to prevent anybody from erecting a skyscraper next to her house. She is paying a big sum of money in order to have space fully and perfectly made useless, and it seems to me she never spent her money more wisely.

In this connection, I might mention a personal experience. I could never see the beauty of skyscrapers in New York, and it was not until I went to Chicago that I realized that a skyscraper could be very imposing and very beautiful to look at, if it had a good frontage and at least half a mile of unused space around it. Chicago is fortunate in this respect, because it has more space than Man-hattan. The tall buildings are better spaced, and there is the possibility of obtaining an unobstructed view of them from a long distance. Figuratively speaking, we, too, are so cramped in our life that we cannot enjoy a free perspective of the beauties of our spiritual life. We lack spiritual frontage. . . .

To the Chinese, therefore, with the fine philosophy that " Nothing matters to a man who says nothing matters," Americans offer a strange contrast. Is life really worth all the bother, to the extent of making our soul a slave to the body? The high spirituality of the philosophy of loafing forbids it. The most characteristic advertisement I ever saw was one by an engineering firm with the big words: " Nearly Right Is Not Enough." The desire for one hundred per cent efficiency seems almost obscene. The trouble with Americans is that when a thing is nearly right, they want to make it still better, while for a Chinese, nearly right is good enough.

The three great American vices seem to be efficiency, punctuality and the desire for achievement and success. They are the things that make the Americans so unhappy and so nervous. They steal from them their inalienable right of loafing and cheat them of many a good, idle and beautiful afternoon. One must start out with a

belief that there are no catastrophes in this world, and that besides
the noble art of getting things done, there is a nobler art of leaving
things undone. On the whole, if one answers letters promptly, the
result is about as good or as bad as if he had never answered them
at all. After all, nothing happens, and while one may have missed
a few good appointments, one may have also avoided a few unpleasant ones. Most of the letters are not worth answering, if you
keep them in your drawer for three months; reading them three
months afterward, one might realize how utterly futile and what
a waste of time it would have been to answer them all. Writing letters really can become a vice. It turns our writers into fine pro-
motion salesmen and our college professors into good efficient business executives. In this sense, I can understand Thoreau's contempt
for the American who always goes to the post office.

   Our quarrel is not that efficiency gets things done and very well
done, too. I always rely on American water taps, rather than on those
made in China, because American water taps do not leak. That is
a consolation. Against the old contention, however, that we must all
be useful, be efficient, become officials and have power, the old
reply is that there are always enough fools left in the world who
are willing to be useful, be busy and enjoy power, and so somehow
the business of life can and will be carried on. The only point is
who are the wise, the loafers or the hustlers? Our quarrel with
efficiency is not that it gets things done, but that it is a thief of time
when it leaves us no leisure to enjoy ourselves and that it frays our
nerves in trying to get things done perfectly. An American editor
worries his hair gray to see that no typographical mistakes appear
on the pages of his magazine. The Chinese editor is wiser than that.
He wants to leave his readers the supreme satisfaction of discovering a few typographical mistakes for themselves. More than that, a
Chinese magazine can begin printing serial fiction and forget about
it halfway. In America it might bring the roof down on the editors,
but in China *it doesn't matter, simply because it doesn't matter.*
American engineers in building bridges calculate so finely and exactly as to make the two ends come together within one tenth of an
inch. But when two Chinese begin to dig a tunnel from both sides

of a mountain, both come out on the other side. The Chinese's firm conviction is that it doesn't matter so long as a tunnel is dug through, and if we have two instead of one, why, we have a double track to boot. Provided you are not in a hurry, two tunnels are as good as one, dug somehow, finished somehow and if the train can get through somehow. And the Chinese are extremely punctual, provided you give them plenty of time to do a thing. They always finish a thing on schedule, provided the schedule is long enough.

The tempo of modern industrial life forbids this kind of glorious and magnificent idling. But worse than that, it imposes upon us a different conception of time as measured by the clock, and eventually turns the human being into a clock himself. This sort of thing is bound to come to China, as is evident for instance in a factory of twenty thousand workers. The luxurious prospect of twenty thousand workers coming in at their own sweet pleasure at all hours is, of course, somewhat terrifying. Nevertheless, this is what makes life so hard and hectic. A man who has to be punctually at a certain place at five o'clock has the whole afternoon from one to five ruined for him already. Every American adult is arranging his time on the pattern of the schoolboy — three o'clock for this, five o'clock for that, six-thirty for change of dress; six-fifty for entering the taxi and seven o'clock for emerging into a hotel room. It just makes life not worth living.

And Americans have now come to such a sad state that they are booked up not only for the following day, or the following week, but even for the following month. An appointment three weeks ahead of time is a thing unknown in China. And when a Chinese receives an invitation card, happily he never has to say whether he is going to be present or not. He can put down on the invitation list " coming " if he accepts, or " thanks " if he declines, but in the majority of cases the invited party merely writes the word " know," which is a statement of fact that he knows of the invitation and not a statement of intention. An American or a European leaving Shanghai can tell me that he is going to attend a committee meeting in Paris on April 19, 1938, at three o'clock and that he will be arriving in Vienna on May 21st by the seven o'clock train. If an afternoon is to be condemned and executed, must we announce its execution so early? Cannot a fellow travel and be lord of himself, arriving when he likes and taking departure when he likes?

But above all, the American's inability to loaf comes directly from his desire for doing things and in his placing action above being. We should demand that there be character in our lives as we demand there be character in all great art worthy of the name. Unfortunately, character is not a thing which can be manufactured overnight. Like the quality of mellowness in wine, it is acquired by standing still and by the passage of time. The desire of American old men and women for action, trying in this way to gain their self-respect and the respect of the younger generation, is what makes them look so ridiculous to an Oriental. Too much action in an old man is like a broadcast of jazz music from a megaphone on top of an old cathedral. Is it not sufficient that the old people *are* something? Is it necessary that they must be forever *doing* something? The loss of the capacity for loafing is bad enough in men of middle age, but the same loss in old age is a crime committed against human nature.

Character is always associated with something old and takes time to grow, like the beautiful facial lines of a man in middle age, lines that are the steady imprint of the man's evolving character. It is somewhat difficult to see character in a type of life where every man is throwing away his last year's car and trading it in for the new model. As are the things we make, so are we ourselves. In 1937 every man and woman look 1937, and in 1938 every man and woman will look 1938. We love old cathedrals, old furniture, old silver, old dictionaries and old prints, but we have entirely forgotten about the beauty of old men. I think an appreciation of that kind of beauty is essential to our life, for beauty, it seems to me, is what is old and mellow and well-smoked.

Sometimes a prophetic vision comes to me, a beautiful vision of a millennium when Manhattan will go slow, and when the American "go-getter" will become an Oriental loafer. American gentlemen will float in skirts and slippers and amble on the sidewalks of Broadway with their hands in their pockets, if not with both hands

stuck in their sleeves in the Chinese fashion. Policemen will exchange a word of greeting with the slow-devil at the crossings, and
the drivers themselves will stop and accost each other and inquire
after their grandmothers' health in the midst of traffic. Someone
will be brushing his teeth outside his shop front, talking the while
placidly with his neighbors, and once in a while, an absent-minded
scholar will sail by with a limp volume rolled up and tucked away
in his sleeve. Lunch counters will be abolished, and people will be
lolling and lounging in soft, low armchairs in an Automat, while
others will have learned the art of killing a whole afternoon in
some café. A glass of orange juice will last half an hour, and
people will learn to sip wine by slow mouthfuls, punctuated by
delightful, chatty remarks, instead of swallowing it at a gulp.
Registration in a hospital will be abolished, "emergency wards"
will be unknown, and patients will exchange their philosophy with
their doctors. Fire engines will proceed at a snail's pace, their staff
stopping on the way to gaze at and dispute over the number of
passing wild geese in the sky. It is too bad that there is no hope
of this kind of millennium on Manhattan ever being realized. There
might be so many more perfect idle afternoons.

APPRECIATION HINTS

1. What is the Chinese theory of leisure? What illustration does Lin Yutang use to make it clear?
2. What does he think are the three great American vices?
3. What does he say about the Chinese attitude toward precision in engineering?
4. What is the Chinese way of handling an invitation?
5. How does he account for the American's inability to loaf?
6. Put the central theme of this essay in a few words.
7. Describe Manhattan when it has learned to loaf. Will such an era ever be possible?
8. Discuss the statement that the Chinese would be a happier people if they were thoroughly Americanized.
9. " Magnificent idling." Cameron Rogers wrote a book about Walt Whitman entitled *The Magnificent Idler.* Can you show how, in some respects, Walt Whitman lived out Lin Yutang's theory?
10. Review your own day to find out what time it affords for " living."
11. What agreements do you observe between Yutang and Morley about answering letters?
12. Write a composition on some topic suggested by this essay. Possible titles: Time for Living, School Activities, What Really Matters, Spiritual Frontage, Streamlined Cars — and Men.
13. Write a composition about a person whom you value for what he (or she) is, rather than for what he (or she) does.
14. Read from *My Country and My People* or from *The Importance of Living.*

That we should practice what we preach is generally admitted; but anyone who preaches what he and his hearers practice must incur the gravest moral disapprobation. Logan Pearsall Smith: *Afterthoughts*

FRANCIS BACON 1561–1626

that follow originated in one of the greatest intellects represented in this book. Nowhere except in parts of the Bible has so much been said in so few words as in the essays of Francis Bacon. What a little wordy writer will take a volume to express Bacon puts in one sentence; thus instead of writing a book about the value of studies he says, " They perfect Nature, and are perfected by experience." The style of Bacon is compact and condensed because it is the expression of the simple truths lying at the heart of questions men have always thought about. At first glance it is amazing that the words of one who could write in Latin as easily as in English are often the words of a child; so that if we read them rapidly we may completely miss the profundity of their meaning. For example, in the essay " Of Youth and Age," we read in the first sentence " A man that is young in years may be old in hours if he has lost no time." This is the language of a child of five, but the wisdom of a man of fifty. Truth seems simple when great minds disclose it to us. Bacon's essays, therefore, are among the books that have to be chewed and digested if they are going to be read at all. Don't treat them lightly!

Bacon would jot down pointed sentences which seemed to sum up his thought on the subject of his meditations. In 1597 he published some of these notes, among them the first version we have of the essay " Of Studies." It shows only eleven sentences, with the paragraph sign in front of most of them. Then after twenty-eight years he published the essay as we have it. When an intellect like Bacon's meditates thirty years and then writes us a message, we ought to read it.

For Bacon's was one of the great intellects of all time. When his public career ended in 1621 with his conviction of accepting bribes, he retired to seclusion and to study. He had attempted to summarize all knowledge in *The Advancement of Learning*, and the *Novum Organum*, written in Latin, founded the modern scientific method of discovering truth by experimentation. The essays appeared in three editions, the last in 1626. He died as the result of a chill caught while he was making the first experiments with frosted foods.

Of Riches

I CANNOT call riches better than the baggage of virtue. The Roman word is better, *impedimenta;* for as the baggage is to an army, so is riches to virtue; it cannot be spared nor left behind, but it hindereth the march; yea, and the care of it sometimes loseth or disturbeth the victory. Of great riches there is no real use, except it be in the distribution; the rest is but conceit. So saith Salomon: *Where much is, there are many to consume it; and what hath the owner but the sight of it with his eyes?* The personal fruition in any man cannot reach to feel great riches: there is a custody of them; or a power of dole and donative [1] of them; or a fame of them; but no solid use to the owner. Do you not see what feigned prices are set upon little stones and rarities? and what works of ostentation are undertaken, because there might seem to be some use of great riches? But then you will say, they may be of use to buy men out of dangers or trouble. Salomon saith: *Riches are as a stronghold in the imagination of the rich man.* But this is excellently expressed, that it is in imagination, and not always in fact. For certainly great riches have sold more men than they have brought out. Seek not proud riches, but such as thou mayest get justly, use soberly, distribute cheerfully, and leave contentedly. Yet have no abstract nor friarly contempt of them. But distinguish, as Cicero saith well of Rabirius

[1] Giving.

Posthumus: *In studio rei amplificandæ apparebat non avaritiæ prædam sed instrumentum bonitati quæri.*[2] Hearken also to Salomon, and beware of hasty gathering of riches: *Qui festinat ad divitias non erit insons.*[3] The poets feign that when Plutus (which is Riches) is sent from Jupiter, he limps and goes slowly; but when he is sent from Pluto, he runs and is swift of foot; meaning, that riches gotten by good means and just labor pace slowly; but when they come by the death of others (as by the course of inheritance, testaments, and the like), they come tumbling upon a man. But it might be applied likewise to Pluto, taking him for the devil. For when riches come from the devil (as by fraud and oppression and unjust means), they come upon speed.

The ways to enrich are many, and most of them foul. Parsimony[4] is one of the best, and yet is not innocent; for it withholdeth men from works of liberality and charity. The improvement of the ground is the most natural obtaining of riches; for it is our great mother's blessing, the earth's; but it is slow. And yet, where men of great wealth do stoop to husbandry, it multiplieth riches exceedingly. I knew a nobleman in England, that had the greatest audits[5] of any man in my time; a great grazier, a great sheepmaster, a great timberman, a great collier, a great cornmaster, a great leadman, and so of iron, and a number of the like points of husbandry: so as the earth seemed a sea to him, in respect of the perpetual importation. It was truly observed by one, that himself came very hardly to a little riches, and very easily to great riches. For when a man's stock is come to that, that he can expect the prime of markets, and overcome those bargains which for their greatness are few men's money, and be partner in the industries of younger men, he cannot but increase mainly. The gains of ordinary trades and vocations are honest, and furthered by two things chiefly: by diligence, and by a good name for good and fair dealing. But the gains of bargains are of a more doubtful nature; when men shall wait upon others' necessity, broke by servants and

[2] In his desire to be rich he seemed to seek not the satisfaction of avarice, but the means of doing good.
[3] The man who runs after riches will lose his innocence.
[4] Miserliness.
[5] Accounts.

instruments to draw them on, put off others cunningly that would be better chapmen, and the like practices, which are crafty and naught.[6] As for the chopping of bargains,[7] when a man buys, not to hold, but to sell over again, that commonly grindeth double, both upon the seller and upon the buyer. Sharings do greatly enrich, if the hands be well chosen that are trusted. Usury is the certainest means of gain, though one of the worst; as that whereby a man doth eat his bread *in sudore vultûs alieni*,[8] and besides, doth plow upon Sundays. But yet, certain though it be, it hath flaws; for that the scriveners and brokers do value unsound men, to serve their own turn. The fortune in being the first in an invention, or in a privilege, doth cause sometimes a wonderful overgrowth in riches; as it was with the first sugar man in the Canaries: therefore if a man can play the true logician, to have as well judgment as invention, he may do great matters; especially if the times be fit. He that resteth upon gains certain, shall hardly grow to great riches: and he that puts all upon adventures, doth oftentimes break and come to poverty: it is good therefore to guard adventures with certainties that may uphold losses. Monopolies, and coemption of wares for resale, where they are not restrained, are great means to enrich; especially if the party have intelligence what things are like to come into request, and so store himself beforehand. Riches gotten by service, though it be of the best rise, yet when they are gotten by flattery, feeding humors, and other servile conditions, they may be placed amongst the worst. As for fishing for testaments and executorships (as Tacitus saith of Seneca, *testamenta et orbos tanquam indagine capi*[9]), it is yet worse; by how much men submit themselves to meaner persons than in service.

Believe not much them that seem to despise riches: for they despise them that despair of them; and none worse, when they come to them. Be not penny-wise; riches have wings, and sometimes they fly away of themselves, sometimes they must be set flying to bring in more. Men leave their riches either to their kindred, or to the public; and moderate portions prosper best in both. A great state left to an

[6] Bad.
[7] Speculation.
[8] Earned by the sweat of another.
[9] Seizing wills and those that need them as it were by hunting.

heir is as a lure to all the birds of prey round about to seize him, if he
be not the better stablished in years and judgment. Likewise glorious
gifts and foundations are like *sacrifices without salt;* and but the
painted sepulchers of alms, which soon will putrefy and corrupt in-
wardly. Therefore measure not thine advancements by quantity, but
frame them by measure: and defer not charities till death; for certainly, if a man weigh it rightly, he that doth so is rather liberal of
another man's than of his own.

Of Studies

STUDIES serve for delight, for
ornament, and for ability. Their chief use for delight is in privateness
and retiring; for ornament, is in discourse; and for ability, is in the
judgment and disposition of business. For expert men can execute
and perhaps judge of particulars, one by one; but the general coun-
sels, and the plots and marshaling of affairs, come best from those
that are learned. To spend too much time in studies is sloth; to use
them too much for ornament is affectation; to make judgment wholly
by their rules is the humor of a scholar. They perfect nature, and are
perfected by experience; for natural abilities are like natural plants,
that need proyning [1] by study; and studies themselves do give forth
directions too much at large, except they be bounded in by experience. Crafty men contemn studies; simple men admire them; and
wise men use them: for they teach not their own use; but that is a
wisdom without them and above them, won by observation. Read
not to contradict and confute; nor to believe and take for granted;
nor to find talk and discourse; but to weigh and consider. Some books
are to be tasted, others to be swallowed, and some few to be chewed
and digested: that is, some books are to be read only in parts; others
to be read, but not curiously; and some few to be read wholly, and
with diligence and attention. Some books also may be read by deputy,
and extracts made of them by others; but that would be only in the
less important arguments, and the meaner sort of books; else distilled

_____
[1] Cultivating.

books are like common distilled waters, flashy things. Reading maketh a full man; conference [2] a ready man; and writing an exact man. And therefore, if a man write little, he had need have a great memory; if he confer little, he had need have a present wit; and if he read little, he had need have much cunning, to seem to know that he doth not. Histories make men wise; poets witty; the mathematics subtile; natural philosophy deep; moral grave; logic and rhetoric able to contend. *Abeunt studia in mores.*[3] Nay, there is no stond [4] or impediment in the wit, but may be wrought out by fit studies: like as diseases of the body may have appropriate exercises. Bowling is good for the stone [5] and reins; shooting for the lungs and breast; gentle walking for the stomach; riding for the head; and the like. So if a man's wit be wandering, let him study the mathematics; for a demonstration, if his wit be called away never so little, he must begin again: if his wit be not apt to distinguish or find differences, let him study the schoolmen; for they are *cymini sectores:* [6] if he be not apt to beat over matters, and to call one thing to prove and illustrate another, let him study the lawyer's case: so every defect of the mind may have a special receipt.

APPRECIATION HINTS

Of Riches

1. What does Bacon mean by calling riches the *impedimenta* of virtue?
2. In the second paragraph he mentions nine ways to become rich. Can you list seven of them?
3. By what means had the nobleman grown rich?
4. What are the two objections Bacon has to getting rich on the interest on money loaned?
5. What are the dangers incurred by the heirs to a great estate?
6. Point out some ways to become rich, condemned by Bacon, but sanctioned by common practice.

[2] Conversation.   [5] Disease of the kidneys.
[3] Studies pass into character. [6] Splitters of cumin-seeds; that is, hair-splitters.
[4] Stand; obstacle.

7. Write a composition on a topic suggested by this essay. Examples: The Baggage of Virtue, Plowing on Sunday, Penny-Wise, Riches Have Wings, Little Stones and Rarities.

Of Studies

1. According to Bacon, what are the purposes of studies?
2. What is the purpose of reading?
3. Into what three classes does he divide books?
4. Why does he prescribe mathematics for a wandering wit?
5. Give examples of books which you would consider proper to be (1) tasted, (2) swallowed, (3) chewed and digested.
6. This essay is remarkable for its compressed style. Make a list of condensed statements.
7. Take one of the condensed statements of this essay and expand it into a composition. Examples: Abeunt Studia in Mores, Reading Maketh a Full Man, Read Not to Believe and Take for Granted.
8. If you like Bacon read " Of Truth," " Of Friendship," " Of Travel," " Of Gardens."

THINKING FOR ONESELF

The multitude of books serves only to show how many false paths there are, and how widely astray a man may wander if he follows any of them. But if he is guided by his genius, he who thinks for himself, who thinks spontaneously and exactly, possesses the only compass by which he can steer aright. A man should read only when his own thoughts stagnate at their source, which will happen often enough even with the best minds. On the other hand, to take up a book for the purpose of scaring away one's own original thoughts is sin against the Holy Ghost. It is like running away from nature to look at a museum of dried plants or gaze at a landscape in copperplate.   Arthur Schopenhauer: *Thinking for Oneself*

COURAGE TO LIVE AND DIE

THE heading for this section is doubly charged with meaning because war has come to a new generation of Americans. As a consequence, well-known messages like Stevenson's dauntless challenge to young men in "Aes Triplex," his praise of life lived with a certain reckless-ness, have in a moment become strangely fresh and personal. So has Tomlinson's sincere and glowing tribute to the heroism in the com-mon man, as he watched the tragedy at the pit mouth of the burning colliery — "greatness is as common as that." And a deeper meaning now imbues the ancient story of Socrates drinking the hemlock, for it is the immortal portrait of a stiff, fearless man standing at his post of duty, and choosing, of his own free will, to die rather than to de-sert it. Most of us, like him, will face our duty in the market place of ordinary life. When the recruiting rush is over, there comes the long pull, testing our courage in the daily grind. Then it is that the memory of Mary White with her natural joy and sparkle and plain goodness is a treasure worth keeping. Not less applicable is Clifton Fadiman's impressive account of the noble courage of a woman in ac-complishing what she set out to do, and her complete indifference to public honors and public adulation. In comparison with the steady il-lumination of the lives of such women as Marie Curie and Helen Keller, how quickly the latest movie star fades and is forgotten!

WILLIAM ALLEN WHITE
1868–

ONE MAY read this essay again and again, always with a fresh sense of its peculiar power. We feel an awed wonder that a father, stunned by the sudden death of his daughter, should have been able, on the day of her burial, so to steady and control himself, to "grip his feeling in his fist," as to write a description of his tomboy saint of a daughter, so clear, so objective, that the child might almost seem to belong to another father. This is no soft and weepy eulogy; it is as if the blow which struck down Mary had clarified her father's vision so that he could write her down exactly as she was. He has handed on to us the gift of knowing this brimming and bubbling spirit, for she lives permanently in this essay. Through it, Mary White has had an influence on many thousands of high-school girls and boys, who otherwise could never have known that she existed. And how Mary would have laughed to know that here, in this book, she was going to be bound up with some of her favorite authors.

Mary White achieved the kind of immortality which would have delighted her — to live in the heart of youth. She had planned to enter Wellesley College in 1922 and graduate in 1926. When the girls in that class read this essay, they enrolled her as one of their number, and in 1926 dedicated the class annual, *Wellesley Legenda* to her memory.

William Allen White is a kind of model of Americanism. His grandfather went to Ohio in a covered wagon; his parents were Kansas pioneers; when he was only twenty-four he bought the Emporia *Gazette* for three thousand borrowed dollars, and paid for it in three years. He wrote the editorials, so soon to be known and copied throughout the country; his wife collected the news; "young Bill lived and crowed and cried in the office waste basket." What White wrote was himself — pungent and humorous, but also honest and straightforward, and always on the side of decency in politics. "White preaches," said his friend Theodore Roosevelt, "what he practices." Offered enviable positions in many parts of the country, he consistently refused them in order to go on doing good in his own way in his own town, Emporia, Kansas.

THE ASSOCIATED PRESS reports carrying the news of Mary White's death declared that it came as the result of a fall from a horse. How she would have hooted at that! She never fell from a horse in her life. Horses have fallen on her and with her — " I'm always trying to hold 'em in my lap," she used to say. But she was proud of few things, and one was that she could ride anything that had four legs and hair. Her death resulted not from a fall, but from a blow on the head which fractured her skull, and the blow came from the limb of an overhanging tree on the parking.

The last hour of her life was typical of its happiness. She came home from a day's work at school, topped off by a hard grind with the copy on the High School Annual, and felt that a ride would refresh her. She climbed into her khakis, chattering to her mother about the work she was doing, and hurried to get her horse and be out on the dirt roads for the country air and the radiant green fields of the spring. As she rode through the town on an easy gallop she kept waving at passers-by. She knew everyone in town. For a decade the little figure with the long pigtail and the red hair ribbon has been familiar on the streets of Emporia, and she got in the way of speaking to those who nodded at her. She passed the Kerrs, walking the horse, in front of the Normal Library, and waved at them; passed another friend a few hundred feet farther on, and waved at her. The horse was walking and as she turned into North Merchant Street she took off her cowboy hat, and the horse swung into a lope. She passed the Tripletts and waved her cowboy hat at them, still moving gaily north on Merchant Street. A *Gazette* carrier passed — a high-school boy friend — and she waved at him, but with her bridle hand; the horse veered quickly, plunged into the parking where the low-hanging limb faced her, and, while she still looked back waving, the blow came. But she did not fall from the horse; she slipped off, dazed a bit, staggered, and fell in a faint. She never quite recovered consciousness.

But she did not fall from the horse, neither was she riding fast. A year or so ago she used to go like the wind. But that habit was broken, and she used the horse to get into the open to get fresh, hard exercise, and to work off a certain surplus energy that welled up in her and needed a physical outlet. That need has been in her heart for years. It was back of the impulse that kept the dauntless, little brown-clad figure on the streets and country roads of this community and built into a strong, muscular body what had been a frail and sickly frame during the first years of her life. But the riding gave her more than a body. It released a gay and hardy soul. She was the happiest thing in the world. And she was happy because she was enlarging her horizon. She came to know all sorts and conditions of men. Charley O'Brien, the traffic cop, was one of her best friends. W. L. Holtz, the Latin teacher, was another. Tom O'Connor, farmer-politician, and Rev. J. H. J. Rice, preacher and police judge, and Frank Beach, music master, were her special friends, and all the girls, black and white, above the track and below the track, in Pepville and Stringtown, were among her acquaintances. And she brought home riotous stories of her adventures. She loved to rollick; persiflage was her natural expression at home. Her humor was a continual bubble of joy. She seemed to think in hyperbole and metaphor. She was mischievous without malice, as full of faults as an old shoe. No angel was Mary White, but an easy girl to live with, for she never nursed a grouch five minutes in her life.

With all her eagerness for the out-of-doors, she loved books. On her table when she left her room were a book by Conrad, one by Galsworthy, *Creative Chemistry* by E. E. Slosson, and a Kipling book.

She read Mark Twain, Dickens, and Kipling before she was ten — all of their writings. Wells and Arnold Bennett particularly amused and diverted her. She was entered as a student in Wellesley in 1922; was assistant editor of the High School Annual this year, and in line for election to the editorship of the Annual next year. She was a member of the executive committee of the High School Y. W. C. A.

Within the last two years she had begun to be moved by an ambition to draw. She began as most children do by scribbling in her schoolbooks, funny pictures. She bought cartoon magazines and took a course — rather casually, naturally, for she was, after all, a child, with no strong purposes — and this year she tasted the first fruits of success by having her pictures accepted by the High School Annual. But the thrill of delight she got when Mr. Ecord, of the Normal Annual, asked her to do the cartooning for that book this spring was too beautiful for words. She fell to her work with all her enthusiastic heart. Her drawings were accepted, and her pride — always repressed by a lively sense of the ridiculousness of the figure she was cutting — was a really gorgeous thing to see. No successful artist ever drank a deeper draft of satisfaction than she took from the little fame her work was getting among her schoolfellows. In her glory, she almost forgot her horse — but never her car.

For she used the car as a jitney bus. It was her social life. She never had a "party" in all her nearly seventeen years — wouldn't have one; but she never drove a block in the car in her life that she didn't begin to fill the car with pick-ups! Everybody rode with Mary White — white and black, old and young, rich and poor, men and women. She liked nothing better than to fill the car full of long-legged high-school boys and an occasional girl, and parade the town. She never had a "date," nor went to a dance, except once with her brother, Bill, and the "boy proposition" didn't interest her — yet. But young people — great, spring-breaking, varnish-cracking, fender-bending door-sagging carloads of "kids" — gave her great pleasure. Her zests were keen. But the most fun she ever had in her life was acting as chairman of the committee that got up the big turkey dinner for the poor folks at the county home; scores of pies, gallons of slaw, jam, cakes, preserves, oranges, and a wilderness of turkey were

loaded in the car and taken to the country home. And, being of a practical turn of mind, she risked her own Christmas dinner by staying
to see that the poor folks actually got it all. Not that she was a cynic;
she just disliked to tempt folks. While there she found a blind Negro
uncle, very old, who could do nothing but make rag rugs, and she
rustled up from her school friends rags enough to keep him busy for a
season. The last engagement she tried to make was to take the guests
at the county home out for a car ride. And the last endeavor of her
life was to try to get a rest room for Negro girls in the high school.
She found one girl reading in the toilet, because there was no better
place for a Negro girl to loaf, and it inflamed her sense of injustice
and she became a nagging harpy to those who she thought could
remedy the evil.

The poor she had always with her, and was glad of it. She hun-
gered and thirsted for righteousness; and was the most impious creature in the world. She joined the Congregational Church without
consulting her parents; not particularly for her soul's good. She never
had a thrill of piety in her life, and would have hooted at a " testimony." But even as a little child she felt the church was an agency
for helping people to more of life's abundance, and she wanted to
help. She never wanted help for herself. Clothes meant little to her.
It was a fight to get a new rig on her; but eventually a harder fight to
get it off. She never wore a jewel and had no ring but her high-school
class ring, and never asked for anything but a wrist watch. She
refused to have her hair up, though she was nearly seventeen.
" Mother," she protested, " you don't know how much I get by with,
in my braided pigtails, that I could not with my hair up." Above every
other passion of her life was her passion not to grow up, to be a child.
The tomboy in her, which was big, seemed to loathe to be put away
forever in skirts. She was a Peter Pan, who refused to grow up.

Her funeral yesterday at the Congregational Church was as she
would have wished it; no singing, no flowers save the big bunch of
red roses from her brother Bill's Harvard classmen — Heavens, how
proud that would have made her! and the red roses from the *Gazette*
force — in vases at her head and feet. A short prayer, Paul's beautiful
essay on " Love," from the thirteenth chapter of First Corinthians,

some remarks about her democratic spirit by her friend, John H. J. Rice, pastor and police judge, which she would have deprecated if she could, a prayer sent down for her by her friend, Carl Nau, and opening the service the slow, poignant movement from Beethoven's *Moonlight Sonata,* which she loved, and closing the service a cutting from the joyously melancholy first movement of Tschaikowski's *Symphonie Pathétique,* which she liked to hear in certain moods on the phonograph; then the Lord's Prayer by her friends in the high school.

That was all.

For her pallbearers only her friends were chosen: her Latin teacher, W. L. Holtz; her high-school principal, Rice Brown; her doctor, Frank Foncannon; her friend, W. W. Finney; her pal at the *Gazette* office, Walter Hughes; and her brother Bill. It would have made her smile to know that her friend, Charley O'Brien, the traffic cop, had been transferred from Sixth and Commercial to the corner near the church to direct her friends who came to bid her good-by.

A rift in the clouds in a gray day threw a shaft of sunlight upon her coffin as her nervous, energetic little body sank to its last sleep. But the soul of her, the glowing, gorgeous, fervent soul of her, surely was flaming in eager joy upon some other dawn.

APPRECIATION HINTS

1. How did the accident fatal to Mary occur?
2. What books were on her table when she went out riding?
3. Tell about her success as a cartoonist.
4. What were some of the good things she did in the community?
5. Why didn't Mary want to have her hair up?
6. Describe her funeral.
7. What is it in the character of Mary which appeals to you most?
8. What are the qualities in her which are representative of the best type of high-school girl?
9. Point out instances which reveal her truly democratic spirit.
10. Make a list of effective phrases; for example, " spring-breaking, varnish-cracking, fender-bending carloads of kids."

11. Write a composition suggested by this essay. Possible titles: A Friend of Mine Like Mary, The Most Generous Person I Know, Reforms Needed in My School, What I Have Learned from Mary White, My Friend — the Traffic Cop.
12. Read William Allen White's " The Country Newspaper " in *Harper's Magazine*, May, 1916, and *A Certain Rich Man*.

THE TORCHBEARER

The present is in every age merely the shifting point at which past and future meet, and we can have no quarrel with either. There can be no world without traditions; neither can there be any life without movement. As Heraclitus knew at the outset of modern philosophy, we cannot bathe twice in the same stream, though, as we know today, the stream still flows in an unending circle. There is never a moment when the new dawn is not breaking over the earth, and never a moment when the sunset ceases to die. It is well to greet serenely even the first glimmer of the dawn when we see it, not hastening towards it with undue speed, nor leaving the sunset without gratitude for the dying light that once was dawn.

In the moral world we are ourselves the light-bearers, and the cosmic process is in us made flesh. For a brief space it is granted to us, if we will, to enlighten the darkness that surrounds our path. As in the ancient torch-race, which seemed to Lucretius to be the symbol of all life, we press forward torch in hand along the course. Soon from behind comes the runner who will outpace us. All our skill lies in giving into his hand the living torch, bright and unflickering, as we ourselves disappear in the darkness.

Havelock Ellis: *The New Spirit*
(The National Home Library Foundation)

CLIFTON FADIMAN 1904-

THE FOLLOWING essay is the only book review in this volume. The author is probably known to all of us as the master of ceremonies and referee, since 1938, of " Information Please." But he is first and foremost a reviewer of books, and one of the best of guides for those who read books and then wish to sum up their impressions about them for the benefit of others. Mr. Fadiman has written about this profession or trade as he calls it, and since he was himself a boy wonder book reviewer, what he says is of great interest to young writers. In the first place he believes that Francis Bacon was mistaken when he said reading maketh a full man. " I suppose I have read five or ten thousand books in the past couple of decades. Every so often I catch myself wondering whether I shouldn t be a sight wiser if I had read only fifteen, and they, the right ones." The good reviewer, he believes, is neither critic nor creative writer and cannot be. " If he is a good reviewer and keeps in the groove fifteen or twenty years he has no more chance of becoming a writer than a pig has of flying. . . . One decent hack, to my mind, is worth a stable of would-be Pegasuses."

And yet, many readers in search of guidance look first to Mr. Fadiman's reviews in the *New Yorker,* and you cannot read this example and still believe that the author is just plying a trade. It was perhaps inevitable that the nobility of the character unfolded in the book should steal the spotlight of the reviewer; the surprising thing is that one who has to read say two books a day, and keep on doing it, can retain this capacity to react freshly and promptly when a great book comes to his desk.

Clifton Fadiman graduated at Columbia University, taught English for two years, and began reviewing for the *New Yorker* in 1933. He edited *I Believe,* a compilation of the personal philosophies of some twenty-one eminent men and women of our time.

" She Did Not Know How to Be Famous "

DESCARTES was unheroic, Leibnitz a fawning courtier, Willard Gibbs a recluse, Gauss [1] cold and secretive. For all his nobility, Pasteur was tainted with chauvinism [2] and race hatred. An infantile religiosity clouded to the end the magnificent minds of Newton and Pascal. Indeed, it is hard to think of many first-rate scientific careers in which some major flaw of character does not show itself, confounding our natural desire for wholehearted hero worship. But the lives of Marie and Pierre Curie, two of the most beautiful lives, I suppose, that have ever been lived, provide an exception. It was almost theatrically apt that this man and woman, with characters of shining purity, should have built their careers around a physical element recognizable by its indestructible and essential radiance.

The life of Madame Curie, who died in 1934, has now been written by Eve, her younger daughter, and sensitively translated by Vincent Sheean. One can give *Madame Curie* no higher praise than to say it is almost worthy of its subject. It is not, I think, as solid a biography as it might be. It does not have that wonderful density of technical information, for example, which made Vallery-Radot's *Pasteur* a classic. It tells you just enough about radium to make

---

[1] All four of these were philosophers or scientists: Descartes a Frenchman; Leibnitz and Gauss, Germans; Josiah Willard Gibbs, a Professor at Yale.

[2] Exaggerated patriotism.

you understand the great achievement of the Curies. But the biography of a scientist should do more. One can only regret that Irène Joliot-Curie (the elder daughter, co-winner of the Nobel Prize) did not collaborate with her sister on the scientific chapters. But aside from this defect, here is a noble and moving biography, which takes due advantage of the fact that the life of Marie Curie might have been conceived not by the accidents of nature but by the patterning brain of a tragic dramatist of genius.

One looks at the frontispiece, a photograph of Marie taken in 1929, when she was sixty-two. The face is lined. From underneath the white and casually arranged hair arcs an abnormally spacious brow. She is dressed in a simple black dress that looks like a laboratory smock. The face is that of a truly beautiful woman, the beauty lying in the bones and in the brain that sends its clear signals through the deep, penetrating eyes. What can Hollywood, when it films this book, do with such a face?

The story of Marie Curie is not merely that of a poor Polish governess who struggled against adversity and became a triumphant success. The story of Marie Curie lies precisely in the fact that she was happiest during her struggles and least happy when a vulgar world acclaimed her. Hers is a success story with an ironic twist. Einstein has said, " Marie Curie is, of all celebrated beings, the only one whom fame has not corrupted." " She did not know how to be famous," says Eve Curie. In one deliberate sentence of her perfectly composed introduction, she strikes to the heart of the secret: " I hope that the reader may constantly feel, across the ephemeral movement of one existence, what in Marie Curie was even more rare than her work or her life: the immovable structure of a character; the stubborn effort of an intelligence; the free immolation of a human being that could give all and take nothing, could even receive nothing; and above all the quality of a soul in which neither fame nor adversity could change the exceptional purity."

Recall that unbelievably dramatic life. She is born Manya Sklodowska, youngest child of a Warsaw physicist and a sensitive, tubercular mother. The childhood is unhappy, torn by the death of mother and eldest sister, rendered overserious by poverty, given a certain tenseness by the fact that she is a member of a subject race, the Poles. She grows up, becomes the conventional intellectual rebel of her time, like "all the little Polish girls who had gone mad for culture." She is intelligent, but nothing yet reveals that "immovable structure" of which her daughter speaks. She becomes a governess, a bit of a bluestocking touched with Tolstoyan sentimentality. Now "the eternal student" begins to rise up in her. The little child who at five stood in rapt awe before her father's case containing the "physics ap-pa-ra-tus" reawakens in the girl of eighteen. Her duties as a governess do not prevent her from studying. She has no money, not even for stamps so that she may write to her brother. But "I am learning chemistry from a book." Back in Warsaw, she is allowed to perform elementary chemical experiments in a real laboratory, and at last, after inconceivable setbacks and economies, after years of weary waiting, she goes to Paris to study at the Sorbonne.

On forty rubles a month Manya (now Marie) Sklodowska lives, studies, learns. Solitude, near-starvation, an unheated garret — none of these things matters, as long as at least a part of her day is spent in the laboratory. Now even the miserable forty rubles cease. She is about to return in despair to Warsaw when she is given a six-hundred-ruble scholarship. A few years afterward, with the first money she earns as a scientist, she returns the amount of the scholarship so that some other poor student may be assisted by it.

In 1894 she meets Pierre Curie, already a physicist of note, a mind "both powerful and noble." In an atmosphere of garrets and laboratories, these two, very grave and serious, conduct their love affair. They marry. On her wedding day, to the generous friend who wishes to give her a bridal dress, she writes, " I have no dress except the one I wear every day. If you are going to be kind enough to give me one, please let it be practical and dark so that I can put it on afterwards to go to the laboratory."

It is a perfect marriage, the marriage not merely of two people who love each other but, what is incomparably more interesting and important, of two great physicists who can help each other. It is Marie, attracted by the uranium researches of Becquerel, who starts herself and her husband on the long, tedious, glorious path at the end of which lies radium. They know that radium and polonium (named by Marie to commemorate her beloved native land) exist, but they must prove it. From 1898 to 1902, in a dilapidated, leaking, freezing shed, with primitive apparatus, with little or no help, unaided by the scientific bureaucracy or by the State, these two gentle fanatics work in an absorption that is like a dream. The government is too busy spending money on armament to buy them the few tons of pitchblende they need. Somehow they get their pitchblende, paying for its transportation themselves out of their insufficient salaries. With "her terrible patience," Marie, doing the work of four strong men, pounds away at her chemical masses, boils, separates, refines, stirs, strains. Somewhere in this inert brown stuff lies radium. Marie loses fifteen pounds during these five years. At last they isolate the element.

All this time they have been bringing up a family. They have had sorrows, family illnesses. Pierre's mother has died of the very disease against which radium is soon to prove a beneficent weapon. All this time no provision is made for these selfless geniuses. The State, as always, cares nothing. Recognition comes first from other countries, from Switzerland, England. "With great merit and even greater modesty," says Montaigne, "one can remain unknown for a long time."

Now the full implications of their work begin to appear. The immovable atom moves; matter is touched with a mysterious life; physics revises its nineteenth-century conceptions of the indestructibility of matter and the conservation of energy. The Curies are triumphant; and their first major decision is to refrain from patenting their radium-extraction process. They give it freely to the world. This gesture alone — or rather the inevitable expression of their characters — is enough to lend their lives a depth that can never attach to a commercial career like that of Edison. The difference between a Curie and an Edison is not merely one of scientific genius, it is a difference of order. The Curies are one kind of human being, Edison was another.

In 1903 the Curies, with Becquerel, receive the Nobel Prize for Physics. The world pursues them. Now they must flee the world. "In science we must be interested in things, not in persons," says Marie, who was never to be interested in herself. One evening, at the height of their fame, as they are about to leave for a banquet, Pierre looks at his wife, with her ash-gray eyes, her ash-blond hair, her exquisite wrists and ankles, and he murmurs, " It's a pity. Evening dress becomes you." Then, with a sigh, he adds, " But there it is, we haven't got time."

They are offered the slimy vulgarity of decorations, ribbons, rosettes. But no laboratory. (Pierre eventually died without getting his laboratory, without being allowed to work properly.) The life of the Curies will remain, forever terrible, as a somber reminder of the stupidity, the greed, even the sadism [3] of the French ruling class of the period.

Then on April 19, 1906, Aeschylean tragedy, cutting Marie's life in two, giving it at the same time a new emotional dimension. Pierre's head is crushed by a van in a street accident, and Marie becomes " a pitiful and incurably lonely woman." She refuses a pension (always the State makes its generous offers too late); she proceeds with the education of her daughters; she takes over Pierre's teaching post and, in a dry, monotonous voice, without making any reference to her predecessor, resumes the lectures at the exact point at which Pierre had left off.

The rest of her life is the story of her marriage with radium. For her laboratory, for science, she will do anything, even try to be " famous." In 1911 she receives the Nobel Prize for Chemistry. During the war she equips, with superhuman energy, a fleet of radiological cars so that the wounded may be helped by X rays. She is no rotogravure ministering angel, no Queen Marie of Rumania. She actually works — works for the State which had done its best in those dark years to prevent her from working. Later, again for the sake of science, she comes to America to receive a gram of radium from the hand of an amiable poker player who could not possibly have understood even the most trivial of the thoughts in Marie Curie's mind. Then, applauded by all America, she goes back to France, and all America turns to the next celebrity, Carpentier, to lavish an identical adulation upon him. Almost blind, her hands and arms scarred,

[3] Perverted cruelty.

pitted, and burned by thirty years of radium emanations, she continues her work almost to the day of her death, caused in part by that very element which she had released for the use of mankind.

Rarely — increasingly rarely — a book appears which reconciles us to belonging to the human race. Here is one.

APPRECIATION HINTS

1. What is the main thought of the first paragraph?
2. How does Fadiman qualify his praise of the book?
3. Explain more fully what the title means.
4. Tell about Marie's earliest studies in science.
5. Tell about her studies in Paris.
6. Describe the conditions in which they worked while they were discovering radium.
7. For what reason does Fadiman place the Curies above Edison?
8. What was Marie's service in the war?
9. Would you call this essay a book review or a brief biography? Why?
10. What are the qualities of character which make us admire Madame Curie?
11. Can you think of other geniuses in modern times who struggled in poverty?
12. What are the purposes of a book review? Which of these purposes does this essay fulfill?
13. Write a composition based on what Einstein said: "Marie Curie is, of all celebrated beings, the only one whom fame has not corrupted." Think of instances in history of people who have deteriorated when they became famous.
14. Write a composition based on some topic suggested by this essay. Possible titles: Early Struggles, My First Experiments in Science, America's Adulations, A Hero for a Moment, Only One Dress.
15. Read "The Reviewing Business" in *Harper's* for October, 1941; and the collection, *Reading I've Liked*.

BY THE COMPASS

The mariner of old said this to Neptune in a great tempest. "O God! thou mayest save me if thou wilt, or if thou wilt thou mayest destroy me; but whether or no, I will steer my rudder true."　　Montaigne: *Of Glory*

H. M. TOMLINSON 1873 –

IF YOU WANT to write supremely well, here is a guide. A fellow craftsman, Christopher Morley, has said that in reading the best essays of Tomlinson, and submitting oneself to the "moving music and magic of that prose, so simple and yet so subtle, one wonders whether poetry is not, after all, an inferior and more mechanic form." Tomlinson himself has answered the question. "There is no difference between prose and poetry," he writes, "only between prose and verse." We may feel when we read some essays that the author is consciously trying to write beautifully or cleverly. We never feel that with Tomlinson. A great Frenchman said, "Le style, c'est l'homme même" — style, that's the man himself. It needed a particular kind of man, with a particular attitude toward life, to see what he saw at the Great Barr colliery fire, and then to put its significance into language.

It was not merely that Tomlinson had grown up in London by the river, had mingled with the Lascars, the Chinese, and the dockwallopers of Thames bank, and had learned to love the plain tough men who do the hard dirty work. There was something in him humane and noble, which illuminated this experience, and enabled him to see in the stevedore and the miner more than we do.

As a boy Henry Major Tomlinson saw the last of the old clipper ships, and loved to watch them beating up the Thames basin and coming into port. His long career as an author started, when, as a young shipping clerk, he began to write sketches of the water front. His wild voyage up the Amazon in a tramp steamer captained by his brother resulted in *The Sea and the Jungle*, 1912, one of the best of modern stories of travel. *Old Junk*, perhaps the best known of his collections of essays, appeared in 1919. In 1927 Mr. Tomlinson published one of the great novels of the decade, largely autobiographical, *Gallions Reach*. His latest novel is *The Day Before*, 1939.

The Pit Mouth

THERE WAS Great Barr, idle, still, and quiet. Through the Birmingham suburbs, out into the raw, bleak winter roads between the hedges, quite beyond the big town smoking with its enterprising labors, one approached the village of calamity with some awe and diffidence. You felt you were intruding; that you were a mere gross interloper, coming through curiosity, that was not excused by the compunction you felt, to see the appearance of a place that had tragedy in nearly all its homes. Young men streamed by on bicycles in the same direction, groups were hurrying there on foot.

The road rose in a mound to let the railway under, and beyond the far dip was the village, an almost amorphous group of mean red dwellings stuck on ragged fields about the dominant colliery buildings. Three high, slim chimneys were leisurely pouring smoke from the grotesque black skeleton structures above the pits. The road ran by the boundary, and was packed with people, all gazing absorbed and quiet into the grounds of the colliery; they were stacked up the hedge banks, and the walls and trees were loaded with boys.

A few empty motorcars of the colliery directors stood about. A carriage horse champed its bit, and the still watchers turned at once to that intrusive sound. Around us, a lucid winter landscape (for it had been raining) ran to the distant encompassing hills which lifted like low ramparts of cobalt and amethyst to a sky of lu-

minous saffron and ice green, across which leaden clouds were moving. The country had that hard, coldly radiant appearance which
always impresses a sad man as this world's frank expression of its
alien disregard; this world not his, on which he has happened, and
must endure with his trouble for a brief time.

As I went through the press of people to the colliery gates, the
women in shawls turned to me, first with annoyance that their
watching should be disturbed, and then with some dull interest.
My assured claim to admittance probably made them think I was
the bearer of new help outside their little knowledge; and they
willingly made room for me to pass. I felt exactly like the interfer-
ing fraud I was. What would I not have given then to be made, for a
brief hour, a nameless miracle worker.

In the colliery itself was the same seeming apathy. There was
nothing to show in that yard, black with soddened cinders and ash
muck, where the new red-brick enginehouses stood, that somewhere half a mile beneath our feet were thirty men, their only exit
to the outer world barred by a subterranean fire. Nothing showed of

the fire but a whitish
smoke from a ventilating
shaft; and a stranger
would not know what that
signified. But the women
did. Wet with the rain
showers, they had been
standing watching that
smoke all night, and were
watching it still, for its un-
ceasing pour to diminish.
Constant and unrelenting, it streamed steadily upward, as though it
drew its volume from central fires that would never cease.

The doors of the office were thrown open, and three figures
emerged. They broke into the listlessness of that dreary place, where
nothing seemed to be going on, with a sudden real purpose, fast but
unhurried, and moved toward the shaft. Three Yorkshire rescue experts — one of them to die later — with the Hamstead manager ex-

plaining the path they should follow below with eager seriousness.
"Figures of fun"! They had muzzles on their mouths and noses,
goggles on their eyes, fantastic helms, and queer cylinders and bags
slung about them. As they went up the slope of wet ash, quick and
full of purpose, their comical gear and coarse dress became suddenly transfigured; and the silent crowd cheered emotionally that
little party of forlorn hope.

They entered the cage, and down they went. Still it was difficult for me to think that we were fronting tragedy, for no danger
showed. An hour and more passed in nervous and dismal waiting.
There was a signal. Some men ran to the pit head carrying hot bricks
and blankets. The doctors took off their coats, and arranged bottles
and tinkling apparatus on chairs stuck in the mud. The air smelt
of iodoform. A cloth was laid on the ground from the shaft to the
enginehouse, and stretchers were placed handy. The women, some
carrying infants, broke rank. That quickly uprunning rope was
bringing the first news. The rope stopped running and the cage appeared. Only the rescue party came out, one carrying a moribund
cat. They knew nothing; and the white-faced women, with hardly
repressed hysteria, took again their places by the enginehouse. So
we passed that day, watching the place from which came nothing
but disappointment. Occasionally a child, too young to know it was
adding to its mother's grief, would wail querulously. There came a
time when I and all there knew that to go down that shaft was to
meet with death. The increasing exhaustion and pouring sweat of
the returning rescue parties showed that. Yet the miners who were
not selected to go down were angry; they violently abused the
favoritism of the officials who would not let all risk their lives.

I have a new regard for my fellows since Great Barr. About you
and me there are men like that. There is nothing to distinguish
them. They show no signs of greatness. They have common talk.
They have coarse ways. They walk with an ugly lurch. Their eyes
are not eager. They are not polite. Their clothes are dirty. They live
in cheap houses on cheap food. They call you "sir." They are the
great unwashed, the mutable many, the common people. The common people! Greatness is as common as that. There are not enough

honors and decorations to go round. Talk of the soldier! *Vale* [1] to Welsby of Normanton! He was a common miner. He is dead. His fellows were in danger, their wives were white-faced and their children were crying, and he buckled on his harness and went to the assault with no more thought for self than great men have in a great cause; and he is dead. I saw him go to his death. I wish I could tell you of Welsby of Normanton.

I left that place where the starshine was showing the grim skeleton of the shaftwork overhead in the night, and where men moved about below in the indeterminate dark like dismal gnomes. There was a woman whose cry, when Welsby died, was like a challenge.

Next morning, in Great Barr, some blinds were down, the street was empty. Children, who could see no reason about them why their fathers should not return as usual, were playing football by the tiny church. A group of women were still gazing at the grotesque ribs and legs of the pit-head staging as though it were a monster without ruth.

November 1907.

APPRECIATION HINTS

1. What are the signs, noted in the first three paragraphs, that told him he was approaching a village of calamity?
2. What was the attitude of the women at the colliery gates toward him?
3. What had happened in the pit?
4. Describe the three rescue experts.
5. What happened above ground when the signal came from below?
6. What was it that gave the author a new regard for his fellows?
7. Describe Great Barr next morning.
8. Is this essay written in long sentences or short? Is there any relation between the length of the author's sentences and what he wants to say?
9. Which of the following expressions best conveys to you the central quality of this essay: (a) accurate reporting of the facts; (b) con-

[1] Farewell

scious effort to write beautifully; (c) the quality of the author, and the way he looks at the world.

10. Pick out any passages which seem to you to support the view that Tomlinson is a great writer of prose.

11. Imagine that you had been reporting the pit fire at Great Barr. What would be the items of "news value" you would have looked for?

12. Write a composition suggested by this essay. Possible titles: First Signs of the Fire, First Aid for the Drowning, A Young Hero, Faces of the Watchers, Greatness Is as Common as That.

13. Read "The Art of Writing," "The Call," "Bed-Books and Night-Lights," all from *Old Junk;* "The Foreshore" and "The Master" from *London River.*

"AS COMMON AS THAT"

In the Afghan War men were wanted for a perilous enterprise — an assault from which there was little chance of returning. It was decided to call for recruits. The colonel of the Scots Guards called out his men, and told them plainly the dangers ahead.

"If any of you wish to volunteer, I will ask you to step out from the ranks three paces."

He then turned his back for a few moments to let them make up their minds. When he faced them again the line was intact. The colonel's eyes blazed with indignation: "The Scots Guards . . . and not one man . . ."

A subaltern came forward and saluted.

"Colonel," said he, "the whole line stepped forward."

Life is no brief candle to me. It is a sort of splendid torch which I have got hold of for the moment, and I want to make it burn as brightly as possible before handing it on to future generations. George Bernard Shaw

ROBERT LOUIS STEVENSON
1850–1894

HERE IS an essay by one of the great champions of youth — of its exuberance, its courage, and even its follies. "For God's sake," Stevenson writes in another essay which you should read, "give me the young man who has brains enough to make a fool of himself . . . Youth is the time to go flashing from one end of the world to the other both in mind and body; to hear the chimes at midnight, to see sunrise in town and country, to write halting verses, to run a mile to see a fire . . . It is better to be a fool than to be dead." Stevenson's heroes were people like Joan of Arc and Columbus, not people like John D. Rockefeller and Benjamin Franklin. And we can see from the following essay, particularly from its last splendid paragraph, that what he found most to admire in the young is the stout heart, the reckless courage it brings to bear on living. It isn't life that counts, it's the courage you bring to it.

One might infer that Stevenson's youth must have been rugged and strenuous. But his whole life was a fight against tuberculosis; he was hopeless in athletics; he was the butt of his schoolmates at Edinburgh Academy, and an idler and failure at Edinburgh University. He was unable to cope with the practical problems of life; his first night in New York City was spent in a twenty-five-cent boardinghouse; in California he was sometimes in desperate need, and worked as a two-dollar-a-week reporter. It was only after his marriage to the American, Mrs. Osbourne, in 1879 that the Stevenson we know and love begins to emerge.

Stevenson has an established place in English literature as poet, novelist, essayist, and letter writer. He became famous with *Treasure Island,* written for his little stepson Lloyd, who had demanded "something interesting," and with *Dr. Jekyll and Mr. Hyde,* written from memories of "a fine bogey tale," which had come to him as half dream, half nightmare. Collections of his essays made during his lifetime are: *An Inland Voyage, Travels with a Donkey, Virginibus Puerisque, Memories and Portraits,* and *Across the Plains.*

Aes Triplex, "triple brass" is a phrase of Horace. He says that the men who first braved the sea in ships must have had hearts bound with three folds of brass.

. . . AS A MATTER of fact, although few things are spoken of with more fearful whisperings than the prospect of death, few have less influence on conduct under healthy circumstances. We have all heard of cities of South America built upon the side of fiery mountains, and how, even in this tremendous neighborhood, the inhabitants are not a jot more impressed by the solemnity of mortal conditions than if they were delving gardens in the greenest corner of England. There are serenades and suppers and much gallantry among the myrtles overhead; and meanwhile the foundation shudders underfoot, the bowels of the mountain growl, and at any moment living ruin may leap sky-high into the moonlight, and tumble man and his merrymaking in the dust. In the eyes of very young people, and very dull old ones, there is something indescribably reckless and desperate in such a picture. It seems not credible that respectable married people, with umbrellas, should find appetite for a bit of supper within quite a long distance of a fiery mountain; ordinary life begins to smell of high-handed debauch when it is carried on so close to a catastrophe; and even cheese and salad, it seems, could hardly be relished in such circumstances without something like a defiance of the Creator. It should be a place for nobody but hermits dwelling in prayer and maceration, or mere born devils drowning care in a perpetual carouse.

And yet, when one comes to think upon it calmly, the situation

of these South American citizens forms only a very pale figure for
the state of ordinary mankind. This world itself, traveling blindly
and swiftly in overcrowded space, among a million other worlds
traveling blindly and swiftly in contrary directions, may very well
come by a knock that would set it into explosion like a penny squib.
And what, pathologically looked at, is the human body with all its
organs, but a mere bagful of petards? [1] The least of these is as dangerous to the whole economy as the ship's powder magazine to the
ship; and with every breath we breathe, and every meal we eat, we
are putting one more of them in peril. If we clung as devotedly as
some philosophers pretend we do to the abstract idea of life, or were
half as frightened as they make out we are, for the subversive accident that ends it all, the trumpets might sound by the hour and no
one would follow them into battle — the blue peter might fly at the
truck, but who would climb into a seagoing ship? Think (if these
philosophers were right) with what a preparation of spirit we should
affront the daily peril of the dinner table: a deadlier spot than any
battlefield in history, where the far greater proportion of our ancestors have miserably left their bones! What woman would ever be
lured into marriage, so much more dangerous than the wildest sea?
And what would it be to grow old? For, after a certain distance,
every step we take in life we find the ice growing thinner below
our feet, and all around us and behind us we see our contemporaries
going through. By the time a man gets well into the seventies, his
continued existence is a mere miracle; and when he lays his old
bones in bed for the night, there is an overwhelming probability
that he will never see the day. Do the old men mind it, as a matter
of fact? Why, no. They were never merrier; they have their grog at
night, and tell the raciest stories; they hear of the death of people
about their own age, or even younger, not as if it was a grisly warning, but with a simple childlike pleasure at having outlived someone
else; and when a draft might puff them out like a guttering candle,
or a bit of a stumble shatter them like so much glass, their old hearts
keep sound and unaffrighted, and they go on, bubbling with laughter, through years of man's age compared to which the valley at

[1] Bombs.

Balaklava was as safe and peaceful as a village cricket green on Sunday. It may fairly be questioned (if we look at the peril only) whether it was a much more daring feat for Curtius [2] to plunge into the gulf than for any old gentleman of ninety to doff his clothes and clamber into bed.

Indeed, it is a memorable subject for consideration, with what unconcern and gaiety mankind pricks on along the Valley of the Shadow of Death. The whole way is one wilderness of snares; and the end of it, for those who fear the last pinch, is irrevocable ruin. And yet we go spinning through it all, like a party for the Derby. Perhaps the reader remembers one of the humorous devices of the deified Caligula: how he encouraged a vast concourse of holiday-makers on to his bridge over Baiae bay, and, when they were in the height of their enjoyment, turned loose the Pretorian guards among the company, and had them tossed into the sea. This is no bad minia-ture of the dealings of nature with the transitory race of man. Only, what a checkered picnic we have of it, even while it lasts! and into what great waters, not to be crossed by any swimmer, God's pale Pretorian throws us over in the end!

We live the time that a match flickers; we pop the cork of a ginger-beer bottle, and the earthquake swallows us on the instant. Is it not odd, is it not incongruous, is it not in the highest sense of human speech, incredible, that we should think so highly of the ginger beer and regard so little the devouring earthquake? The love of Life and the fear of Death are two famous phrases that grow harder to understand the more we think about them. It is a well-known fact that an immense proportion of boat accidents would never happen if people held the sheet in their hands instead of making it fast; and yet, unless it be some martinet of a professional mariner or some landsman with shattered nerves, every one of God's creatures makes it fast. A strange instance of man's unconcern and brazen boldness in the face of death!

We confound ourselves with metaphysical phrases, which we

[2] There was a tradition that about 360 B.C. a gulf opened in the Forum of Rome which could not be closed except by sacrifice. Curtius mounted on his horse, and plunged in. The abyss closed.

import into daily talk with noble inappropriateness. We have no idea of what death is, apart from its circumstances and some of its consequences to others; and although we have some experience of living, there is not a man on earth who has flown so high into abstraction as to have any practical guess at the meaning of the word *life*. All literature, from Job and Omar Khayam to Thomas Carlyle or Walt Whitman, is but an attempt to look upon the human state with such largeness of view as shall enable us to rise from the consideration of living to the Definition of Life. And our sages give us about the best satisfaction in their power when they say that it is a vapor, or a show, or made out of the same stuff with dreams. Philosophy, in its more rigid sense, has been at the same work for ages; and after a myriad bald heads have wagged over the problem, and piles of words have been heaped one upon another into dry and cloudy volumes without end, philosophy has the honor of laying before us, with modest pride, her contribution toward the subject: that life is a Permanent Possibility of Sensation. Truly a fine result! A man may very well love beef, or hunting, or a woman; but surely, surely, not a Permanent Possibility of Sensation! He may be afraid of a precipice, or a dentist, or a large enemy with a club, or even an undertaker's man; but not certainly of abstract death. We may trick with the word life in its dozen senses until we are weary of tricking; we may argue in terms of all the philosophies on earth; but one fact remains true throughout — that we do not love life, in the sense that we are greatly preoccupied about its conservation; that we do not, properly speaking, love life at all, but living. . . . To be deeply interested in the accidents of our existence, to enjoy keenly the mixed texture of human experience, rather leads a man to disregard precautions, and risk his neck against a straw. For surely the love of living is stronger in an Alpine climber roping over a peril, or a hunter riding merrily at a stiff fence, than in a creature who lives upon a diet and walks a measured distance in the interest of his constitution.

There is a great deal of very vile nonsense talked upon both sides of the matter; tearing divines reducing life to the dimensions of a mere funeral procession, so short as to be hardly decent; and melancholy unbelievers yearning for the tomb as if it were a world

too far away. Both sides must feel
a little ashamed of their performances now and again, when they
draw in their chairs to dinner. Indeed, a good meal and a bottle of
wine is an answer to most stand-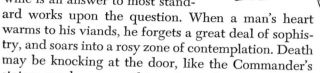
ard works upon the question. When a man's heart
warms to his viands, he forgets a great deal of sophis-
try, and soars into a rosy zone of contemplation. Death
may be knocking at the door, like the Commander's
statue; we have something else in hand, thank God, and let him
knock. Passing bells are ringing the world over. All the world over,
and every hour, someone is parting company with all his aches
and ecstasies. For us also the trap is laid. But we are so fond of life
that we have no leisure to entertain the terror of death. It is a honeymoon with us all through, and none of the longest. Small blame to
us if we give our whole hearts to this glowing bride of ours — to the
appetites, to honor, to the hungry curiosity of the mind, to the pleasure of the eyes in nature, and the pride of our own nimble bodies.

We all of us appreciate the sensations; but as for caring about
the Permanence of the Possibility, a man's head is generally very
bald, and his senses very dull, before he comes to that. Whether we
regard life as a lane leading to a dead wall — a mere bag's end, as
the French say — or whether we think of it as a vestibule or gym-
nasium, where we wait our turn and prepare our faculties for some
more noble destiny; whether we thunder in a pulpit, or pule in little
atheistic poetry books, about its vanity and brevity; whether we look
justly for years of health and vigor, or are about to mount into a
bath chair, as a step toward the hearse; in each and all of these views
and situations there is but one conclusion possible: that a man should
stop his ears against paralyzing terror, and run the race that is set
before him with a single mind. No one surely could have recoiled
with more heartache and terror from the thought of death than our
respected lexicographer; [3] and yet we know how little it affected his
conduct, how wisely and boldly he walked, and in what a fresh and

[3] Samuel Johnson.

lively vein he spoke of life. Already an old man, he ventured on his Highland tour; and his heart, bound with triple brass, did not recoil before twenty-seven individual cups of tea. As courage and intelligence are the two qualities best worth a good man's cultivation, so it is the first part of intelligence to recognize our precarious estate in life, and the first part of courage to be not at all abashed before the fact. A frank and somewhat headlong carriage, not looking too anxiously before, not dallying in maudlin regret over the past, stamps the man who is well armored for this world.

And not only well armored for himself, but a good friend and a good citizen to boot. We do not go to cowards for tender dealing; there is nothing so cruel as panic; the man who has least fear for his own carcass, has most time to consider others. That eminent chemist who took his walks abroad in tin shoes, and subsisted wholly upon tepid milk, had all his work cut out for him in considerate dealings with his own digestion. So soon as prudence has begun to grow up in the brain, like a dismal fungus, it finds its first expression in a paralysis of generous acts. The victim begins to shrink spiritually; he develops a fancy for parlors with a regulated temperature, and takes his morality on the principle of tin shoes and tepid milk. The care of one important body or soul becomes so engrossing that all the noises of the outer world begin to come thin and faint into the parlor with the regulated temperature; and the tin shoes go equably forward over blood and rain. To be otherwise is to ossify; and the scruplemonger ends by standing stock-still. Now the man who has his heart on his sleeve, and a good whirling weathercock of a brain, who reckons his life as a thing to be dashingly used and cheerfully hazarded, makes a very different acquaintance of the world, keeps all his pulses going true and fast, and gathers impetus as he runs, until, if he be running toward anything better than wildfire, he may shoot up and become a constellation in the end. Lord look after his health, Lord have a care of his soul, says he; and he has the key of the position, and swashes through incongruity and peril toward his aim. Death is on all sides of him with pointed batteries, as he is on all sides of all of us; unfortunate surprises gird him round; mim-mouthed friends and relations hold up their hands in quite a little elegiacal synod about his path: and what cares he for all this? Being a true lover of living, a fellow with something pushing and spontaneous in his inside, he must, like any other soldier, in any other stirring, deadly warfare, push on at his best pace until he touch the goal. "A peerage or Westminster Abbey!" cried Nelson in his bright, boyish, heroic manner. These are great incentives; not for any of these, but for the plain satisfaction of living, of being about their business in some sort or other, do the brave, serviceable men of every nation tread down the nettle danger, and pass flying over all the stumbling blocks of prudence. Think of the heroism of Johnson, think of that superb indifference to mortal limitation that set him upon his dictionary, and carried him through triumphantly until the end! Who, if he were wisely considerate of things at large, would ever embark upon any work much more considerable than a halfpenny post card? Who would project a serial novel, after Thackeray and Dickens had each fallen in mid-course? Who would find heart enough to begin to live, if he dallied with the consideration of death?

And, after all, what sorry and pitiful quibbling all this is! To forgo all the issues of living, in a parlor with a regulated temperature — as if that were not to die a hundred times over, and for ten years at a stretch! As if it were not to die in one's own lifetime, and without even the sad immunities of death! As if it were not to die, and yet to be the patient spectators of our own pitiable change! The Permanent Possibility is preserved, but the sensations carefully held at arm's length, as if one kept a photographic plate in a dark chamber. It is better to lose health like a spendthrift than to waste it like a miser. It is better to live and be done with it, than to die daily in the sickroom. By all means begin your folio; even if the doctor does not give you a year, even if he hesitates about a month, make one brave push and see what can be accomplished in a week. It is not only in finished undertakings that we ought to honor useful labor. A spirit goes out of the man who means execution, which outlives the most untimely ending. All who have meant good work with their whole hearts, have done good work, although they may die before they have the time to sign it. Every heart that has beat strong and cheerfully has left a hopeful impulse behind it in the world, and bettered the tradition of mankind. And even if death catch people, like an open pitfall, and in mid-career, laying out vast projects, and planning monstrous foundations, flushed with hope, and their mouths full of boastful language, they should be at once tripped up and silenced: is there not something brave and spirited in such a termination? and does not life go down with a better grace, foaming in full body over a precipice, than miserably straggling to an end in sandy deltas? When the Greeks made their fine saying that those whom the gods love die young, I cannot help believing they had this sort of death also in their eye. For surely, at whatever age it overtake the man, this is to die young. Death has not been suffered to take so much as an illusion from his heart. In the hot-fit of life, a-tiptoe on the highest point of being, he passes at a bound on to the other side. The noise of the mallet and chisel is scarcely quenched, the trumpets are hardly done blowing, when, trailing with him clouds of glory, this happy-starred, full-blooded spirit shoots into the spiritual land.

APPRECIATION HINTS

1. What does Stevenson say about the life of people living near volcanoes?
2. What does he say about the dangers of ordinary living?
3. What does he say about efforts to find meaning in the word *life?*
4. What does Stevenson mean by saying that we do not love life, but living?
5. What conclusion does he arrive at about the proper attitude toward life?
6. For what reason does he call prudence a " dismal fungus "?
7. Describe the attitude of the brave serviceable man toward living.
8. What qualities in Mary White would Stevenson have admired?
9. List effective phrases and sentences which impressed you; for example, " God's pale Pretorian."
10. Mention passages in this essay which seem to reflect Stevenson's own experience.
11. What is it that makes the last so splendid a paragraph?
12. Write a composition suggested by this essay. Possible titles: Taking

the Risk, We Made the Sheet Fast, The Timid Soul, Live All Your Life, The Philosopher at Dinner.

13. If you like Stevenson read " An Apology for Idlers " and " Crabbed Age and Youth " from *Virginibus Puerisque.* Other essays you might like are " Walking Tours," " Random Memories," and " The Ideal House."

You don't learn to hold your own in the world by standing on guard, but by attacking, and getting well hammered yourself.   G. B. Shaw: *Getting Married*

DEFINITIONS

Barometer. *An ingenious instrument which indicates what kind of weather we are having.*

Bore. *A person who talks when you wish him to listen.*

Coward. *One who in a perilous emergency thinks with his legs.*

Egotist. *A person of low taste, more interested in himself than in me.*

Patience. *A minor form of despair, disguised as a virtue.*

Ambrose Bierce: *The Devil's Dictionary*
(Albert and Charles Boni, Inc.)

Once, to an old Scotch carpenter, I boasted with scant tact of ten ancestors on the Mayflower *and that every drop of my blood had been on American soil for more than two centuries. He replied:*

" Tell me this — how many nights sat ye up decidin' ye'd no be born Chinese? "   John Palmer Gavit

PLATO 428?–348? B.C.

THIS EXTRACT from one of Plato's most famous dialogues reports a conversation between Socrates, just out of prison and still rubbing away the pains left by his ankle chains, and his friends who had lately been admitted to the courthouse, after waiting since dawn at its gates. The conversation begins early on one of the longest days of summer, and it ends at sunset, for that is the death hour set by the laws of Athens. While the long day is drawing to its close, the officer of the Eleven is pounding the deadly hemlock seeds in his mortar. Now the cup of poison is prepared, the sun is on the mountains, and the officer courteously presents the drink to Socrates and, bursting into tears, withdraws. Then we witness the final scene of this sublimely simple and moving story.

Plato, then twenty-nine, was not present at the scene because of illness, but there is no reason to think that his account of what happened is not substantially correct. In regard to what is said, in this as in other dialogues, Plato employs Socrates as his chief character, and puts into his mouth opinions and arguments which are Plato's. The dialogue from which the following extract is taken is the *Phaedo,* and its central object is to make the doctrine of immortality reasonable.

Socrates wrote nothing. His youth and manhood were spent in the most splendid period of Greek history. We know that he was a brave soldier, and saved the life of Alcibiades at the battle of Potidaea. While Plato was still a little child, Socrates had begun that cross-examination of Athenians which at last brought him the hemlock. In 399 B.C. he was put on trial for corrupting the youth of Athens, found guilty, and, by a judges' vote of 281 to 220 condemned to death. Socrates might have saved himself by consenting to stop demanding that his countrymen give an account of their lives. " I cannot hold my peace," he said, " for that would be to disobey God." Knowing nothing certainly of what comes after death, he resolutely chose to die rather than desert the post at which God had placed him.

Phaedo. I will endeavor to relate the whole to you from the beginning. On the preceding days I and the others were constantly in
the habit of visiting Socrates, meeting early in the morning at the
courthouse where the trial took place, for it was near the prison.
Here then we waited every day till the prison was opened, conversing with each other; for it was not opened very early, but, as soon as
it was opened we went in to Socrates, and usually spent the day with
him. On that occasion however, we met earlier than usual; for on the
preceding day, when we left the prison in the evening, we heard that
the ship had arrived from Delos.[1] We therefore urged each other to
come as early as possible to the accustomed place; accordingly we
came, and the porter, who used to admit us, coming out, told us to
wait, and not enter until he called us. " For," he said, " the Eleven [2]
are now freeing Socrates from his bonds, and announcing to him
that he must die today." But in no long time he returned, and bade
us enter.

When we entered, we found Socrates just freed from his bonds,
and Xantippe, you know her, holding his little boy and sitting by
him. As soon as Xantippe saw us, she wept aloud and said such
things as women usually do on such occasions, as " Socrates, your
friends will now converse with you for the last time and you with

[1] This was the sacred ship sent annually on a mission to Apollo at Delos.
While it was away no one could be put to death.
[2] The executive officers of Athens.

them." But Socrates, looking toward Crito, said, " Crito, let someone take her home." Upon which some of Crito's attendants led her away, wailing and beating herself.

But Socrates sitting up in bed, drew up his leg, and rubbed it with his hand, and as he rubbed it, said: " What an unaccountable thing, my friends, that seems to be, which men call pleasure; and how wonderfully related toward that which appears to be its contrary, pain; in that they will not both be present to a man at the same time, yet, if anyone pursues and attains the one, he is almost always compelled to receive the other, as if they were both united together from one head.

" And it seems to me," he said, " that if Aesop had observed this he would have made a fable from it, how the deity, wishing to reconcile these warring principles, when he could not do so, united their heads together, and from hence whomsoever the one visits the other attends immediately after; as appears to be the case with me, since I suffered pain in my leg before the chain, but now pleasure seems to have succeeded " . . .

" He who is to give you the poison," said Crito, " told me some time ago, that I should tell you to speak as little as possible. For he says that men become heated by speaking, and that nothing of this kind ought to interfere with the poison, and that otherwise, those who did so were compelled to drink two or three times."

To which Socrates replied, " Let him alone, and let him attend to his business, and prepare to give it me twice, or if occasion requires, even thrice."

" I was almost certain what you would say," answered Crito, " but he has been some time pestering me."

" Never mind him," he rejoined.

" But now I wish to render an account to you of the reason why a man who has really devoted his life to philosophy, when he is about to die, appears to me, on good grounds, to have confidence, and to entertain a firm hope that the greatest good will befall him in the other world, when he has departed this life. . . . There is great hope for one who arrives where I am going, there, if anywhere, to acquire that in perfection for the sake of which we have taken so much pains during our past life; so that the journey now appointed me is set out upon with good hope, and will be so by any other man who thinks that his mind has been as it were purified. . . .

"For wisdom alone is the right coin for which we ought to barter all things; and for this, and with this everything is in reality bought and sold, fortitude, temperance, and justice; and in a word, true virtue subsists with wisdom, whether pleasures and fears, and everything else of the kind are present or absent; but when separated from wisdom, and changed one from another, consider whether such virtue is not a mere outline, and in reality servile, possessing neither soundness nor truth, but the really true virtue is a purification from all such things, and temperance, justice, fortitude, and wisdom itself, are a kind of initiatory purification . . . I have, to the utmost of my ability, left no means untried, but I have endeavored to the utmost of my power to be of the number of those who have pursued philosophy rightly. But whether I have endeavored rightly, and have in any respect succeeded, on arriving there I shall know clearly, if it please God, very shortly, as it appears to me . . .

"The soul of a philosopher would reason thus, and would not think that philosophy ought to set it free, and that when it is freed it should give itself up again to pleasures and pains, to bind it down again, and make her work void, weaving a kind of Penelope's web the reverse way.[3] On the contrary, effecting a calm of the passions, and following the guidance of reason, and being always intent on this, contemplating that which is true and divine, and not subject to opinion, and being nourished by it, it thinks that it ought to live in this manner as long as it does live, and that when it dies it shall go to a kindred essence, and one like itself, and shall be freed from human evils. From such a regimen as this the soul has no occasion to fear, while it strictly attends to these things, lest being torn to pieces at its departure from the body it should be blown about and dissipated by the winds, and no longer have an existence anywhere . . .

---

[3] Penelope, to preserve her virtue, undid at night the work she wove by day; the soul weaves again the web of lusts which philosophy has been unraveling to set her free.

"Let us not, Phaedo, admit into our souls the notion, that there appears to be nothing sound in reasoning, but much rather that we are not yet in a sound condition, and that we ought vigorously and strenuously to endeavor to become sound, you and the others, on account of your whole future life; but I, on account of my death, since I am in danger at the present time, of not behaving as becomes a philosopher, with respect to this very subject, but as a wrangler like those who are utterly uninformed. For they, when they dispute about anything, care nothing at all for the subject about which the discussion is, but are anxious about this, that what they have themselves advanced shall appear true to the persons present. And I seem to myself on the present occasion to differ from them only in this respect; for I shall not be anxious to make what I say appear true to those who are present, except that it may happen by the way, but that it may appear certainly to be so to myself. . . . If nothing remains to one that is dead, I shall at least during the interval before death, be less disagreeable to those present by my lamentations. But this ignorance of mine will not continue long, for that would be bad, but will shortly be put an end to. . . . Do you however, if you will be persuaded by me, pay little attention to Socrates, but much more to the truth, and if I appear to you to say anything true, assent to it, but if not, oppose me with all your might, taking good care that in my zeal I do not deceive both myself and you, and like a bee depart leaving my sting behind. . . .

"To affirm positively, indeed, that these things are exactly as I have described them, does not become a man of sense; that however either this, or something of the kind, takes place with respect to our souls and their habitations — since our soul is certainly immortal — this appears to me most fitting to be believed, and worthy the hazard for one who trusts in its reality; for the hazard is noble, and it is right to allure ourselves with such things, as with enchantments; for which reason I have prolonged my story to such a length. On account of these things, then, a man ought to be confident about his soul, who during this life has disregarded all the pleasures and ornaments of the body as foreign from his nature, and who, having thought that they do more harm than good, has zealously applied himself to the acquirement of knowledge, and who having adorned his soul not with a foreign but its own proper ornament, temperance, justice, fortitude, freedom, and truth, thus waits for his passage to Hades, as one who is ready to depart whenever destiny shall summon him. You then," he continued, "Simmias and Cebes, and the rest, will each of you depart at some future time; but now destiny summons me, as a tragic writer would say, and it is nearly time for me to betake myself to the bath; for it appears to me to be better to drink the poison after I have bathed myself, and not to trouble the women with washing my dead body."

When he had thus spoken, Crito said, "So be it, Socrates, but what commands have you to give to these or to me, either respecting your children, or any other matter, in attending to which we can most oblige you?"

"What I always say, Crito," he replied, "nothing new; that by taking care of yourselves you will oblige both me and mine, and yourselves, whatever you do, though you should not now promise it; but if you neglect yourselves, and will not live as it were in the footsteps of what has been now and formerly said, even though you should promise much at present, and that earnestly, you will do no good at all."

"We will endeavor then so to do," he said; "but how shall we bury you?"

"Just as you please," he said, "if only you can catch me, and I do not escape from you." And at the same time smiling gently, and looking round on us, he said; "I cannot persuade Crito, my friends, that I am that Socrates who is now conversing with you, and who methodizes each part of the discourse; but he thinks that I am he whom he will shortly behold dead, and asks how he should bury me. But that which I some time since argued at length, that when I have drunk the poison I shall no longer remain with you, but shall depart to some happy state of the blessed, this I seem to have urged to him in vain, though I meant at the same time to console both you and myself. Be ye then my sureties to Crito," he said, "in an obligation contrary to that which he made to the judges; for he undertook that I should remain; but do you be sureties that, when I die, I shall not remain, but shall depart, that Crito may more easily bear it, and when he sees my body either burnt or buried, may not be afflicted for me, as if I suffered some dreadful thing, nor say at my interment that Socrates is laid out, or is carried out, or is buried. For be well assured," he said, " most excellent Crito, that to speak improperly is not only culpable as to the thing itself, but likewise occasions some injury to our souls. You must have a good courage then, and say that you bury my body, and bury it in such a manner as is pleasing to you, and as you think is most agreeable to our laws."

When he had said thus he rose, and went into a chamber to bathe, and Crito followed him, but he directed us to wait for him. We waited, therefore, conversing among ourselves about what had been said, and considering it again, and sometimes speaking about our calamity, how severe it would be to us, sincerely thinking that, like those who are deprived of a father, we should pass the rest of our life as orphans. When he had bathed, and his children were brought to him, for he had two little sons and one grown up, and the women belonging to his family were come, having conversed with them in the presence of Crito, and given them such injunctions as he wished, he directed the women and children to go away, and then returned to us. And it was now near sunset; for he spent a considerable time within. But when he came from bathing he sat down, and did not speak much afterward; then the officer of the Eleven came in, and standing near him, said, " Socrates, I shall not have to find that fault with you that I do with others, that they are angry with me, and curse me, when, by order of the archons, I bid them drink the poison. But you, on all other occasions during the time you have been here, I have found to be the most noble, meek, and excellent man of all that ever came into this place: and, therefore, I am now well convinced that you will not be angry with me, for you know who are to blame, but with them. Now, then, for you know what I came to announce to you, farewell, and endeavor to bear what is inevitable as easily as possible." And at the same time, bursting into tears, he turned away and withdrew.

And Socrates, looking after him, said, " And thou, too, farewell, we will do as you direct." At the same time turning to us, he said,

"How courteous the man is; during the whole time I have been here he has visited me, and conversed with me sometimes, and proved the worthiest of men; and now how generously he weeps for me. But come, Crito, let us obey him, and let someone bring the poison, if it is ready pounded, but if not, let the man pound it."

Then Crito said, "But I think, Socrates, that the sun is still on the mountains, and has not yet set. Besides, I know that others have drunk the poison very late, after it had been announced to them, and have supped and drunk freely, and some even have enjoyed the objects of their love. Do not hasten then, for there is yet time."

Upon this Socrates replied, "These men whom you mention, Crito, do these things with good reason, for they think they shall gain by so doing, and I too with good reason shall not do so; for I think I shall gain nothing by drinking a little later, except to become ridiculous to myself, in being so fond of life, and sparing of it when none any longer remains. Go then," he said, "obey, and do not resist."

Crito having heard this, nodded to the boy that stood near. And the boy having gone out, and stayed for some time, came, bringing with him the man that was to administer the poison, who brought it ready pounded in a cup. And Socrates, on seeing the man, said, "Well, my good friend, as you are skilled in these matters, what must I do?"

"Nothing else," he replied, "than when you have drunk it walk about, until there is a heaviness in your legs, then lie down; thus it will do its purpose." And at the same time he held out the cup to Socrates. And he having received it very cheerfully, Echecrates, neither trembling, nor changing at all in color or countenance, but, as he was wont, looking steadfastly at the men, said, "What say you of this potion, with respect to making a libation to anyone, is it lawful or not?"

"We only pound so much, Socrates," he said, "as we think sufficient to drink."

"I understand you," he said, "but it is certainly both lawful and right to pray to the gods, that my departure hence thither may be happy; which therefore I pray, and so may it be." And as he said this he drank it off readily and calmly. Thus far, most of us were with difficulty able to restrain ourselves from weeping, but when we saw him drinking, and having finished the draft, we could do so no longer; but in spite of myself the tears came in full torrent, so that, covering my face, I wept for myself, for I did not weep for him, but for my own fortune, in being deprived of such a friend. But Crito, even before me, when he could not restrain his tears, had risen up. But Apollodorus, even before this had not ceased weeping, and then bursting into an agony of grief, weeping and lamenting, he pierced the heart of everyone present, except Socrates himself. But he said, " What are you doing, my admirable friends? I indeed, for this reason chiefly, sent away the women, that they might not commit any folly of this kind. For I have heard that it is right to die with good omens. Be quiet, therefore, and bear up."

When we heard this we were ashamed, and restrained our tears. But he, having walked about, when he said that his legs were growing heavy, lay down on his back; for the man so directed him. And at the same time he who gave him the poison, taking hold of him, after a short interval examined his feet and legs; and then having pressed his foot hard, he asked if he felt it: he said that he did not. And after this he pressed his thighs; and thus going higher, he showed us that he was growing cold and stiff. Then Socrates touched himself, and said, that when the poison reached his heart he should then depart. But now the parts around the lower belly were almost cold; when uncovering himself, for he had been covered over, he said, and they were his last words, " Crito, we owe a cock to Aesculapius; pay it, therefore, and do not neglect it."

" It shall be done," said Crito, " but consider whether you have anything else to say."

To this question he gave no reply; but shortly after he gave a convulsive movement, and the man covered him, and his eyes were fixed; and Crito, perceiving it, closed his mouth and eyes.

This, Echecrates, was the end of our friend, a man, as we may say, the best of all of his time that we have known, and moreover, the most wise and just.

APPRECIATION HINTS

1. Why had they met at the prison earlier than usual?
2. What comment does Socrates make about the chain-wounds on his leg?
3. What is the purpose of the discourse of Socrates to his friends?
4. For what reason does Socrates think that he should be confident about his soul after death?
5. What directions does Socrates give about his burial?
6. What discussion takes place about the time when he should drink the poison?
7. What is he to do after drinking the poison?
8. What were the last words of Socrates?
9. What evidence is there in this selection that, to Socrates, philosophy was something that controlled conduct?
10. Discuss Socrates' idea that pain and pleasure are " united together from one head."
11. Previously Socrates' friends had tried to persuade him to escape from prison. What do you think were his reasons for refusing?
12. Write a composition on some subject suggested by this extract. Possible titles: Keeping Calm in a Crisis, Socrates' Idea of Wisdom, A Working Philosophy, Xantippe, The Jailbird and the Jailer.

*What a piece of work is a man! how noble in reason!
how infinite in faculty! in form and moving how express
and admirable! in action how like an angel! in apprehension how like a god!*   Shakespeare: *Hamlet*

THOMAS DE QUINCEY
1785–1859

TWO THINGS should be noted before you read this strange essay. One is that De Quincey's world was that twilight world of dreams, which you are conscious of in " The Vision of Sudden Death." His daughter tells us that her father's one chance of producing anything good came between nine o'clock at night and five o'clock in the morning. The other thing to note is that to De Quincey all literature was either " literature of knowledge," appealing to the reason, or " literature of power," appealing to the emotions. He thought this last was the great literature " triumphant forever as long as the language exists in which it speaks." In this essay the effect of the night collision between a gig and a stagecoach going thirteen miles an hour is far more terrific than the ordinary report of the destruction of a bus by an express train. It is not our reason but our emotion that he plays upon.

The most vivid description of Thomas De Quincey comes from a contemporary, Thomas Carlyle. " He was a pretty little creature, full of wire-drawn ingenuities, bankrupt enthusiasms, bankrupt pride, with the finest silver-tongued low voice and most elaborately gentle winding courtesies. What wouldn't one give to have him in a box, and take him out to talk! . . . One of the smallest man figures I ever saw; shaped like a pair of tongs, and hardly above five feet in all. When he sat, you would have taken him, by candlelight, for the beautifullest little child . . . had there not been something too that said, Lo, this child has been in hell."

What that hell had been you may read in *Confessions of an English Opium-Eater*. The happiest years of his life were spent at Dove Cottage in the English Lake District. But after that, his life was a continual struggle to keep ahead of the bailiff; he had at times to seek refuge in the debtors' sanctuary at Holyrood in Edinburgh, where he and his family had gone to live.

De Quincey's nearest of kin in American literature is Poe, but the Englishman lives exclusively in his splendid and sonorous prose. He wrote by sound. For this reason we do not find order or logical arrangement in De Quincey, but a prose which at its best reminds us of Milton or of the Bible.

The Vision of Sudden Death

THE INCIDENT, so memorable in itself by its features of horror, and so scenical by its grouping for the eye, which furnished the text for this reverie upon sudden death occurred to myself in the dead of night, as a solitary spectator, when seated on the box of the Manchester and Glasgow mail, in the second or third summer after Waterloo. . . . Wearied with the long detention at a gloomy hotel, I walked out about eleven o'clock at night for the sake of fresh air, meaning to fall in with the mail and resume my seat at the post office. The night, however, being yet dark, as the moon had scarcely risen, and the streets being at that hour empty so as to offer no opportunities for asking the road, I lost my way; and did not reach the post office until it was considerably past midnight; but, to my great relief (as it was important for me to be in Westmoreland by the morning), I saw in the huge saucer eyes of the mail, blazing through the gloom, an evidence that my chance was not yet lost. Past the time it was, but, by some rare accident, the mail was not even yet ready to start. . . .

Having mounted the box, I took a small quantity of laudanum, having already traveled two hundred and fifty miles, — viz., from a point seventy miles beyond London. In the taking of laudanum there was nothing extraordinary. But by accident it drew upon me the special attention of my assessor on the box, the coachman. And in *that* also there was nothing extraordinary. But by accident, and with

great delight, it drew my own attention to the fact that this coachman was a monster in point of bulk, and that he had but one eye. In
fact, he had been foretold by Vergil as

Monstrum, horrendum, informe, ingens, cui lumen ademptum.[1]

He answered to the conditions in every one of the items: — 1, a monster he was; 2, dreadful; 3, shapeless; 4, huge; 5, who had lost an
eye. . . . But what was Cyclops doing here? Had the medical men
recommended northern air, or how? I collected, from such explanations as he volunteered, that he had an interest at stake in some suit
at law now pending at Lancaster; so that probably he had got himself transferred to this station for the purpose of connecting with his
professional pursuits an instant readiness for the calls of his lawsuit.

Meantime, what are we stopping for? Surely we have now
waited long enough. Oh, this procrastinating mail, and this procrastinating post office! Can't they take a lesson upon that subject from
me? Some people have called *me* procrastinating. Yet you are witness, reader, that I was kept here waiting for the post office. . . .
But at last all is finished. Sound your horn, guard. Manchester, good-
by; we've lost an hour by your criminal conduct at the post office;
which, however, though I do not mean to part with a serviceable
ground of complaint, and one which really *is* such for the horses, to
me secretly is an advantage, since it compels us to look sharply for
this lost hour amongst the next eight or nine, and to recover it (if we
can) at the rate of one mile extra per hour. Off we are at last, and at
eleven miles per hour; and for the moment I detect no changes in
the energy or in the skill of Cyclops. . . .

On this occasion the usual silence and solitude prevailed along
the road. Not a hoof nor a wheel was to be heard. And to strengthen
this false luxurious confidence in the noiseless roads, it happened
also that the night was one of peculiar solemnity and peace. . . .
Obliquely upon our left we were nearing the sea, which also must,
under the present circumstances, be repeating the general state of
halcyon repose. The sea, the atmosphere, the light, bore each an

---

[1] Vergil is describing Polyphemus, the Cyclops, whose eye was put out
by Ulysses.

orchestral part in this universal lull. Moonlight and the first timid tremblings of the dawn were by this time blending; and the blendings were brought into a still more exquisite state of unity by a slight silvery mist, motionless and dreamy, that covered the woods and fields, but with a veil of equable transparency. Except the feet of our own horses, which, running on a sandy margin of the road, made but little disturbance, there was no sound abroad. In the clouds and on the earth prevailed the same majestic peace. . . .

Suddenly, from thoughts like these I was awakened to a sullen sound, as of some motion on the distant road. It stole upon the air for a moment; I listened in awe; but then it died away. Once roused, however, I could not but observe with alarm the quickened motion of our horses. Ten years' experience had made my eye learned in the valuing of motion; and I saw that we were now running thirteen miles an hour. . . . Any carriage that we could meet would be frail and light in comparison of ourselves. And I remark this ominous accident of our situation. We were on the wrong side of the road. . . .

Under this steady though rapid anticipation of the evil which *might* be gathering ahead, ah! what a sullen mystery of fear, what a sigh of woe, was that which stole upon the air, as again the far-off sound of a wheel was heard? A whisper it was — a whisper from, perhaps, four miles off — secretly announcing ruin that, being foreseen, was not the less inevitable; that, being known, was not, therefore, healed. What could be done — who was it that could do it — to check the storm flight of these maniacal horses? Could I not seize the reins from the grasp of the slumbering coachman? You, reader, think that it would have been in *your* power to do so. And I quarrel not with your estimate of yourself. But, from the way in which the coachman's hand was vised between his upper and lower thigh, this was impossible. Easy, was it? See, then, that bronze equestrian statue. The cruel rider has kept the bit in his horse's mouth for two centuries. Unbridle him for a minute, if you please, and wash his mouth with water. Easy was it? Unhorse me, then, that imperial rider; knock me those marble feet from those marble stirrups of Charlemagne.

The sounds ahead strengthened, and were now too clearly the sounds of wheels. Who and what could it be? Was it industry in a taxed cart? Was it youthful gaiety in a gig? Was it sorrow that loitered, or joy that raced? For as yet the snatches of sound were too intermitting, from distance, to decipher the character of the motion. Whoever were the travelers, something must be done to warn them. Upon the other party rests the active responsibility, but upon *us* — and woe is me! that *us* was reduced to my frail opium-shattered self — rests the responsibility of warning. Yet, how should this be accomplished? Might I not sound the guard's horn? Already, on the first thought, I was making my way over the roof of the guard's seat. But this, from the accident which I have mentioned, of the foreign mails being piled upon the roof, was a difficult and even dangerous attempt to one cramped by nearly three hundred miles of outside traveling. And, fortunately, before I had lost much time in the attempt, our frantic horses swept round an angle of the road which opened upon us that final stage where the collision must be accomplished and the catastrophe sealed. All was apparently finished. The court was sitting; the case was heard; the judge had finished; and only the verdict was yet in arrear.

Before us lay an avenue straight as an arrow, six hundred yards, perhaps, in length; and the umbrageous trees, which rose in a regular line from either side, meeting high overhead, gave to it the character of a cathedral aisle. These trees lent a deeper solemnity to the early light; but there was still light enough to perceive, at the farther end of this Gothic aisle, a frail reedy gig, in which were seated a young man, and by his side a young lady. Ah, young sir! what are you about? If it is requisite that you should whisper your communication to this young lady — though really I see nobody, at an hour and on a road so solitary, likely to overhear you — is it therefore requisite that you should carry your lips forward to hers? The little carriage is creeping on at one mile an hour; and the parties within it, being thus tenderly engaged, are naturally bending down their heads. Between them and eternity, to all human calculation, there is but a minute and a half. . . .

Suddenly he rose; stood upright; and by a powerful strain upon the reins, raising his horse's forefeet from the ground, he slewed him round on the pivot of his hind legs, so as to plant the little equipage in a position nearly at right angles to ours. Thus far his condition was not improved, except as a first step had been taken toward the possibility of a second. If no more were done, nothing was done; for the little carriage still occupied the very center of our path, though in an altered direction. Yet even now it may not be too late; fifteen of the seventy seconds may still be unexhausted; and one almighty bound may avail to clear the ground. Hurry then, hurry! for the flying moments — *they* hurry. Oh, hurry, hurry, my brave young man! for the cruel hoofs of our horses — *they* also hurry! Fast are the flying moments, faster are the hoofs of our horses. But fear not for *him*, if human energy can suffice; faithful was he that drove to his terrific duty; faithful was the horse to *his* command. One blow, one impulse given with voice and hand, by the stranger, one rush from the horse, one bound as if in the act of rising to a fence, landed the docile creature's forefeet upon the crown or arching center of the road. The larger half of the little equipage had then cleared our overtowering

shadow: *that* was evident even to my own agitated sight. But it mattered little that one wreck should float off in safety if upon the wreck that perished were embarked the human freightage. The rear part of the carriage — was *that* certainly beyond the line of absolute ruin? What power could answer the question? Glance of eye, thought of man, wing of angel, which of these had speed enough to sweep between the question and the answer, and divide the one from the other? Light does not tread upon the steps of light more indivisibly than did our all-conquering arrival upon the escaping efforts of the gig. *That* must the young man have felt too plainly. His back was now turned to us; not by sight could he any longer communicate with the peril; but, by the dreadful rattle of our harness, too truly had his ear been instructed that all was finished as regarded any effort of *his*. Already in resignation he had rested from his struggle; and perhaps in his heart he was whispering, " Father, which art in heaven, do Thou finish above what I on earth have attempted." Faster than ever mill-race we ran past them in our inexorable flight. Oh, raving of hurricanes that must have sounded in their young ears at the moment of our transit. Even in that moment the thunder of collision spoke aloud. Either with the swinglebar [2] or with the haunch of our near leader, we had struck off the wheel of the little gig, which stood rather obliquely and not quite so far advanced as to be accurately parallel with the near wheel. The blow, from the fury of our passage, resounded terrifically. I rose in horror to gaze upon the ruins we might have caused. From my elevated station I looked down, and looked back upon the scene, which in a moment told its own tale, and wrote all its records on my heart forever.

Here was the map of the passion that now had finished. The horse was planted immovably, with his forefeet upon the paved crest of the central road. He of the whole party might be supposed untouched by the passion of death. The little cany carriage — partly, perhaps, from the violent torsion of the wheels in its recent movement, partly from the thundering blow we had given it — as if it sympathized with human horror, was all alive with tremblings and shiverings. The young man trembled not, nor shivered. He sat like a rock. But *his* was the steadiness of agitation frozen into rest by horror. As yet he dared not to look around; for he knew that, if anything remained to do, by him it could no longer be done. And as yet he knew not for certain if their safety were accomplished. But the lady ——

[2] Swingletree, the pivoted crossbar to the ends of which the traces are attached.

But the lady ——! Oh, Heavens! will that spectacle ever depart from my dreams, as she rose and sank upon her seat, sank and rose, threw up her arms wildly to heaven, clutched at some visionary object in the air, fainting, praying, raving, despairing? Figure to yourself, reader, the elements of the case; suffer me to recall before your mind the circumstances of that unparalleled situation. From the silence and deep peace of this saintly summer night — from the pathetic blending of this sweet moonlight, dawnlight, dreamlight — from the manly tenderness of this flattering, whispering, murmuring love — suddenly as from the woods and fields — suddenly as from the chambers of the air opening in revelation — suddenly as from the ground yawning at her feet, leaped upon her, with the flashing of cataracts, Death the crowned phantom, with all the equipage of his terrors, and the tiger roar of his voice.

The moments were numbered; the strife was finished; the vision was closed. In the twinkling of an eye, our flying horses had carried us to the termination of the umbrageous aisle; at the right angles we wheeled into our former direction; the turn of the road carried the scene out of my eyes in an instant, and swept it into my dreams forever.

APPRECIATION HINTS

1. When did this dream or reverie come to De Quincey?
2. Describe the coachman.
3. Describe the road and the night.
4. What is it that gives him uneasiness as the coach drives on?
5. Why cannot he do anything to avert the catastrophe?
6. Describe the gig and its occupants.
7. What did the driver of the gig do to avert a collision?
8. Tell what happened.
9. What did De Quincey see as he looked back upon the scene?
10. What is there about this essay that gives the impression that it is not quite real?
11. How does the style of De Quincey differ from that of Stevenson or Tomlinson?
12. Do you recall among your own dreams any which involved an impending catastrophe?

13. Write a composition on a topic suggested by this essay. Possible titles: My Nightmare, The Moment Before the Crash, The Sleeping Driver, The Ride in the Moonlight, Wrong Side of the Road, Between Sleeping and Waking.
14. Read "The Confessions of an English Opium Eater," "Murder as One of the Fine Arts," Joan of Arc."

BEAUTY

Among all the ugly mugs of the world we see now and then a face made after the divine pattern. Then a wonderful thing happens to us; The Blue Bird sings, the golden Splendour shines, and for a queer moment everything seems meaningless save our impulse to follow these fair forms, to follow them to the clear Paradises they promise.

Plato assures us that these moments are not (as we are apt to think them) mere blurs and delusions of the senses, but divine revelations; that in a lovely face we see imaged, as in a mirror, the Absolute Beauty; it is Reality flashing on us in the cave where we dwell amid shadows and darkness. Therefore we should follow these fair forms, and their shining footsteps will lead us upward to the highest heaven of Wisdom. The poets, too, keep chanting this great doctrine of Beauty in grave notes to their golden strings. Its music floats up through the skies so sweet, so strange, that the very Angels seem to lean from their stars to listen.

But, O Plato, O Shelley, O Angels of Heaven, what scrapes you do get us into!

Logan Pearsall Smith: *Trivia*

HELEN KELLER 1880– NO READER is ignorant of the facts concerning the adventurous life of Helen Keller. Left deaf and blind at nineteen months after an illness, she was also dumb, since there seemed no way to teach her to speak. But today she is known everywhere for her achievements, because Miss Anne Sullivan (Mrs. John A. Macy) made her a part of the world of people by teaching her how to communicate with the world about her. Forty-six years of devotion have earned Mrs. Macy the title of "the other half of Helen Keller." A wise aunt of Helen's said of the little girl who was blind, deaf, and dumb, "This child has more sense than all the Kellers if there is ever any way to reach her mind." In 1887, Miss Sullivan came to Tuscumbia, Alabama, where Helen Keller was born, to take charge of the child's training. The first task was to gain Helen's love, so that she would accept her mentor's control. How the first word, "water," was learned is a thrilling story. Miss Sullivan says: "One day we went to the pump house. I made Helen hold her mug under the spout while I pumped. As the cold water gushed forth, I spelled 'w-a-t-e-r' several times. All the way back to the house she was highly excited, and learned the name of every object she touched. In a few hours she had added thirty new words to her vocabulary."

Miss Keller's life and interests may be read in *The Story of My Life* (1902) and *The World I Live in* (1908). Certainly one agrees with Mark Twain's statement: "You are a wonderful creature — you and your other half together — Miss Sullivan, I mean, for it took the pair of you to make a complete and perfect whole."

There are many records of men and women who made physical handicaps steppingstones to splendid strength, but none of any other who had such heavy handicaps as Helen Keller, and none of any who won to a higher intellectual and spiritual power. What follows is a somewhat condensed form of an essay that appeared in the *Atlantic Monthly*.

Three Days to See

I HAVE often thought it would be a blessing if each human being were stricken blind and deaf for a few days at some time during his early adult life. Darkness would make him more appreciative of sight; silence would teach him the joys of sound.

Now and then I have tested my seeing friends to discover what they see. Recently I asked a friend, who had just returned from a long walk in the woods, what she had observed. "Nothing in particular," she replied.

How was it possible, I asked myself, to walk for an hour through the woods and see nothing worthy of note? I who cannot see find hundreds of things to interest me through mere touch. I feel the delicate symmetry of a leaf. I pass my hands lovingly about the smooth skin of a silver birch, or the rough, shaggy bark of a pine. In spring I touch the branches of trees hopefully in search of a bud, the first sign of awakening Nature after her winter's sleep. Occasionally, if I am very fortunate, I place my hand gently on a small tree and feel the happy quiver of a bird in full song.

At times my heart cries out with longing to see all these things. If I can get so much pleasure from mere touch, how much more beauty must be revealed by sight. And I have imagined what I should most like to see if I were given the use of my eyes, say, for just three days. . . .

I should divide the period into three parts. On the first day, I should want to see the people whose kindness and gentleness and companionship have made my life worth living. First I should like to gaze long upon the face of my dear teacher, Mrs. Anne Sullivan Macy, who came to me when I was a child and opened the outer world to me. I should want not merely to see the outline of her face, so that I could cherish it in my memory, but to study that face and find in it the living evidence of the sympathetic tenderness and patience with which she accomplished the difficult task of my education. I should like to see in her eyes that strength of character which has enabled her to stand firm in the face of difficulties, and that compassion for all humanity which she has revealed to me so often.

I do not know what it is to see into the heart of a friend through that "window of the soul," the eye. I can only "see" through my finger tips the outline of a face. I can detect laughter, sorrow, and many other obvious emotions. I know my friends from the feel of their faces. But I cannot really picture their personalities by touch. I know their personalities, of course, through other means, through the thoughts they express to me, through whatever of their actions are revealed to me. But I am denied that deeper understanding of them which I am sure would come through sight of them, through watching their reactions to various expressed thoughts and circumstances, through noting the immediate and fleeting reactions of their eyes and countenance.

Friends who are near to me I know well, because through the months and years they reveal themselves to me in all their phases; but of casual friends I have only an incomplete impression, an impression gained from a handclasp, from spoken words which I take from their lips with my finger tips, or which they tap into the palm of my hand.

How much easier, how much more satisfying it is for you who can see to grasp quickly the essential qualities of another person by watching the subtleties of expression, the quiver of a muscle, the flutter of a hand. But does it ever occur to you to use your sight to see into the inner nature of a friend or acquaintance? Do not most of you seeing people grasp casually the outward features of a face and let it go at that?

For instance, can you describe accurately the faces of five good friends? Some of you can, but many cannot. As an experiment, I have questioned husbands of long standing about the color of their wives' eyes, and often they express embarrassed confusion and admit that they do not know. And, incidentally, it is a chronic complaint of wives that their husbands do not notice new dresses, new hats, and changes in household arrangements.

The eyes of seeing persons soon become accustomed to the routine of their surroundings, and they actually see only the startling and spectacular. But even in viewing the most spectacular sights the eyes are lazy. Court records reveal every day how inaccurately "eyewitnesses" see. A given event will be "seen" in several different ways by as many witnesses. Some see more than others, but few see everything that is within the range of their vision.

Oh, the things that I should see if I had the power of sight for just three days!

The first day would be a busy one. I should call to me all my dear friends and look long into their faces, imprinting upon my mind the outward evidences of the beauty that is within them. I should let my eyes rest, too, on the face of a baby, so that I could catch a vision of the eager, innocent beauty which precedes the individual's consciousness of the conflicts which life develops.

And I should like to look into the loyal, trusting eyes of my dogs — the grave, canny little Scottie, Darkie, and the stalwart, understanding Great Dane, Helga, whose warm, tender, and playful friendships are so comforting to me.

On that busy first day I should also view the small simple things of my home. I want to see the warm colors in the rugs under my feet, the pictures on the walls, the intimate trifles that transform a house into home. My eyes would rest respectfully on the books in raised type which I have read, but they would be more eagerly interested in the printed books which seeing people can read, for during the long night of my life the books I have read and those which have been read to me have built themselves into a great shining lighthouse, revealing to me the deepest channels of human life and the human spirit.

In the afternoon of that first seeing day, I should take a long walk in the woods and intoxicate my eyes on the beauties of the world of Nature, trying desperately to absorb in a few hours the vast splendor which is constantly unfolding itself to those who can see. On the way home from my woodland jaunt my path would lie near a farm so that I might see the patient horses plowing in the field (perhaps I should see only a tractor!) and the serene content of men living close to the soil. And I should pray for the glory of a colorful sunset. . . .

The next day — the second day of sight — I should arise with the dawn and see the thrilling miracle by which night is transformed into day. I should behold with awe the magnificent panorama of light with which the sun awakens the sleeping earth.

This day I should devote to a hasty glimpse of the world, past and present. I should want to see the pageant of man's progress, the kaleidoscope of the ages. How can so much be compressed into one day? Through the museums, of course. Often I have visited the New York Museum of Natural History to touch with my hands many of the objects there exhibited, but I have longed to see with my eyes the condensed history of the earth and its inhabitants displayed there — animals and the races of men pictured in their native environment; gigantic carcasses of dinosaurs and mastodons which roamed the earth long before man appeared, with his tiny stature and powerful brain, to conquer the animal kingdom; realistic presentations of the processes of evolution in animals, in man, and in the implements which man has used to fashion for himself a secure home on this planet; and a thousand and one other aspects of natural history.

My next stop would be the Metropolitan Museum of Art, for just as the Museum of Natural History reveals the material aspects of the world, so does the Metropolitan show the myriad facets of the human spirit. Throughout the history of humanity the urge to artistic expression has been almost as powerful as the urge for food, shelter, and procreation. And here, in the vast chambers of the Metropolitan Museum, is unfolded before me the spirit of Egypt, Greece, and

Rome, as expressed in their art. I know well through my hands the sculptured gods and goddesses of the ancient Nile land. I have felt copies of Parthenon friezes, and I have sensed the rhythmic beauty of charging Athenian warriors. Apollos and Venuses and the Wingèd Victory of Samothrace are friends of my finger tips. The gnarled, bearded features of Homer are dear to me, for he, too, knew blindness.

My hands have lingered upon the living marble of Roman sculpture as well as that of later generations. I have passed my hands over a plaster cast of Michelangelo's inspiring and heroic Moses; I have sensed the power of Rodin; I have been awed by the devoted spirit of Gothic wood carving. These arts which can be touched have meaning for me, but even they were meant to be seen rather than felt, and I can only guess at the beauty which remains hidden from me. I can admire the simple lines of a Greek vase, but its figured decorations are lost to me.

So on this, my second day of sight, I should try to probe into the soul of man through his art. The things I knew through touch I should now see. More splendid still, the whole magnificent world of painting would be opened to me, from the Italian Primitives, with their serene religious devotion, to the Moderns, with their feverish visions. I should look deep into the canvases of Raphael, Leonardo da Vinci, Titian, Rembrandt. I should want to feast my eyes upon the warm colors of Veronese, study the mysteries of El Greco, catch a new vision of Nature from Corot. Oh, there is so much rich meaning and beauty in the art of the ages for you who have eyes to see! . . .

The evening of my second day of sight I should spend at a theater or at the movies. Even now I often attend theatrical performances of all sorts, but the action of the play must be spelled into my hand by a companion. But how I should like to see with my own eyes the fascinating figure of Hamlet, or the gusty Falstaff amid colorful Elizabethan trappings! How I should like to follow each movement of the graceful Hamlet, each strut of the hearty Falstaff! And since I could see only one play, I should be confronted by a many-horned dilemma, for there are scores of plays I should want to see. You who have eyes can see any you like. How many of you, I wonder, when you gaze at a play, a movie, or any spectacle, realize and give thanks for the miracle of sight which enables you to enjoy its color, grace, and movement?

I cannot enjoy the beauty of rhythmic movement except in a sphere restricted to the touch of my hands. I can vision only dimly the grace of a Pavlowa, although I know something of the delight of rhythm, for often I can sense the beat of music as it vibrates through the floor. I can well imagine that cadenced motion must be one of the most pleasing sights in the world. I have been able to gather something of this by tracing with my fingers the lines in sculptured marble; if this static grace can be so lovely, how much more acute must be the thrill of seeing grace in motion.

One of my dearest memories is of the time when Joseph Jefferson allowed me to touch his face and hands as he went through some of the gestures and speeches of his beloved Rip Van Winkle. I was able to catch thus a meager glimpse of the world of drama, and I shall never forget the delight of that moment. But, oh, how much I must miss, and how much pleasure you seeing ones can derive from watching and hearing the interplay of speech and movement in the unfolding of a dramatic performance! If I could see only one play, I should know how to picture in my mind the action of a hundred plays which I have read or had transferred to me through the medium of the manual alphabet. . . .

The following morning, I should again greet the dawn, anxious to discover new delights, for I am sure that, for those who have eyes which really see, the dawn of each day must be a perpetually new revelation of beauty.

This, according to the terms of my imagined miracle, is to be my third and last day of sight. I shall have no time to waste in regrets or longings; there is too much to see. The first day I devoted to my friends, animate and inanimate. The second revealed to me the history of man and Nature. Today I shall spend in the workaday world of the present, amid the haunts of men going about the business of life. And where can one find so many activities and conditions of men as in New York? So the city becomes my destination.

I start from my home in the quiet little suburb of Forest Hills,

Long Island. Here, surrounded by green lawns, trees, and flowers, are neat little houses, happy with the voices and movements of wives and children, havens of peaceful rest for men who toil in the city. I drive across the lacy structure of steel which spans the East River, and I get a new and startling vision of the power and ingenuity of the mind of man. Busy boats chug and scurry about the river — racy speedboats, stolid, snorting tugs. If I had long days of sight ahead, I should spend many of them watching the delightful activity upon the river.

I look ahead, and before me rise the fantastic towers of New York, a city that seems to have stepped from the pages of a fairy story. What an awe-inspiring sight, these glittering spires, these vast banks of stone and steel — structures such as the gods might build for themselves! This animated picture is a part of the lives of millions of people every day. How many, I wonder, give it so much as a second glance? Very few, I fear. Their eyes are blind to this magnificent sight because it is so familiar to them.

I hurry to the top of one of those gigantic structures, the Empire State Building, for there, a short time ago, I " saw " the city below through the eyes of my secretary. I am anxious to compare my fancy with reality. I am sure I should not be disappointed in the panorama spread out before me, for to me it would be a vision of another world.

Now I begin my rounds of the city. First, I stand at a busy corner, merely looking at people, trying by sight of them to understand something of their lives. I see smiles, and I am happy. I see serious determination, and I am proud. I see suffering, and I am compassionate.

I stroll down Fifth Avenue. I throw my eyes out of focus so that I see no particular object but only a seething kaleidoscope of color. I am certain that the colors of women's dresses moving in a throng must be a gorgeous spectacle of which I should never tire. But perhaps if I had sight I should be like most other women — too interested in styles and the cut of individual dresses to give much attention to the splendor of color in the mass. And I am convinced, too, that I should become an inveterate window-shopper, for it must be a delight to the eye to view the myriad articles of beauty on display.

From Fifth Avenue I make a tour of the city — to Park Avenue, to the slums, to factories, to parks where children play. I take a stay-at-home trip abroad by visiting the foreign quarters. Always my eyes are open wide to all the sights of both happiness and misery so that I may probe deep and add to my understanding of how people work and live. My heart is full of the images of people and things. My eye passes lightly over no single trifle; it strives to touch and hold closely each thing its gaze rests upon. Some sights are pleasant, filling the heart with happiness; but some are miserably pathetic. To these latter I do not shut my eyes, for they, too, are part of life. To close the eye on them is to close the heart and mind.

My third day of sight is drawing to an end. Perhaps there are many serious pursuits to which I should devote the few remaining hours, but I am afraid on the evening of that last day I should again run away to the theater, to a hilariously funny play, so that I might appreciate the overtures of comedy in the human spirit.

At midnight my temporary respite from blindness would cease, and permanent night would close in on me again. Naturally in those three short days I should not have seen all I wanted to see. Only when darkness had again descended upon me should I realize how much I had left unseen. . . .

Perhaps this short outline of how I should spend three days of sight does not agree with the program you would set for yourself if you knew that you were about to be stricken blind. I am, however, sure that if you actually faced that fate your eyes would open to things you had never seen before, storing up memories for the long night ahead. You would use your eyes as never before. Everything you saw would become dear to you. Your eyes would touch and embrace every object that came within your range of vision. Then, at last, you would really see, and a new world of beauty would open itself before you.

I who am blind can give one hint to those who see — one admonition to those who would make full use of the gift of sight: Use your eyes as if tomorrow you would be stricken blind. And the same method can be applied to the other senses. Hear the music of voices, the song of a bird, the mighty strains of an orchestra, as if you would be stricken deaf tomorrow. Touch each object you want to touch as if tomorrow your tactile sense would fail. Smell the perfume of flowers, taste with relish each morsel, as if tomorrow you could never smell and taste again. Make the most of every sense; glory in all the facets of pleasure and beauty which the world reveals to you through the several means of contact which Nature provides. But of all the senses, I am sure that sight must be the most delightful.

APPRECIATION HINTS

1. How does Helen Keller occasionally hear a bird's song?
2. What is the chief thing she would do on her first day?
3. What would she do on the afternoon of the first day?
4. To what purpose would she devote the second day?
5. Where would she go to accomplish this purpose?
6. How would she spend the evening?
7. How did she once learn something about acting?
8. How would she spend her last day?
9. Trace her proposed tour of sight-seeing.
10. Imagine yourself in the same condition as Helen Keller. How would you plan your three days?
11. Imagine yourself deaf since birth. What would you plan if you had three days to hear?
12. Stevenson makes a distinction in "Aes Triplex" between life and living. What new light on that distinction is shed by this essay?
13. Write a composition on a topic suggested by this essay. Possible titles: Eyes Have They But They See Not, Feeling Music, Remembered Faces, My City's Busiest Corner, Window-Shopping.

When Voltaire arrived in England in 1727, he found that feeling ran so high against the French, that on the streets of London he was in grave peril. One day during a walk a crowd of angry citizens shouted, "Kill him! Hang the Frenchman!"

Voltaire stopped, faced the crowd, and cried, "Englishmen! You want to kill me because I am a Frenchman! Am I not punished enough, in not being an Englishman?"

The crowd cheered wildly, and provided him safe conduct back to his dwelling. Christian Science Monitor

LIVING ISSUES OF TODAY AND TOMORROW

MOST OF THE ESSAYS of the preceding section are definite in pointing to values in life which are more precious than life itself. But are we today quite sure what the basic values are for which we are willing to die? Courage to die — for what?

The essays in this section help us to come to a clear answer to that question. All the authors who speak to us in this section are convinced that in modern American life basic values have deteriorated. All the writers point to some way in which they can be recovered. Archibald MacLeish, the distinguished poet and Librarian of Congress, bids us look at the men who made our country and be like them; Dorothy Thompson pleads for a humane understanding of the men who do the work of America, so that they may once more hold their heads up like the pioneers; Lewis Mumford calls on all hands to save the only thing that is worth saving — the spirit of America; Dorothy Canfield shows us something of the ancient virtues of our forefathers, still preserved by plain countryfolk, but lost and smothered by the rush of the great cities; Pearl Buck points to the great unused fund of energy in many American women, which is paralyzed by their vaunted privileges; and Stuart Chase gives us hope and courage when he points to what the people of America can do when they set to work and build things fit to realize the visions of the founders. Walter Lippmann treats systematically with what he thinks our schools and colleges ought to have done — and haven't. His essay is not humorous, and it is not easy reading. But it is a challenge to thought for everyone who wants really to be educated.

ARCHIBALD MacLEISH
1892–

USUALLY the most-likely-to-succeed votes at commencement time don't mean much. But the Yale seniors of 1915 guessed right when they picked Archibald MacLeish as the most brilliant and versatile man in the class. His great ambition was to be a poet; and that ambition was combined in recent years with an urgent inner compulsion to arouse his fellow countrymen to a revived faith in democracy so that they might be able to defend it. He saw that the challenge was coming. MacLeish was in the A.E.F. of the First World War and came out a captain of field artillery " with no distinction," he says, " except that his brother Kenneth had been a grand flier and had been killed."

The versatility which MacLeish's classmates had recognized is seen in his experiments in combining the arts of the poet and the broadcaster. *Air Raid* has been called by critics the best play ever written for broadcasting. We hear the matter-of-fact reporting of the announcer telling about the maneuvers of the bombers, and feel at the same time the approach of an appalling doom. In his earlier *The Fall of the City* the poet had broken ground in this adaptation of verse to radio, and was saying in a different medium what he says in " Look to the Spirit within You " — namely, that man's fate is still at issue.

Archibald MacLeish was educated at Hotchkiss and Yale and then at the Harvard Law School. Though he " could never believe in the law," he built up a successful practice in Boston after the war but abandoned it to write poetry. He won the Pulitzer Prize with the play *Conquistador* in 1932, published *Land of the Free* in 1938, a book of " photographs illustrated by a poem." The photographs are superb illustrations of poverty-stricken life in a land of plenty. MacLeish was appointed Librarian of the Congressional Library in 1939. His constant theme is that we have not fulfilled the dream of the founders of the Union, and, indeed, have almost lost it.

Look to the Spirit within You

THE ISSUE before the American people depends more surely on our souls than on our weapons; for the enemy which attacks us attacks not with planes alone or tanks or arms, but with violence of belief. The issue is whether those who believe in democracy can bring against that invading faith a stronger, more resisting ardor of their own.

After the Battle of France we learned, in the words of a group of distinguished scholars, that the enemy " were stronger in arms because they were stronger in heart. It was their fanatical faith that gave them wings and fire."

Before the Battle of France we had thought ourselves spectators of a war in Europe. After it, we knew the war was not in Europe but nearer — in the darker and more vulnerable countries of men's hearts.

The real issue is one to be fought in the hard and stony passes of the human spirit — the strict Thermopylaes of time where even if a man is killed he cannot die. And democracy itself is neither gold nor steel nor corn nor silk, nor fatness and indifference and an empty heart, but winter on the Massachusetts Bay and cold at Trenton and the gunfire in Kentucky and the hungry ground. The real issue is between the frenzy of a herded, whipped-up crowd-begotten cause, and the single man's belief in liberty of mind and spirit, and his willingness to sacrifice his comforts and his earnings for its sake.

For three centuries of time and on two continents, democracy has been a faith more powerful than any other. It is so still. All our history has made this plain. Whenever we have given ourselves to creating upon this continent a life in which every man might have the freedom of his mind, we have been confident of our future and asked no questions either of ourselves or anyone.

A century ago when the 400-foot side-wheelers with the crystal chandeliers and the mahogany bars and the eight-course dinners and the filigree funnels, with their sparks like crazy stars, went hooting and slapping up the Ohio and the Hudson and the Mississippi, the Americans had no questions about themselves. They had a job to do. They had the toughest job a people ever undertook — the job of clearing and settling and tying together with ships and roads and rails and words and names the largest area lived on as a single social unit by any nation, at any time. They had the job of creating on an undiscovered continent a country where a hundred million men could live in freedom from the rest of the world and from each other. And while they had that job to do they asked no questions. They knew what men they were. They were the smartest, toughest, luckiest, leanest, all-around knowingest nation on God's green earth. Their way of living was the handsomest way of living human beings had ever hit. Their institutions were the institutions history had been waiting for. If you had told them anyone else had a harder hold on the earth than they did, or anyone else believed in himself more than they believed in themselves, they would have laughed in your face. And gone on working.

Who they were, what they were, never bothered the Americans. They had all the origins of Europe in their veins before the century was over — all the races a man ever heard of and a lot more beside. Races didn't bother the Americans. They were something a lot better than any race. They were a People. They were the first self-constituted, self-declared, self-created People in the history of the world. And their manners were their own business. And so were their politics. And so, but ten times more so, were their souls.

You could see for yourself who and what an American was. He was a man who had the luck to be born on this continent where the heat was hotter and the cold was colder and the sun was brighter and the nights were blacker and the distances were farther and the faces were nearer and the rain was more like rain and the mornings were more like mornings than anywhere else on earth.

An American was a man who knew which way to take to reach tomorrow. An American was a man who could let himself in and let himself out and nobody asked him " please " — not even the President. An American was a man who never asked anyone anything, who he was or where he came from or what he did, because it was answer enough — in America — to be a man.

That was the way it used to be in this country. That was the way it was while the people of this country were clearing the quarter sections for a free man's fields.

That is the way it *can* be, once again. For democracy is never a thing done. Democracy is always something that a nation must be doing. The quarter sections which were freedom a hundred years ago are now not freedom. Freedom will be somewhere else. But the labor of creating freedom is the same. And the cause is the same. And the faith is the same. And the consequence.

Those who fear for America, thinking of France, can give themselves an answer. Democracy in America will not fall like a rotten apple if it is democracy in action, not democracy accomplished and piled up in goods and gold. For democracy in action — the unending labor of creating freedom for every man — is a cause for which the stones themselves will fight.

There are those, and they are not few, who tell us now that liberty must retire, that democracy must retire, that labor must retire, that the Jews must retire and not be seen and not be Jews, that anything that any man might question must retire, that the nation must be unified along the cautious shores of silence and beyond dissent.

Let them look out at others who retired, others who waited, others who drew back.

Let them look back upon the history of this people.

In the wars of the spirit there is no defense but to attack. For in the wars of democracy, of the human spirit, it is faith which will decide the issue. And faith cannot be faith against but *for*.

APPRECIATION HINTS

1. What is the central theme of MacLeish's essay?
2. What reason does he give for the fall of France?
3. Describe the main job of the American people a century ago.
4. Tell about their faith in themselves.
5. Show how the conception of freedom changes from time to time.
6. What must democracy do in order to continue?
7. This essay was written in February, 1941. In what respect have events since then shown that MacLeish was right?
8. Select examples from history to show that belief in one's cause is the strongest of weapons.
9. Explain fully the meaning of the title.
10. By giving examples of things that have to be done show that the tasks of our democracy are different now from what they were a hundred years ago.
11. Write a composition on a topic suggested by this essay. Possible titles: Our Job, What I Believe, The Old Days on the Mississippi, Others Who Retired, Now We Are a People, After the War.
12. Read *Land of the Free, The Fall of the City, Air Raid.*

As I would not be a slave, *so I would not be a* master. *This expresses my idea of democracy. Whatever differs from this, to the extent of the difference, is no democracy.*   Abraham Lincoln

"How does it feel to be President?" an Illinois friend asked Abraham Lincoln.
"Well, I'm like the man they rode out of town on a rail. He said if it wasn't for the honor of it he would just as soon walk."

Carl Sandburg: *The People, Yes*
(Harcourt, Brace and Company)

DOROTHY CANFIELD FISHER   HILLSBORO is the
1879–   village of Arling-
ton in Vermont, where Mrs. Fisher's ancestors settled in 1764 on
land which their descendants have owned ever since. There is surely
no one who can speak with more intimate knowledge about the
values of village life in New England than she. In fact when the
editors of the *Nation* wanted to choose someone to describe Vermont
for their book called *These United States,* they chose Dorothy Canfield. In this essay she takes us behind the false front put on by a
village for its summer visitors — the mask of tennis courts, golf
courses, summer hotels, and picture post cards which hide or distort
its real life. And this is good to see, particularly for the city born
and bred, because it was this kind of community which produced the
rugged American character praised by Archibald MacLeish. The essay is one of a series of about twenty-five sketches of village people
who take time to live. For those whose eyes are blinded by the dust
and heat of the cities, she reveals large vistas behind the front of the
little villages we drive through. No one since Lowell has interpreted
the rural Yankee more faithfully.

But it was only after Dorothy Canfield's marriage that she went
to live on the old farm at Arlington. She was born in Lawrence, Kansas, where her father was a college professor. He was later president
of several state universities, and his daughter thus came to know
various college towns. She studied later at Columbia and received
a doctor's degree. In 1915 appeared *The Bent Twig,* one of her best
novels, and the year after there came some more stories about Hillsboro people. The First World War found her doing relief work in
France. Mrs. Fisher has always been interested in education, has
served, as the first woman member, on the Vermont Board of Education, and has stoutly defended the small school where each student
must take a share in the responsibility. Her latest book, *Seasoned
Timber,* 1939, is a novel of Vermont life.

Town and Country

SOMETIMES people from Hillsboro leave our forgotten valley, high among the Green Mountains, and "go down to the city," as the phrase runs. They always come back exclaiming that they should think New Yorkers would just die of loneliness, and crying out in an ecstasy of relief that it does seem so good to get back where there are some folks. After the desolate isolation of city streets, empty of humanity, filled only with hurrying ghosts, the vestibule of our church after morning service fills one with an exalted realization of the great numbers of the human race. It is like coming into a warmed and lighted room, full of friendly faces, after wandering long by night in a forest peopled only with flitting shadows. In the phantasmagoric pantomime [1] of the city, we forget that there are so many real people in all the world, so diverse, so unfathomably human as those who meet us in the little post office on the night of our return to Hillsboro.

Like any other of those gifts of life which gratify insatiable cravings of humanity, living in a country village conveys a satisfaction which is incommunicable. A great many authors have written about it, just as a great many authors have written about the satisfaction of being in love, but in the one, as in the other case, the essence of the thing escapes. People rejoice in sweethearts because all humanity craves love, and they thrive in country villages because

[1] Stage play of imaginary people.

they crave human life. Now the living spirit of neither of these things can be caught in a net of words. All the foolish, fond doings of lovers may be set down on paper by whatever eavesdropper cares to take the trouble, but no one can realize from that record anything of the glory in the hearts of the unconscious two. All the queer grammar and insignificant surface eccentricities of village character may be ruthlessly reproduced in every variety of dialect, but no one can guess from that record the abounding flood of richly human life which pours along the village street.

This tormenting inequality between the thing felt and the impression conveyed had vexed us unceasingly until one day Simple Martin, the town fool, who always says our wise things, said one of his wisest. He was lounging by the watering trough one sunny day in June, when a carriage of "summer folk" from Winfield over the mountain stopped to water their horses. They asked him, as they always, always ask all of us, "For mercy's sake, what do you people *do* all the time, away off here, so far from everything."

Simple Martin was not irritated, or perplexed, or rendered helplessly inarticulate by this question, as the rest of us had always been. He looked around him at the lovely, sloping lines of Hemlock Mountain, at the Necronsett River singing in the sunlight, at the familiar, friendly faces of the people in the street, and he answered in astonishment at the ignorance of his questioners, "*Do?* Why, we jes' *live!* "

We felt that he had explained us once and for all. We had known that, of course, but we hadn't before, in our own phrase, "sensed it." We just live. And sometimes it seems to us that we are the only people in America engaged in that most wonderful occupation. We know, of course, that we must be wrong in thinking this, and that there must be countless other Hillsboros scattered everywhere, rejoicing as we do in an existence which does not necessarily make us carefree or happy, which does not in the least absolve us from the necessity of working hard (for Hillsboro is unbelievably poor in money), but which does keep us alive in every fiber of our sympathy and thrilling with the consciousness of the life of others.

A common and picturesque expression for a common experience

runs, "It's so noisy I can't hear myself think." After a visit to New York we feel that its inhabitants are so deafened by the constant blare of confusion that they can't feel themselves live. The steady sufferers from this complaint do not realize their condition. They find it on the whole less trouble *not* to feel themselves live, and they are most uneasy when chance forces them to spend a few days (on shipboard, for instance) where they are not protected by ceaseless and aimless activity from the consciousness that they are themselves. They cannot even conceive the bitter-sweet, vital taste of that consciousness as we villagers have it, and they cannot understand how arid their existence seems to us without this unhurried, penetrating realization of their own existence and of the meaning of their acts. We do not blame city dwellers for not having it, we ourselves lose it when we venture into their maelstrom. Like them, we become dwarfed by overwhelming numbers, and shriveled by the incapacity to "sense" the humanity of the countless human simulacra about us. But we do not stay where we cannot feel ourselves live! We hurry back to the shadow of Hemlock Mountain, feeling that to love life one does not need to be what is usually called happy, one needs only to live.

It cannot be, of course, that we are the only community to discover this patent fact; but we know no more of the others than they of us. All that we hear from that part of America which is not Hillsboro is the wild yell of excitement going up from the great cities,

where people seem to be doing everything that was ever done or thought of except just living. City dwellers make money, make reputations (good and bad), make museums and subways, make charitable institutions, make with a hysteric rapidity, like excited spiders, more and yet more complications in the mazy labyrinths of their lives, but they never make each other's acquaintances . . . and that is all that is worth doing in the world.

We who live in Hillsboro know that they are to be pitied, not blamed, for this fatal omission. We realize that only in Hillsboro and places like it can one have "deep, full life and contact with the vitalizing stream of humanity." We know that in the very nature of humanity the city is a small and narrow world, the village a great and wide one, and that the utmost efforts of city dwellers will not avail to break the bars of the prison where they are shut in, each with his own kind. They may look out from the windows upon a great and varied throng, as the beggar munching a crust may look in at a banqueting hall, but the people they are forced to live with are exactly like themselves; and that way lies not only monomonia but an ennui that makes the blessing of life savorless. . . .

The pathetic feature of this universal inexperience among city dwellers of real life and real people is that it is really entirely enforced and involuntary. At heart they crave knowledge of real life and sympathy with their fellow men as starving men do food. In Hillsboro we explain to ourselves the enormous amount of novel reading and playgoing in the great cities as due to a perverted form of this natural hunger for human life. If people are so situated they can't get it fresh, they will take it canned, which is undoubtedly good for those in the canning business; but we feel that we who have better food ought not to be expected to treat their boughten canned goods very seriously. We can't help smiling at the life-and-death discussions of literary people about their preferences in style and plot and treatment . . . their favorite brand on the can, so to speak.

To tell the truth, all novels seem to us badly written, they are so faint and faded in comparison to the brilliant colors of the life which palpitates up and down our village street, called by strangers, " so quaint and sleepy-looking." What does the author of a novel do for you, after all, even the best author? He presents to you people not nearly so interesting as your next-door neighbors, makes them do things not nearly so exciting as what happened to your grandfather, and doles out to you in meager paragraphs snatches of that comprehending and consolatory philosophy of life, which long ago you should have learned to manufacture for yourself out of every incident in your daily routine. Of course, if you don't know your next-door neighbors, and have never had time to listen to what happened to your grandfather, and are too busy catching trains to philosophize on those subjects if you did know them, no more remains to be said. By all means patronize the next shop you see which displays in its show windows canned romances, adventures, tragedies, farces, and the like line of goods. Live vicariously, if you can't at first hand; but don't be annoyed at our pity for your method of passing blindfold through life.

And don't expect to find such a shop in our village. To open one there would be like trying to crowd out the great trees on Hemlock Mountain by planting a Noah's-Ark garden among them. Romances, adventures, tragedies, and farces . . . why, we are the characters of those plots. Every child who runs past the house starts a new story, every old man whom we leave sleeping in the burying ground by the Necronsett River is the ending of another . . . or perhaps the beginning of a sequel. Do you say that in the city a hundred more children run past the windows of your apartment than along our solitary street, and that funeral processions cross your every walk abroad? True, but they are stories written in a tongue incomprehensible to you. You look at the covers, you may even flutter the leaves and look at the pictures, but you cannot tell what they are all about. You are like people bored and yawning at a performance of a tragedy by Sophocles, because the actors speak in Greek. So dreadful and moving a thing as a man's sudden death may happen before your eyes, but you do not know enough of what it means to be moved by it. For you it is not really a man who dies. It is the abstract idea of a man, leaving behind him abstract possibilities of a wife and children. You knew nothing of him, you know nothing of them, you shudder, look the other way, and hurry along, your heart a little more blunted to the sorrows of others, a little more remote from your fellows even than before.

All Hillsboro is more stirred than that, both to sympathy and active help, by the news that Mrs. Brownell has broken her leg. It means something unescapably definite to us, about which we not only can, but must take action. It means that her sickly oldest daughter will not get the care she needs if somebody doesn't go to help out; it means that if we do not do something that bright boy of hers will have to leave school, just when he is in the way of winning a scholarship in college; it means, in short, a crisis in several human lives, which by the mere fact of being known calls forth sympathy as irresistibly as sunshine in May opens the leaf buds.

Just as it is only one lover in a million who can continue to love his mistress during a lifetime of absolute separation from her, so it is one man in a million who can continue his sympathy and interest in his fellow men without continual close contact with them. The divine feeling of responsibility for the well-being of others is diluted and washed away in great cities by the overwhelming impersonal flood of vast numbers; in villages it is strengthened by the sight, apparent to the dullest eyes, of immediate personal and visible application. In other words, we are not only the characters of our unwritten stories, but also part authors. Something of the final outcome depends upon us, something of the creative instinct of the artist is stirred to life within every one of us . . . however unconscious of it in our countrified simplicity we may be. The sympathy we feel for a distressed neighbor has none of the impotent sterility of a reader's sympathy for a distressed character in a book. There is always a chance to try to help, and if that fail, to try again and yet again. Death writes the only *Finis* to our stories, and since a chance to start over again has been so unfailingly granted us here, we cannot but feel that Death may mean only turning over another page. . . .

APPRECIATION HINTS

1. What did the villagers mean by saying, when they came home from New York, that " it was good to get back where there are some folks "?
2. What was the occasion of Simple Martin's remark?
3. What does the author mean by saying that New Yorkers " can't feel themselves live "?
4. What is the " one thing worth doing " which city dwellers never do?
5. What does the author mean by the natural hunger for human life *canned?*
6. Comment on the reason for the different effect of a man's sudden death (a) in a city, (b) in a village.

7. Why did Mrs. Brownell's broken leg mean a crisis in the village?
8. Why does not Hillsboro need a bookshop?
9. Describe some village you know like Hillsboro.
10. It is nearly thirty years since this essay was written. Find out whether the drift of population is still toward the big towns or away from them.
11. Stevenson also has something to say about life in the essay in this volume. Would he have been happy in Hillsboro? How did his ideal of living differ from Mrs. Fisher's?
12. Write a composition on some topic suggested by this essay. Possible titles: A Village Character, The Village Store, Noises of a Big City, Canned Life, My City Neighbor, My Village Neighbor.
13. Read "Petunias: That's for Remembrance," "The Portrait of a Philosopher," "The Bed Quilt," "The Heyday in the Blood," all from *Hillsboro People*.

A. E. Housman's chief scorn was directed against pretentious scholarship, and one of his victims drew this devastating sentence: "Nature, not content with denying to Mr. X the faculty of thinking, has endowed him with the faculty of writing."

Louis Untermeyer: *A Treasury of Great Poems*

It is not so important to be serious as it is to be serious about the important things. The monkey wears an expression of seriousness which would do credit to any college student, but the monkey is serious because he itches.

Robert Maynard Hutchins

I find that a great part of the information I have was acquired by looking up something and finding something else on the way. F.P.A.: *Diary of Our Own Samuel Pepys*

PEARL BUCK 1892– OUT OF the forty-six essays in this book, the following is one of seven written by women, and perhaps this marked disproportion is partially explained by Pearl Buck as she writes about the vast reservoir of energy and ability in American women which finds no outlet. Four of the other essays by women are applicable to all readers of both sexes, and Winifred Kirkland's essay is pointed, one might say poked, at men. Pearl Buck's essay is addressed to women, and boys might perhaps read the title and say, " That's not for me — let's skip it." But have you not heard a young man say, "When I marry, my wife's not going to have to work "? How many of you boys agree? The condition of American women described in this challenging essay could never have come about except through the assent and encouragement of men. Hence " America's Gunpowder Women " should be read by boys and girls with equal interest.

What this internal gunpowder is, the essay tells us. Only a section of the original essay is here reprinted. Earlier in the essay Pearl Buck divides American women into three groups: talented women, who keep on at their chosen work because they can't help it; women who find complete satisfaction in the work of the household; and third, the largest group, women who have surplus time, energy, and ability which they do not know how to use, or the conventions of society forbid them to use. These are Pearl Buck's " gunpowder women."

It required a writer who had had opportunities to observe the status of women in other parts of the world to point out this dangerous vacuum found peculiarly in the lives of American women. Contrary to the prevailing opinion that the privileges of American women are something for all to be proud of, the author pronounces them a curse. Pearl Buck, now Mrs. Richard J. Walsh, grew up in China, the child of American missionaries. After graduating at Randolph-Macon College, she returned to China to spend there ten years as the wife of an American missionary. She suddenly achieved fame as an interpreter of Oriental civilization with her novel *The Good Earth,* which received the Pulitzer Prize in 1932. She is the third American to receive the Nobel Prize.

America's Gunpowder Women

THE VICIOUS RESULT of privilege is that the creature who receives it becomes incapacitated by it as by a disease. Privilege is a serious misfortune anywhere and the more serious because American women do not realize that the privilege they boast is really their handicap and not their blessing. I am sure they do not realize it, because in the agreement and disagreement I had with my former article nearly all the women said, reproachfully, if they disagreed, "You seem to forget that women in America are the most privileged on earth," and, apologetically, if they agreed, "Of course I know women in America are the most privileged on earth, but —"

And every time this was said, in either fashion, a certain bit of Chinese history came warningly into my mind. This is the history:

Centuries ago when astute China was about to be conquered by the naïve and childlike Manchus, the Chinese used a weapon which gave them the final and actual victory, though the Manchus never knew it. When they were conquered the Chinese said, in effect, to the Manchus, "You are our superiors. Therefore we will perform all unpleasant tasks for you. You shall live in palaces apart and there enjoy yourselves. Sums of money will be set aside for you. You need not labor or strive. We will do everything for you. We want you only to be happy and enjoy yourselves."

The Manchus were delighted with this. They laid aside their weapons, went joyfully to the fine palaces the Chinese gave them, and began to spend their lives in pleasure. In a short time the Chinese were ruling their own country again as they always had and the Manchus were as good as dead. Easy food and drink and plenty of leisure had reduced them to complete ineffectuality, just as the Chinese had planned it.

Now, therefore, whenever I hear an American woman begin brightly, " Well, anyway, we are the most privileged. . . ." I remember the Manchus and am troubled. There is something sinister in this matter of privilege.

And yet it is true — I cannot deny it, though I wish I could — the women of the United States are the most privileged in the world. We have never even had a very serious struggle to achieve our privileges, at least any struggle comparable to that of women in other enlightened countries. Privileges have been bestowed upon us, thanks largely to the inflated value which pioneer times gave to American women. That inflation still lasts, although happily it is decreasing. For the moment when American women hit what commercially is called an all-time low they will be forced to wake up, and then perhaps they will put an honest value on themselves, and thus the struggle which other women have made or are making will begin and the result ought to be valuable to everybody. But that moment has not yet arrived, and meanwhile women go on under the handicap of privilege.

Of course many women in other countries, not understanding any more than we do the effect of unearned privilege, envy American women.

I suppose thousands of Oriental women have said to me at one time or another, " How lucky you are to be an American woman! You have freedom and equality with man. Your parents do not groan when you are born and your brothers do not look down on you as less than they. You can go to school. You need not even marry if you do not wish to — at least, you need never marry someone you do not like."

I agreed to all of this and I still agree to it. I had rather be an

American woman than a woman of any other country in the world because everything lies ahead of us still, as women. But if I had a chance now at those Oriental women, after these years spent among my own countrywomen, I'd answer something like this:

"You know, it's true we are very free. We can be anything we like, we American women — lawyers, doctors, artists, scientists, engineers, anything. But, somehow, we're not! "

"You're not! " the Oriental woman would say, astonished. "Why not? Do you mean the doors are open and you don't go out? "

"Well, we go out — " I would have to acknowledge. "I suppose most of us go out in some sort of work if we don't marry first; but we secretly hope to marry first, so that we need not, or we want to work just a year or two, and then come back into the home and shut the door and be secure in the old way."

"Don't you want to be independent, to be free to come and go

as you like? " the Oriental woman cries. "Ah, if I could support myself, know I need not obey father, mother, husband, son all my life — "

"Oh, we American women don't obey any-one," I tell her quickly. "Our husbands support us in the home, but we don't obey them. We do come and go as we like. Of course we work in our own way at house and children, and for a few years we are even quite busy. But we have a great many ways to save labor, and the schools take our children early and then we have a great deal of leisure — at least, *you* would think us very leisured."

"Then what do you do? " the Oriental woman asks blankly.

"We amuse ourselves somehow," I reply.

"You are fed and clothed for that? " she asks.

"Yes," I reply. "Many of us — and we all expect it."

She cannot understand this, and indeed it is difficult to understand and I cannot explain it to her. Why, in a country where everything is free to women and women are so privileged, is it remarkable when a woman is first-rate in anything? But it is. Thanks to our privileges which compel us to no effort, it is the truth that men excel us, numerically as well as actually, at everything except childbearing, and doubtless if men had to bear children they would soon find some better way of doing it. And women, seeing themselves outstripped without understanding why they are, and yet feeling themselves as able as men, grow discontented and join the crowded ranks of the gunpowder women.

The home of course has been the stronghold of this privilege. Behind its sheltering walls women have taken full advantage of every privilege — the privilege of security, the privilege of noncompetitive work, the privilege of privacy. Yes, of privileges women have had plenty, and yet most of them have been denied the one great blessing of man's life — the necessity to go out into the world and earn their bread directly. And this one blessing is worth all privileges put together; for by it man has been compelled to put forth his utmost effort, whetting his brain and sharpening his ambition, and so he has accomplished much.

For Nature is not unjust. She does not steal into the womb and like an evil fairy give her good gifts secretly to men and deny them to women. Men and women are born free and equal in ability and brain. The injustice begins after birth. The man is taught that he must develop himself and work, lest he and his woman starve. But the woman is taught merely to develop such things as will please the man, lest she starve because he does not want to feed her. Because of this one simple, overwhelming fact, men have been the producers, the rulers, and even the artists.

For necessity makes artists too. Many a talent is born without its mate, energy, and so comes to nothing unless energy is somehow created to develop the talent. Necessity is the magic of this creation for the man; for if he has talent he will, if driven desperately enough, apply his compelled energy to his talent and become at least a fair artist — for genius still remains the combination of highest natural talent and highest natural energy of a quality which functions without outside stimulus — and this combination is rare.

" But," a gunpowder woman retorted to this yesterday, " a man can combine his talent with his breadwinning." She looked round on the walls of her comfortable prison. I could feel her thinking, " If I had been free I might have been a great painter."

To which I retorted, " How do you know it is not as easy to combine housekeeping and art as it is to make art a business? You have never tried it because you never had to."

No, the man is lucky. By compulsion of society and public opinion, if he has any ability and pride, he simply must work. Nothing excuses him. Home cannot be his escape. And in desperation he somehow begins to try to make a living by what he wants to do. And whether he succeeds or fails in it, he has no refuge from work, hard and endless, and full of insecurity. He bears, indeed, the brunt of that heaviest load of all — insecurity.

The curse of too many women has been that they have this privilege of refuge in the home. Behind closed doors they may or must work, it is true, but according to their own hours and ways. They escape all the discipline of concentration upon one task, often uncongenial, hour after hour, year after year, the mental discipline of hard creative thinking, the ruthless discipline of social organization. I have been both breadwinner and housekeeper, and I know that breadwinning is infinitely more tedious, more taxing, more nerveracking, than housekeeping. Indeed, cooking, cleaning, caring for children, if you know necessary bills are pretty certainly going to be paid, is almost a soporific and as good as play after the insecurity of competition in business and the arts. For safe in the home a woman becomes used to flitting from one thing to another, and her mind forgets or never learns how to concentrate or perhaps to work at all. There, leaning upon another's efforts, she becomes lazy, if not physically lazy, lazy in that core of her being which is the source of life and development, so that when her children are grown — and in a few years they are — and her mechanical tasks are over, she is fit for nothing more. She has excused herself from a life of labor because of these short-lived tasks, which, necessary as they are for a time, should never have been considered adequate for her whole self. . . .

APPRECIATION HINTS

1. What incident in Chinese history was suggested to the author by the statement that " American women are the most privileged in the world "?
2. What does she mean by " the inflated value which pioneer times gave to American women "?
3. Give the gist of the conversation between the Chinese woman and the author about the use of freedom by American women.
4. At the end of the conversation what is it that the Chinese woman can't understand?
5. What is the reason for the discontent which crowds the ranks of the gunpowder women?
6. What is the one great blessing of man's life?
7. Which is the harder occupation, breadwinning or housekeeping?
8. Explain the full significance of the title.
9. Think of some women you know who are housekeepers, and, in addition, find something useful to do in the work of the world.
10. Do you think that the Japanese have reduced the number of gunpowder women in America? Why?
11. Can you list some American women (a) who are *first-rate* in their profession today; (b) first-rate in professions in earlier days?
12. What is your own plan to fit yourself to do some work?
13. Write a composition on some topic suggested by this essay. Possible titles: Am I Privileged, A Great American Woman, My Plan, Woman's Part in the War, The Curse of Privilege, My Gunpowder.
14. If you are interested in what women can do in times of war, look up in a recent biographical dictionary the names Sun Yat Sen and Chiang Kai-shek, and write a paper about women's part in the defense of China.
15. Read *The Good Earth*, Pearl Buck's best novel, and her essay on " America's Medieval Women " in *Harper's Magazine*, August, 1938.

How awful to reflect that what people say of us is true!
Logan Pearsall Smith

DOROTHY THOMPSON 1894– THIS ESSAY was delivered as an address in October, 1938, when the fall of France still seemed far distant. Before you read this typical utterance of Dorothy Thompson, jot down in order the important events since October, 1938, which led gradually up to our entry into the war, so that you may check up on the statements and prophecies of this " Cassandra." Though there is a considerable difference in time between the essays of Dorothy Thompson, Archibald MacLeish, and Lewis Mumford in this section, it is interesting to notice the similarities in what they have to say.

In 1940, when Lewis Mumford was writing, the weather had become much rougher, the old ship was still leaking, the crew still in their bunks, and it was time for all hands to save ship. But it ought to be noticed that in none of these essays are the authors primarily concerned about what should be done by political or military action. They are concerned with making the crew aware of the value of the ship and its cargo, and that the cargo is their own. All of these essays call for a new clearness in the citizen and the body politic, — for something necessary now, but even more necessary when the storm has passed. It is because they apply to our attitude during the war, and even more to our attitude toward what will have to be done after the war that they are included in this book.

This essay goes directly to the heart of working America. Cassandra's prophecies were never believed; three years after this address, strikes in defense industries were threatening the nation's efforts. But Dorothy Thompson calls for no anti-strike laws; she wants to deal with causes, not symptoms, and asks first for a decent respect for the factory worker as a human being.

For years Dorothy Thompson has been calling on America to realize the tremendous forces loose in the world. She had watched them growing as she studied in Vienna. For eight years she was a foreign correspondent, and was chief of Central European Service at Berlin from 1924 to 1928. Since then she has been one of the best known political commentators, and began conducting her syndicated column *On The Record* for the New York *Herald Tribune* in 1936.

America Faces Tomorrow's World

PEOPLE have recently called my attention to the fate of a well-known and rather disagreeable lady named Cassandra,[1] who, having predicted the worst, eventually met a bad end. But I would reply to those who dislike the observation of disagreeable facts in the words of Pericles, who uttered them, you will remember, in a funeral oration for war victims, on the Causes of Athenian Greatness: "Happiness is freedom, and freedom is courage."

The measure of optimism with which America can face tomorrow's world *may* be the measure of her ignorance. If it is, then like Athens we may expect to fall into the slavery of a new Sparta. But if our courage is equal to our native love of freedom, then we may escape that fate, and not only escape it but have a new birth of freedom, and in that new birth give hope, as once we did, to all the world.

I am aware that in uttering "freedom" I am using an almost forgotten, almost forbidden word. Other words have come to take its place: democracy; equality; security; social justice; efficiency: these are the current words.

It has a quaint, old-fashioned ring, the word "freedom." But if

[1] A daughter of Priam and Hecuba, who was endowed with the gift of prophecy, but condemned never to be believed. She was enslaved by Agamemnon after the fall of Troy.

I use it now, I use it in the firm faith that tomorrow — in some tomor-row — that word will be spoken again, with a passion that has not inflamed it for a century.

It is muttered today, among millions who have lost it and realize too late how dear it was. Under the iron heel of miasmatic [2] despot-isms, in which neighbors spy on neighbors, in which men and women disappear for reasons never known, in which children march in uniform, and masses chant in drilled hosannas, in which new altars are erected for enforced worship, under a hooked cross or a crossed hammer and sickle, in which journalists are all press agents and press agents all propagandists, where even the lover's passion is not safe from the interference of the State, a word is whispered . . . it passes from mouth to mouth, muttered out of the side of drawn lips . . . it flashes through a brain, still functioning behind an outstretched arm. And that word is not Democracy! It is not even Truth, or Justice, or Socialism. It is Svoboda! Libertà! Freiheit! — Freedom.

And it is the great American word. Recently I have been read-ing again some of our great state papers. It struck me as interesting that the word "democracy" never occurs in either the Declaration of Independence or the Constitution of the United States.

We are not a free people because we are democratic. We are a democratic people because we were born free. Out of freedom, de-mocracy develops naturally. Out of democracy, and in its name, any-thing may develop, even despotism.

If I seek to revive this word in disrepute, this great American word "freedom," it is because I observe that "democracy" is suffer-ing assaults and defeats on all fronts. The word has become the very symbol of weakness. It covers so many conceptions of life and society that it has become a neutral word, almost a neuter word, and de-mocracy a sort of no-man's-land, between more aggressive and seem-ingly vigorous forms of social existence. Once it was defined by Lin-coln as government of the people, by the people, and for the people. Now, it apparently becomes corrupted into just one of the trilogy, government *for* the people, and every despot under the sun claims

2 Poisonous.

he has a mandate from the people to rule *for* them, and calls him-self, therefore, a democrat. We are told that Communism is adminis-tered in behalf of the proletariat, and that they being most numerous are the people, hence Russia is a democracy. Hitler and Mussolini claim to head democracies because at periodic intervals their actions are ratified by plebiscites, and because both systems depend on mass support.

The leading positive connotation of the word today is egali-tarianism, a form of government in which all are equal, and, par-ticularly, economically equal — economically leveled. But on that ground, present-day Germany, Italy and Russia are all far more democratic than the United States, Great Britain, the Scandinavian countries or France. The citizens of the former are more econom-ically equal than those of the latter. I will give you a definition of these great totalitarian states that will hold water, however you look at it. They are democracies without freedom! They are mass states, directed by mass organization and mass propaganda and enjoying mass support. They are democracies of a sort, even though they are also despotisms. And I warn you that they are revolutionary states. They represent the revolution of the twentieth century.

This revolution, which, wherever it occurs, develops the same pattern — collectivism, managed and dominated by a monolithic [3] political party — has not just happened. It has social and historical reasons for coming into being. I would put first among them the awakening of the most poor and insecure to the realization that their political liberties could be used to force the richer members of the community to make economic concessions, as the rich in the past have used their political power to sanction exploitation.

The first crime against freedom came with the machine, with large-scale production, with, therefore, work for wages. In the days of crafts and small industries, the workman was a man who owned his own tools and performed his work for a price which he, as an in-dividual, could set. He could save, and there were numerous ways in which he could invest his money with a chance of winning se-curity for the future. He could, for instance, set himself up in a small

[3] Single, like a pillar made of one stone.

business, and by thrift and accumulated savings increase and prosper. But with large-scale machine industry the numbers of such men diminished. Business required larger and larger amounts of capital, and depended increasingly on credit, which was available only to those who already had large accumulations. Most men worked for such large businesses or organizations, and their work was treated as a commodity, like any other commodity, determined by the market. If the market was good, a man's work was wanted; if the market declined, his work was rejected, and from one day to another, from one hour to another, he could be dropped into worklessness.

Now, the very idea of freedom rests on a profound respect for humanity. It rests in a profound conception of human dignity. It rests in the belief in human brotherhood. It is deeply religious, or, if you prefer, ethical and moral in its basis. The idea of freedom derives from the conception of man as the child of God, as enormously valuable, as a person, as a human soul. And a man's work, or a woman's, is the very essence of his personality. We actually create ourselves through what we do. The skills which we develop under the discipline of work actually add to our stature as human beings. Work is life, and work is growth. To be unemployed is to rust, to have one's ego humiliated, to be cut off from the exercise of generosity, to be isolated, to be damned. And yet work, the very expression of the personality and the source of life itself, was treated as though it were a *thing*, to be bought and sold according to the market price of the day.

The advent of the machine would, in any case, have wrought a revolution in the world of work. For the workman often became a mere cog in a vast process. You can go into any factory and watch a man do nothing for six or seven hours a day except put rings on pistons as they move past on a never-pausing belt. Yet that too could be compensated for, if only the imagination were awakened to see that little process as part of something quite miraculous, which brings comfort and even luxury to millions — as part of a communal work endeavor.

But the technological revolution, accompanied by the damnable idea of work as a commodity, detached, as it were, from the worker himself, resulted in two things: enormous insecurity for the worker, and a pernicious but inevitable attitude toward work itself — an attitude of irresponsibility, lack of pride in work, lack of joy in work. The worker himself adopted the attitude of the employer — why should he not? If work was a *thing*, determined by the market, then his business was the business of all traders — to get as much as he could for as little as he could give. Where once the ancient guilds of workers took upon themselves responsibility for the quality of workmanship of their numbers, the modern trade union confines itself exclusively to bargaining for a price for this commodity, which is men's hands and brains, and blood, and food, and the lives of their children.

Where once there was joy and community in work, sullenness and hostility replaced it. And the class conflict arose, and in some countries became so acute that a deadlock was reached, between men bargaining for the commodity of their lives and the employers and managers, whose willingness to undertake heavy responsibilities and risks depends upon the possibility of operating at *some* profit. When many such deadlocks become general, then there is economic breakdown, and when such economic breakdowns occur in too rapid succession, the people scream for someone to take the responsibility and restore order.

And they turn to the government — that is to say to the State. The State becomes one great work monopoly. The worker must work at what he is told, in the way he is told, or he is thrown into prison. Since you cannot run a great monopoly of life and industry by the votes of its members, the citizen loses all his political rights.

Even his religious life, even his love life is interfered with. For if a man has a concept of God, he may remember that he is a man, and an individual. So the State tries to gather up into itself those dangerous religious and aesthetic impulses, that yearning after beauty, that picture that a man has of something better than himself, on which to pattern his life and lend meaning to it. The boss becomes God, too, and his subjects are trained in all the ritual of idolatry.

Such a structure, like all forms of slavery and vassalage, rests on force; force is of its very nature, and it is of its very nature that it be organized like an army, and as an army must go forth to conquer.

People can only be held together in this sort of rigid unity, if they are held together *against* something. This sort of state requires a perennial enemy. First, the bourgeoisie — in Russia — or the Jews, in Germany. But the internal enemies are soon eliminated, by terror. Then one must seek new ones — internally or externally. And the more powerful and efficient of these states, Italy, Germany and Japan, are seeking them externally, and with a common tactic; operating in spheres of influence agreed upon between them, they today menace the whole world.

Japan's aims do not stop short of all Asia, Germany's aims do not stop short of all Europe, and with the conquest of Czechoslovakia she has put herself in the position which Bismarck described when he said, "Who is master of Prague is master of Europe." For the time being, at least, Hitler dictates the policy of London and Paris, without a war, by the very fear of war. And in order to save something for themselves, it is possible that the last of the big European democracies will attempt to divert the attention of Germany and Italy toward another place, and that other place is the western hemisphere.

The first menace which threatens us from this source is the menace of our own internal discontent, which will be, and is being, played upon. There is a hypnotic quality about success. I have observed that in the last month the friends of Nazism have grown greatly in this country. I observe that it has become fashionable in some circles to begin to observe a Jewish menace and an apprehension of Communism. What a comfort these circles are to those who would divide our house against itself, the more easily to render it vulnerable! I observe amongst our workers a terrible fear that the same society that in England and France flirted with the Fascists to their countries' undoing in humiliating defeat is also sympathetic to them here, and that this apprehension drives the workers, too, to more extreme positions.

But restore and make concrete America's own great revolutionary tradition, and this fear will be replaced with courage and action, and this courage and action will give hope and faith to millions, not only here but throughout the earth! The way toward our own internal unity is implicit in the American philosophy, to which, too long, we have been untrue. The worker must be restored to his prestige and self-respect as an individual. And the only way to do that is to give him a definite stake in the industry in which he works, to make him again a man who works for himself and for his family, instead of for the boss, with a definite, *legal* right to a *legal* share of the profits which his work produces. For this country must radically strengthen its defenses, and greatly increase its production, if we are to survive in the next years, and unless we choose to do this by slavery we must do it with the ardent collaboration of free men, whose work is done freely, competently, joyfully and pridefully, in the knowledge that the profits of that work will be justly distributed to those who create them. We must end the conception of work as a commodity and establish it for what it is, a great individual and co-operative effort in behalf of a free people and a free community, to be done with ardor and with love, in the service of a great ideal.

That nation, those people, who first make freedom real again, translating the word into a way of life, will make the great *moral* revolution, founded on respect for the individual, honor for the personality, and individual and social responsibility. And whatever may be the revolution of today, that, I am sure, is the revolution of the future.

APPRECIATION HINTS

1. What does the author say about the word " freedom "?
2. What does she say about the word " democracy "?
3. In what sense of the word is Germany more " democratic " than the United States?
4. What is the author's definition of the totalitarian states?
5. What is one reason she gives for the revolution coming into being?
6. Explain how the machine has robbed workmen of their freedom.
7. From what central idea does the conception of personal freedom spring?
8. What does she mean by " the worker adopted the attitude of the employer " toward work?

9. What is the final result of continual conflict between workers and employers?
10. What is Dorothy Thompson's proposal for restoring prestige and self-respect to the individual workingman?
11. What changes in " tomorrow's world " in America do you think will be necessary?
12. What statements or predictions made in this 1938 address have been verified?
13. Do you know any industries in which workers share in the profits?
14. Can you recall some scenes in one of Chaplain's films which show the effects of monotonous work in a factory?
15. Explain what is meant by " work " being regarded as a " commodity," and show some of the consequences.
16. Write a composition based on a topic suggested by this essay. Possible titles: What " Freedom " Means to Me, Making Fords, The Village Blacksmith, What I Want to Work At, How I Got a Job, In the Factory.
17. Read *Men and Machines*, by Stuart Chase.

FREEDOM—THE GREAT AMERICAN WORD

Sir, I know the uncertainty of human affairs, but I see, I see clearly, through this day's business. You and I, indeed, may rue it. We may not live to the time when this Declaration shall be made good. We may die; die colonists; die slaves; die, it may be, ignominiously and on the scaffold. Be it so.

Be it so. If it be the pleasure of Heaven that my country shall require the poor offering of my life, the victim shall be ready, at the appointed hour of sacrifice, come when that hour may. But while I do live, let me have a country, and that a free country. . . .

Sir, before God, I believe the hour is come. My judgment approves this measure, and my whole heart is in it. All I have, and all that I am, and all that I hope, in this life, I am now ready to stake upon it; and I leave off as I began, that live or die, survive or perish, I am for the Declaration. John Adams in 1776

STUART CHASE 1888– THIS ESSAY describes an example of government facing the world of tomorrow. In the building of the Grand Coulee Dam the American people has demonstrated that pioneer spirit of which Archibald MacLeish speaks, the spirit which tackles a big tough job in order to make a country fit for free men to live in. A New Englander who well knows that the age of the old individual pioneering has closed looks down from the canyon's rim at the Colorado a thousand feet below, and at the progress of the colossal task of chaining it for the service of men. In this essay we feel his pride and share it, as he recognizes a great example of the national will at work — democracy in action — to promote the health and happiness of men. "We may be poor at shuffling stocks and bonds, but, by the eternal, we can build dams! "

This essay is a good one to read, not merely because Stuart Chase always has something to say, and knows how to say it, but because he has spent the last twenty years in emphasizing and interpreting to us the living issues of today and tomorrow. We know these books come from an able man; we like them, and look for them because, whether right or wrong, they come from a man honest and incorruptible. Indeed it is Stuart Chase's awareness of the damage done to the inner integrity of men and women by the prevailing ethics of politics and business that inspires him to speak out.

Stuart Chase graduated at Harvard with the class of 1910, which produced five other famous men. He worked in his father's accounting firm, became a Certified Public Accountant, investigated several American industries under the Federal Trade Commission, including the meat packers. *A Honeymoon Experiment*, 1916, records the studies in unemployment made by the newly-married Chases, when they presented themselves in a strange city as a couple out of work. *The Tragedy of Waste* appeared in 1925. *The Economy of Abundance* in 1934, *Idle Money Idle Men* in 1940. Stuart Chase likes high mountains and clean-cut thinking; he dislikes billboards and high-pressure salesmen.

Great Dam

IN A desert in Egypt has stood for six thousand years the most massive structure ever built by man. In a desert in the State of Washington a new champion arises. The Great Pyramid weighs some 7,000,000 tons — say 120 *Queen Marys* piled together and squashed solid. The Grand Coulee Dam on the Columbia River already exceeds this total. When it is finished it will weigh 23,000,000 tons, more than thrice the heft of Cheops.

One of these masses is built of cut stone, the other of poured concrete. One took 50,000 men twenty years to build, the other will take 5,000 men six years, in a task not only three times greater but vastly more complex and dangerous. Both structures relied on the labor of those who would otherwise have been unemployed. Egyptian peasants in the off season built Cheops; American workingmen and engineers shelved by a great depression are building Grand Coulee. Pyramids were houses for the dead. Dams are centers of energy for the living. It is better, I think, to live in the age of the Great Dams than in the age of the Great Pyramids.

Owners of stocks and bonds in utility companies, to judge by their dinner-table conversation, prefer pyramids. It is still too early, however, to calculate the final effect of cheap hydroelectric power on utility earnings. In the Tennessee Valley, to date, power from government dams has so stimulated consumption that some private utilities in the South are said to be doing the best business in their history. The big dams, however, are not primarily power projects, I believe, but something more fundamental. In the last hundred years, man has all but wrecked the balance of nature in the North American continent. Flood, drought, dust storms, erosion, the destruction of forest and grass cover, are making severe inroads on the organic stability of the United States. Some 10,000,000 Americans have already lost their living from natural resources. The most important function of the great dams will be to restore equilibrium. . . .

I reached the site from Spokane by motor in about two hours. We crossed a dry, rolling plain, with a few prosperous farms and the scars of much erosion. It is always difficult for an Easterner to realize that east of the Cascade Mountains, which are not far from the coast, large sections of Washington and Oregon are natural cow country, arid as the Great Plains. . . . The sky has a luminous quality such as you see in the Southwest, but the landscape is comparatively dull. Suddenly the plain bursts open! We halt at the rim of a canyon and look down into the depths. At the bottom, one thousand feet below, the Columbia is doing a hairpin turn, twisting from a southwest flow to a northeast flow. The canyon is scarred with excavations, and just beyond the twist is the line of the dam. This is an urgent river, white-foamed and charging, quite different from the murky, placid Mississippi.

We wind down a steep switchback road to the bottom. Four years ago there was a sheep path here, one sorry peach orchard, and a crude ferry to take the sheep across to pasture. Charlie Osborne ran the orchard, and Sam Seaton ran the ferry. They constituted the total population of the canyon. The walls and river looked much as they did after the last ice sheet moved north.

They look different now. When American engineers move, they move. Government dams are said to lack the incentive of private profit. Then what incentive has driven the colossal, earth-changing force which has been loosed here? There is a dump pile that could swallow the Empire State Building. There is a conveyor system, of the general dimensions of Brooklyn Bridge, to carry gravel from the dump pile to the cement mixers. The mixers would dwarf a Minneapolis grain elevator. There are three distinct towns where as many as 15,000 people have lived — workers and their families.

The dam is low and straight, shouldered deep into scarred granite walls on either side of the canyon. The river pours through a series of cement grooves in the center, arranged like huge building blocks. To the right and left, the walls are higher, and on the downside the emplacements for the twin powerhouses have been made ready. On top of the dam I see an object which looks like a red box for thumbtacks, but which turns out, on closer inspection, to be a standard box freight car. Only then do I begin to grasp the sheer magnitude of the mass.

Most of it is already under water. The big job has been done. The cofferdams which shunted the river now to the east and then to the west, so that bedrock might be bared and the foundations poured, have been removed. They were as long as the dam at Muscle Shoals. On the great swelling foundation it now remains to build up the narrower top another three hundred feet; up to those marks on either side of the canyon walls where the big signs are posted: SAFETY PAYS. Pour, pour, pour, for three more years.

The big job, the hard job, is done. It took thousands of sweating men; it took forty lives. Nothing like it has ever been accomplished in the world before. Grand Coulee is anchored for millennia in its granite cradle, its joints grouted by cement and water, under high pressure, to form one monolithic mass. Norris Dam is a toy compared to this. Boulder looks more dramatic, arched and dead white in its narrower, blue-black canyon; but, for all its greater height, its bulk is only a third as great.

This dam, on the second largest river on the continent, may remain the grandest structure ever built by man for a thousand years to come. It has been designed to take the Columbia at full flood over the upper spillways — one million cubic feet per second, five times the flow of Niagara, and three times the height of the fall. That will be a sight to travel round the world to see! Will she hold? She will. We Americans may be poor hands at shuffling stocks and bonds and credit instruments in a manner to keep the economic structure from collapsing, but, by the eternal, we can build dams. . . .

We climb into the car again, and wind up the west canyon wall to the rim. Leading off to the south is another canyon, or coulee, which is dry. The bottom is perhaps seven hundred feet above where the river is now. It is about two miles wide, with sheer rock walls on either side. In the middle is a great mesa called Steamboat Rock. The walls are stained with orange and red lichens, and snow lies in the fissures. This is dramatic scenery, worthy of New Mexico. We follow the canyon down some thirty miles, where it ends in a 400-foot precipice, curved in a great bow three miles wide. These are the famous " Dry Falls." At the bottom are a few small pools of water, and many rattlesnakes. . . .

It is in the higher canyon that the storage reservoir is to be situated. *This technically is the " Grand Coulee."* A 70-foot earth dam will be built at either end, stretching from wall to wall. Steamboat Rock will become a flat-topped island. A battery of giant pumps, just behind the river dam on the west side, will lift water from the lower lake up into the Grand Coulee. The vertical distance is 280 feet. The balancing reservoir will then feed the irrigation area off to the south, by gravity canals, of which the longest will run for one hundred miles. Thus men are doing in a smaller way what the Ice Age did in a bigger way — spreading the waters of the Columbia over the plains below the Dry Falls. . . .

After flowing through the dam, the river turns west and then south in a great bend, and forms the westerly boundary of the proposed irrigation area. But to get water into the area the river must be tapped much farther upstream. A man named Billy Clapp, eating ham and eggs in a cafeteria in the little town of Ephrata, in 1918, is credited with solving the riddle. He thumped the table with his coffee cup and proposed to duplicate the geology of the Ice Age. They called him a crackpot until Colonel Goethals,[1] after a careful survey, checked the plan. Hoover and Coolidge then fell into line. It remained for Roosevelt actually to start the dirt flying.

The area to be irrigated is almost as large as Connecticut. It is estimated that two grand canals coming down from the balancing reservoir, one to the west, one to the east, with their feeders, can transform 1,200,000 acres from semidesert to a garden spot. The skeptic can cross the river, drive a few miles to the west and see the Yakima Valley, as lush a garden spot as you please, already reclaimed from desert by irrigation. In 1900 there were 13,000 people in the Yakima Valley; now there are 110,000.

First and last, Yakima and many other irrigation projects have had a lot of trouble with land speculators. These fast-moving gentlemen discount the future work of farmer and God. They harness the farmer with a staggering debt burden before he plants a crop. At Grand Coulee for once the dirt farmer will get a break. Congress has passed a law forbidding land speculators to practice here. The area will be condemned and valued as desert land. The bona fide settler will pay desert prices — say $7.50 an acre. If he later sells, it must be at desert-land valuation — plus his tangible improvements. The farmer will be charged by the government, without interest, for his share of the irrigation investment, plus his share of the maintenance cost of getting water on his land. A single man will be entitled to not more than forty acres; a family to not more than eighty. A total family investment for land, water costs, house, barn, tools, machinery, electric-power connection, has not been determined. Estimates run from $8,000 to $10,000. . . .

How about the financial and business aspect? Where is the money coming from? Who's going to pay for it? Why bring in more

[1] American military engineer responsible for the construction of the Panama Canal and Muscle Shoals.

agricultural land when farmers all over the country have gone broke because they have produced so much? Who is going to use a billion kilowatts of farm power from the dam — grasshoppers, prairie dogs? If even part of the power is used, what is going to happen to the widows and orphans who have put their hard-earned savings into utility securities?

These are relevant questions. But they are not all the questions. The impartial conclusion as to the social and economic justification of Grand Coulee can be arrived at only after *all* the relevant questions have been taken into consideration. For instance: Why do Chambers of Commerce in the Northwest enthusiastically support the project? Why did Goethals, Hoover, and Coolidge favor it? If there are 10,000,000 unemployed persons in the country who should be given work if possible, is it better to put them at building battle-ships, raking leaves, or constructing new energy stations for food, water, conservation, recreation, and electric power? If men must be fed anyway, is it better to get something useful for the taxpayer's money, or to get nothing, and let the men rot into the ranks of the unemployables? If investors in private power companies are really damaged, may it not be better to compensate them directly than to deny cheap power to millions of consumers?

What is going to happen to the 100,000 migrants from the dust bowl into the Northwest? Many of them are excellent farmers. Is it better to give them new land for the lands they have lost, and let them at least feed themselves, or to allow them to haunt the bread lines, the relief stations, and the factory doors of the Pacific States, while their families drift from bad to worse? I have seen them. I have talked to them. They want to be given a chance to go to work. They look to these new projects as the Israelites looked to Canaan.

Where are the crop surpluses which cause most of the trouble? In wheat, cotton, corn, and tobacco. What irrigated crops are grown in the Northwest? Apples, pears, nuts, celery, alfalfa, grapes, dairy products, and specialty livestock. Are American consumers surfeited with these products? They are not. They may be surfeited in some areas with hog and hominy, corn pone and sowbelly, but not with apples, celery, tomatoes, butter, and such products rich in vitamins.

I do not mean that market surpluses never occur in these crops, but that they are smaller and are usually consumable.

Has the consumption of power in the Northwest grown at the rate of 9.5 per cent, compounded annually, in recent years? It has. Is population growing in this area? Owing to one of the greatest migrations in history, it is growing rapidly. Even if the growth rate of power consumption is cut in half, will all of the power from Grand Coulee be absorbed? Every kilowatt-hour, in less than fifteen years. Are there possibilities of new electrochemical industries in the region? In Idaho is the largest known deposit of phosphate rock in the world. Power is needed to turn it into fertilizer. Does increased power use follow a lowering of rates? Almost always. Does the cost of power drop with increased load? Almost always. Is it a good idea to build up more regional self-sufficiency, saving long freight hauls and excessive interdependence? Is it economic to mine ore in Washington and send it to Pittsburgh to be refined, to Bridgeport to be machined, and back to Washington to be consumed as a finished product? Is it wholesome or desirable to have the West and South in perpetual hock to New York?

These, also, are relevant questions. I have indicated answers to some of them. Others require more study than they have yet received. Perhaps, on balance, the great dams are not justified by the financial beliefs of 1928. Perhaps they are not altogether sound, self-liquidating investments at 6 per cent. But this, sigh as we may, is 1940, and, for better or worse, a different world. Nineteen fifty promises to be stranger still. We can never go back to 1928.

We are going hell-bent for somewhere, the like of which, financially, has never been seen before. This is also true of Europe under the impact of the war. Concrete dams in granite cradles are solid. They are not like debentures and mortgages, which go up in smoke. Even companies owning skyscrapers go up in smoke, but the steel and concrete never quiver. In a time of disturbing transition, it may not be a bad idea to build solid things that add to the long-range wealth and energy of the people; that reduce flood and drought, water the desert, conserve soil, supply " protective " foods, and release great blocks of light, heat, and power.

I may be wrong. Right or wrong, no American can stand below the spillways of the Grand Coulee and not be proud to belong to the nation which could rear this mighty thing.

APPRECIATION HINTS

1. Compare the magnitude of the work necessary to make the Grand Pyramid with that needed to make the Grand Coulee Dam.
2. What is the chief purpose of the great dams?
3. Describe the situation of the dam in relation to the river.
4. Describe the situation and the function of the " Grand Coulee " in relation to the dam.
5. How will the dirt farmer at Grand Coulee " get a break "?
6. What are some of the questions connected with the building of the Grand Coulee Dam?
7. Which crop surpluses cause most trouble? What crops are needed in greater quantity?
8. What is going to happen to the migrants from the dust bowl?
9. Perhaps there is someone in the group who has seen the Grand Coulee Dam since 1940 and can describe what it looks like now.
10. What other great reservoirs of power and water has the Federal Government already finished, or is planning to construct?
11. In view of the needs of today, are such works justified? Why?
12. What are some of the other great examples of American skill in engineering?
13. Read again the second paragraph of this essay, and write a composition on the purpose of great structures of this kind. Has your town any " houses for the dead "? Has the United States? What is their value? How are they different from the Great Pyramids?
14. Write a composition on a topic suggested by this essay. Possible titles: A Great Piece of Engineering, The Dust Bowl, The View from on Top, When I Was an Engineer, Damming the Stream, Give the Farmer a Break.
15. Read " The Luxury of Integrity " in *The Nemesis of American Business;* " Six Modest Proposals " in *Idle Money Idle Men.* You would also be interested in *The Tyranny of Words.*

I wonder that some people I know do not refuse to look at the new moon out of respect for that ancient institution — the old one.

Douglas Jerrold

WALTER LIPPMANN 1889–

TRAVELERS were beginning a long journey, driving westward on a road which led, they had been told, to a beautiful land. At a place where the highway divided they took the left fork, because men working on the road told them that was the right way. Besides, it was smoother and newer than the other. For hours they drove along it; but the landscape was disturbing, and the sun did not seem to be in the right quarter. A road surveyor stood by the wayside, and the travelers stopped and asked whether this was the way to the happy land they sought. " I'm sorry," he replied, " but you took the wrong fork sixty miles back."

That is the central thought of the following essay if we make these substitutions. Instead of the travelers' automobile, imagine a colossal bus with the eight million students in our high schools and colleges on board; instead of the road traveled, the course of American education; instead of sixty miles, sixty years; instead of the road surveyor, Walter Lippmann.

But the essay is not so simple as this little fable might indicate. It is the hardest reading in this book — a real test of your power to read. The chief reason for your making every effort to understand what the essay means is that *you are on the bus.* Lincoln Steffens was on the bus; and in his *Autobiography* — his " search for meanings " — he tells how he looked in vain in schools and colleges for someone to tell him where the bus was going. When one is lost, the first thing is to know it. Mr. Lippmann in this essay is not concerned to point out the exact road we should take to rejoin the highway; he wants us to realize first that we have taken the wrong road in education. If the bus has lost its way, everyone who is traveling on it, and everyone who is helping to drive it should know, for their own sakes and for the sake of their children present or to come. And there is another reason for urging you to master this essay. If Mr. Lippmann's thesis is correct, it helps to explain such a phenomenon as Hitler, and shows the danger that the future may breed scourges even more terrible unless education can once more humanize mankind. It will help you to understand the essay if, after you have read it over, you try to answer the first sixteen questions placed at the end.

This challenge comes from a notably thoughtful and able mind. Walter Lippmann is best known to the public through his column entitled *Today and Tomorrow*, read three times a week by eight million people. He graduated with honors in three years at Harvard, where he was a friend of the great psychologist, William James. As a young man, Lippmann helped Lincoln Steffens in the investigation of corruption in business and municipal government and aided in cleaning up the crooked politics of Schenectady, New York. He was called to Washington to be secretary to Newton D. Baker, Secretary of War under Woodrow Wilson, and later joined the staff of the New York *World* in 1921, and of the New York *Herald Tribune* in 1931. He is the author of *A Preface to Politics*, 1913, and *A Preface to Morals*, 1929. In the latter book Mr. Lippmann tries to help us construct a credible basis for our ideals.

This essay was originally delivered under the auspices of the Phi Beta Kappa Society at the annual meeting of the American Association for the Advancement of Science at the University of Pennsylvania in December, 1940.

Education vs. Western Civilization

IT WAS once the custom in the great universities to propound a series of theses which, as Cotton Mather [1] put it, the student had to " defend manfully." I should like to revive this custom by propounding a thesis about the state of education in this troubled age.

The thesis which I venture to submit to you is as follows:

That during the past forty or fifty years those who are responsible for education have progressively removed from the curriculum of studies the Western culture which produced the modern democratic state;

That the schools and colleges have, therefore, been sending out into the world men who no longer understand the creative principle of the society in which they must live;

That, deprived of their cultural tradition, the newly educated Western men no longer possess in the form and substance of their own minds and spirits, the ideas, the premises, the rationale, the logic, the method, the values or the deposited wisdom which are the genius of the development of Western civilization;

That the prevailing education is destined, if it continues, to destroy Western civilization and is in fact destroying it;

[1] Cotton Mather (1663–1728), son of one of the early presidents of Harvard, was a Puritan writer and preacher.

That our civilization cannot effectively be maintained where it still flourishes, or be restored where it has been crushed, without the revival of the central, continuous, and perennial culture of the Western world;

And that, therefore, what is now required in the modern educational system is not the expansion of its facilities or the specific reform of its curriculum and administration but a thorough reconsideration of its underlying assumptions and of its purposes.

I realize quite well that this thesis constitutes a sweeping indictment of modern education. But I believe that the indictment is justified and that there is a prima facie case for entertaining this indictment.

Universal and compulsory modern education was established by the emancipated democracies during the 19th century. "No other sure foundation can be devised," said Thomas Jefferson, "for the preservation of freedom and happiness." Yet as a matter of fact during the 20th century the generations trained in these schools have either abandoned their liberties or they have not known, until the last desperate moment, how to defend them. The schools were to make men free. They have been in operation for some sixty or seventy years and what was expected of them they have not done. The plain fact is that the graduates of the modern schools are the actors in the catastrophe which has befallen our civilization. Those who are responsible for modern education — for its controlling philosophy — are answerable for the results.

They have determined the formation of the mind and education of modern men. As the tragic events unfold they cannot evade their responsibility by talking about the crimes and follies of politicians, businessmen, labor leaders, lawyers, editors and generals. They have conducted the schools and colleges and they have educated the politicians, businessmen, labor leaders, lawyers, editors and generals. What is more they have educated the educators.

They have had money, lots of it, fine buildings, big appropriations, great endowments and the implicit faith of the people that the school was the foundation of democracy. If the results are bad, and indubitably they are, on what ground can any of us who are in any

way responsible for education disclaim our responsibility or decline
to undertake a profound searching of our own consciences and a
deep re-examination of our philosophy. . . .

The institutions of the Western world were formed by men who
learned to regard themselves as inviolable persons because they were
rational and free. They meant by rational that they were capable of
comprehending the moral order of the universe and their place in
this moral order. They meant when they regarded themselves as free
that within that order they had a personal moral responsibility to
perform their duties and to exercise their corresponding rights. From
this conception of the unity of mankind in a rational order the Western world has derived its conception of law — which is that all men
and all communities of men and all authority among men are subject
to law, and that the character of all particular laws is to be judged
by whether they conform to or violate, approach or depart from the
rational order of the universe and of man's nature. From this conception of law was derived the idea of constitutional government and
of the consent of the governed and of civil liberty. Upon this conception of law our own institutions were founded.

This, in barest outline, is the specific outlook of Western men.
This, we may say, is the structure of the Western spirit. This is the
formation which distinguishes it. The studies and the disciplines
which support and form this spiritual outlook and habit are the creative cultural tradition of Europe and the Americas. In this tradition
our world was made. By this tradition it must live. Without this tradition our world, like a tree cut off from its roots in the soil, must die
and be replaced by alien and barbarous things.

It is necessary today in a discussion of this sort to define and
identify what we mean when we speak of Western culture. This is
in itself ominous evidence of what the official historian of Harvard
University has called " the greatest educational crime of the century
against American youth, — depriving him of his classical heritage."
For there will be many, the victims of this educational crime, who
will deny that there is such a thing as Western culture.

Yet the historic fact is that the institutions we cherish — and now

know we must defend against the most determined and efficient attack ever organized against them — are the products of a culture
which, as Gilson put it,

is essentially the culture of Greece, inherited from the Greeks by the Romans, transfused by the Fathers of the Church with the religious teachings
of Christianity, and progressively enlarged by countless numbers of artists,
writers, scientists and philosophers from the beginning of the Middle Ages
up to the first third of the nineteenth century.

The men who wrote the American Constitution and the Bill of
Rights were educated in schools and colleges in which the classic
works of this culture were the substance of the curriculum. In these
schools the transmission of this culture was held to be the end and
aim of education.

Modern education, however, is based on a denial that it is necessary or useful or desirable for the schools and colleges to continue
to transmit from generation to generation the religious and classical
culture of the Western world. It is, therefore, much easier to say
what modern education rejects than to find out what modern education teaches. Modern education rejects and excludes from the curriculum of necessary studies the whole religious tradition of the
West. It abandons and neglects as no longer necessary the study of
the whole classical heritage of the great works of great men.

Thus there is an enormous vacuum where until a few decades
ago there was the substance of education. And with what is that
vacuum filled: it is filled with the elective, eclectic,[2] the specialized,
the accidental and incidental improvisations and spontaneous curi-
osities of teachers and students. There is no common faith, no common body of principle, no common body of knowledge, no common
moral and intellectual discipline. Yet the graduates of these modern
schools are expected to form a civilized community. They are expected to govern themselves. They are expected to have a social conscience. They are expected to arrive by discussion at common purposes. When one realizes that they have no common culture is it
astounding that they have no common purpose? That they worship

[2] Made up of selected material.

false gods? That only in war do they unite? That in the fierce struggle for existence they are tearing Western society to pieces? They
are the graduates of an educational system in which, though attend-
ance is compulsory, the choice of the subject matter of education
is left to the imagination of college presidents, trustees and professors, or even to the whims of the pupils themselves. We have established a system of education in which we insist that while everyone
must be educated, yet there is nothing in particular that an educated
man must know.

For it is said that since the invention of the steam engine we live
in a new era, an era so radically different from all preceding ages
that the cultural tradition is no longer relevant, is in fact misleading.
I submit to you that this is a rationalization, that this is a pretended
reason for the educational void which we now call education. The
real reason, I venture to suggest, is that we reject the religious and
classical heritage, first, because to master it requires more effort than
we are willing to compel ourselves to make, and, second, because it
creates issues that are too deep and too contentious to be faced with
equanimity. We have abolished the old curriculum because we are
afraid of it, afraid to face any longer in a modern democratic society
the severe discipline and the deep, disconcerting issues of the nature
of the universe, and of man's place in it and of his destiny.

I recognize the practical difficulties and the political danger of
raising these questions and I shall not offer you a quick and easy
remedy. For the present discussion all I am concerned with is that
we should begin to recognize the situation as it really is and that we
should begin to search our hearts and consciences.

We must confess, I submit, that modern education has renounced the idea that the pupil must learn to understand himself,
his fellow men and the world in which he is to live as bound together
in an order which transcends his immediate needs and his present
desires. As a result the modern school has become bound to conceive
the world as a place where the child, when he grows up, must com-
pete with other individuals in a struggle for existence. And so the
education of his reason and of his will must be designed primarily
to facilitate his career.

By separating education from the classical religious tradition the school cannot train the pupil to look upon himself as an inviolable person because he is made in the image of God. These very words, though they are the noblest words in our language, now sound archaic. The school cannot look upon society as a brotherhood arising out of a conviction that men are made in a common image. The teacher has no subject matter that even pretends to deal with the elementary and universal issues of human destiny. The graduate of the modern school knows only by accident and by hearsay whatever wisdom mankind has come to in regard to the nature of men and their destiny.

For the vital core of the civilized tradition of the West is by definition excluded from the curriculum of the modern, secular, democratic school. The school must sink, therefore, into being a mere training ground for personal careers. Its object must then be to equip individual careerists and not to form fully civilized men. The utility of the schools must than be measured by their success in equipping specialists for successful rivalry in the pursuit of their separate vocations. Their cultural ideal must then be to equip the individual to deal practically with immediate and discrete difficulties, to find by trial and error immediately workable and temporarily satisfactory expedients.

For if more than this were attempted the democratic secular school would have to regard the pupil as having in him not merely an ambition but a transcendent relationship [3] that must regulate his ambition. The schools would have to regard science as the progressive discovery of this order in the universe. They would have to cultivate Western tradition and transmit it to the young, proving to them that this tradition is no mere record of the obsolete fallacies of the dead but that it is a deposit of living wisdom.

But the emancipated democracies have renounced the idea that the purpose of education is to transmit the Western culture. Thus there is a cultural vacuum, and this cultural vacuum was bound to produce, in fact it has produced, progressive disorder. For the more men have become separated from the spiritual heritage which binds

[3] A relationship with a divine force outside himself.

them together, the more has education become egoist, careerist,[4] specialist and asocial.[5]

In abandoning the classical religious culture of the West the schools have ceased to affirm the central principal of the Western philosophy of life — that man's reason is the ruler of his appetites. They have reduced reason to the role of servant to man's appetites. The working philosophy of the emancipated democracies is, as a celebrated modern psychologist has put it, that " the instinctive impulses determine the *end* of all activities . . . and the most highly developed mind *is but* the instrument by which those impulses seek their satisfaction."

The logic of this conception of the human reason must lead progressively to a system of education which sharpens the acquisitive and domineering and possessive instincts. And in so far as the instincts, rather than reason, determine the ends of our activity the end of all activity must become the accumulation of power over men in the pursuit of the possession of things. So when parents and taxpayers in a democracy ask whether education is useful for life they tend by and large to mean by useful that which equips the pupil for a career which will bring him money and place and power.

The reduction of reason to an instrument of each man's personal career must mean also that education is emptied of its content. For what the careerist has to be taught are the data that he may need in order to succeed. Thus all subjects of study are in principle of equal value. There are no subjects which all men belonging to the same civilization need to study. In the realms of knowledge the student elects those subjects which will presumably equip him for success in his career; for the student there is then no such thing as a general order of knowledge which he is to possess in order that it may regulate his specialty.

And just as the personal ambition of the student rather than social tradition determines what the student shall learn, so the inquiry and the research of the scholar becomes more and more disconnected from any general and regulating body of knowledge.

---

[4] Devoted to preparing one for a career.
[5] Not concerned with how our own actions affects others.

It is this specialized and fundamentally disordered development of knowledge which has turned so much of man's science into the means of his own destruction. For as reason is regarded as no more than the instrument of men's desires, applied science inflates enormously the power of men's desires. Since reason is not the ruler of these desires, the power which science places in men's hands is ungoverned.

Quickly it becomes ungovernable. Science is the product of intelligence. But if the function of the intelligence is to be the instrument of the acquisitive, the possessive and the domineering impulses, then these impulses, so strong by nature, must become infinitely stronger when they are equipped with all the resources of man's intelligence.

That is why men today are appalled by the discovery that when modern man fights he is the most destructive animal ever known on this planet; that when he is acquisitive he is the most cunning and efficient; that when he dominates the weak he has engines of oppression and of calculated cruelty and deception no antique devil could have imagined.

And, at last, education founded on the secular [6] image of man must destroy knowledge itself. For if its purpose is to train the intelligence of specialists in order that by trial and error they may find a satisfying solution of particular difficulties, then each situation and each problem has to be examined as a novelty. This is supposed to be " scientific." But in fact it is a denial of that very principle which has made possible the growth of science.

For what enables men to know more than their ancestors is that they start with a knowledge of what their ancestors have already learned. They are able to do advanced experiments which increase knowledge because they do not have to repeat the elementary experiments. It is tradition which brings them to the point where advanced experimentation is possible. This is the meaning of tradition. This is why a society can be progressive only if it conserves its tradition.

---

[6] Man as concerned only with the present world, or with things not religious.

The notion that every problem can be studied as such with an open and empty mind, without preconception, without knowing what has already been learned about it, must condemn men to a chronic childishness. For no man, and no generation of men, is capable of inventing for itself the arts and sciences of a high civilization. No one, and no one generation, is capable of rediscovering all the truths men need, of developing sufficient knowledge by applying a mere intelligence, no matter how acute, to mere observation, no matter how accurate. The men of any generation, as Bernard of Chartres put it, are like dwarfs seated on the shoulders of giants. If we are to " see more things than the ancients and things more distant " it is " due neither to the sharpness of our sight nor the greatness of our stature " but " simply because they have lent us their own."

For individuals do not have the time, the opportunity or the energy to make all the experiments and to discern all the significance that have gone into the making of the whole heritage of civilization. In developing knowledge men must collaborate with their ancestors. Otherwise they must begin, not where their ancestors arrived but where their ancestors began. If they exclude the tradition of the past from the curricula of the schools they make it necessary for each generation to repeat the errors rather than to benefit by the successes of its predecessors.

Having cut him off from the tradition of the past, modern secular education has isolated the individual. It has made him a careerist — without social connection — who must make his way — without benefit of man's wisdom — through a struggle in which there is no principle of order. This is the uprooted and incoherent modern " free man " that Mr. Bertrand Russell has so poignantly described, the man who sees

surrounding the narrow raft illumined by the flickering light of human comradeship, the dark ocean on whose rolling waves we toss for a brief hour; from the great night without, a chill blast breaks in upon our refuge; all the loneliness of humanity amid hostile forces is concentrated upon the individual soul, which must struggle alone, with what of courage it can command, against the whole weight of the universe that cares nothing for its hopes and fears.

This is what the free man, in reality merely the freed and up-rooted and dispossessed man, has become. But he is not the stoic that Mr. Russell would have him be. To "struggle alone" is more than the freed man can bear to do. And so he gives up his freedom and surrenders his priceless heritage, unable as he is constituted to overcome his insoluble personal difficulties and to endure his awful isolation.

APPRECIATION HINTS

1. Which of the three following statements best summarizes this essay?
  (a) The main purpose of education should be to make us able to earn a living
  (b) The main purpose of education should be to make us useful citizens of the United States.
  (c) The main purpose of education should be to make us acquainted with what men have learned in the past and with the values they have found to be permanent.
2. What important part of the curriculum has been removed during the last 60 years?
3. Why is this part of the curriculum important in our education?
4. When was universal and compulsory high-school education established? For what purpose? What evidence is there that that purpose has not been accomplished?
5. What did the founders of our institutions mean when they declared man to be *rational* and *free*? Free for what?
6. If men are rational and free, what is the object of the laws they write?
7. What were the origins of "Western culture"?
8. What was the substance of the curriculum in the schools where the writers of the Constitution of the United States studied?
9. What three reasons does Mr. Lippmann give for the abandonment of the classical heritage in our education?
10. What has been put into the "cultural vacuum" left in the curriculum by the removal of this classical heritage?
11. What is the central principle of the Western philosophy of life which modern education has ignored?
12. What principle has been substituted for it?
13. How does Mr. Lippmann explain the fact that so much of man's science has become the means of his destruction?
14. For what reason does he think that our education as it is must eventually destroy knowledge itself?

15. What is meant by the statement that the men of any generation are dwarfs seated on the shoulders of giants?

16. Why is it impossible to study every problem with an open and empty mind?

17. Do you think that " all subjects of study are in principle of equal value "? If not, which are the most important? Why?

18. Discuss the statement that there is nothing in particular that an educated man needs to know.

19. In what way has your education been a training in " a common body of knowledge "?

20. On what principle do you plan to select your future studies?

21. Discuss the following questions: Should all boys and girls go to high school? Should there be one course of study for all students in the senior high school? If not, what studies should be common to all students? Should there be different kinds of high schools to fit different kinds of boys and girls?

22. Write a composition based on your own education. Suggestions: My Reasons for Wanting to be Educated, The Studies I Think Essential, What Kind of Education Is Most Useful for Life? Man's Science as the Means of Man's Destruction, Dwarfs on the Shoulders of Giants.

Quarry the granite rock with razors, or moor the vessel with a thread of silk; then may you hope with such keen and delicate instruments as human knowledge and human reason to contend against those giants, the passion and the pride of man.

Cardinal Newman: *The Idea of a University*

Who can ever maintain that he alone is absolutely right? Man's field of vision is minute; language is an imperfect instrument; the problems of life burst all formulas.

Antoine de Saint Exupéry

LEWIS MUMFORD 1895-

IN THE light of what has happened since, this vivid picture of a leaky ship in a hurricane drawn by Lewis Mumford in 1940 to symbolize our country in a chaotic world is intensely interesting to read. A shock has made us recognize the truth of what he was vainly trying to teach us, and to do all we can to trim ship. This is one of the final chapters in the second of the stirring books in which Mr. Mumford has called on us to awake before it is too late. In the first of them, *Men Must Act*, published in 1939, he advocated a positive policy of nonintercourse with the avowed enemies of democracy; in the second, *Faith for Living*, he issued a call to arms against spiritual confusion and inertia. For he is mainly concerned that the internal spirit of America shall recover its original vigor; as he writes in this essay " nothing is lost if the spirit lives." His message is that to recover this spiritual health we must restore the ties of the family, rectify our attitude toward the soil, reform and refine ourselves.

Lewis Mumford is one of the youngest and one of the most influential critics of American life and literature. He is interested in social reforms not for their own sake but because of their effect on our culture. He is an authority on architecture, and he made proposals in *The Culture of the Cities* for the betterment of our cities of today and of tomorrow.

Lewis Mumford was born on Long Island and educated in New York City. He has lectured at The New School of Social Research, and has held Guggenheim Fellowships in 1932 and 1938. In 1942 he became a professor at Stanford University. He began his critical career writing for the *Fortnightly Dial*, and in this field his most notable work is *Herman Melville*, 1929. Mr. Mumford has been the adviser and helper of many young writers.

All Hands Save Ship!

WHEN A SHIP is battling through a storm of hurricane violence and has sprung leaks that the pumps cannot keep up with, there is sometimes one chance of keeping it afloat: throwing overboard its heavy cargo. No matter how precious that cargo may be, its weight may cause the ship to sink. If it is to ride the storm and save the lives aboard, Captain and crew must, with quick zeal, throw overboard all those things which, in calmer weather, might have been brought to their destination. And when the call, "All hands save ship!" is given, everyone must drop his familiar routine and bear a hand. At that moment all private choices vanish.

Plainly we are now in the midst of such a storm: and plainly, too, our ship is a leaky one. We would like to save everything that we value in our civilization, the small dear toys of our children no less than the canister of food, the deck chairs we relaxed in no less than our life belts. But the inexorable conditions we face will not permit it. We must save what is most worth saving, that which will ultimately serve our humanity, that which will guarantee that our children will have toys again, and the aged a place where they may quietly stretch their feet.

In short: we must save the vessel itself; our civilization and the institutions and habits of free men. Some day our children, perhaps only our great-grandchildren, will find a safe anchorage in quiet waters, within sight of a green coast and white buildings, and the sea gulls circling and the smell of grass floating over the waters.

This saying is harder than the figure of the storm-tossed vessel indicates; unless one remembers that those who stick to their posts in a storm to work the vessel may be caught in an avalanche of water and swept overboard. Unless they stick to their posts, no matter what cold terrors they face, the boat will sink. For we cannot do our job if we seek first to save our lives or even to protect our children's lives, once they are old enough to take their turn at the watch. We cannot save bodies. We can only save the spirit that makes those bodies significant.

In the long run it will not matter for humanity if London is ruined as completely as the heart of Rotterdam, provided that those who die in the ruins pass on to the survivors the spirit that is capable of building a greater London. Nothing whatever is saved if only the bodies and the buildings are saved: to crumble stone by stone; to die, drop by drop.

Similarly, nothing is lost if the spirit lives; for a little leaven will leaven the whole loaf. It is not those who sought safety first or who surrendered quickest who will carry on the work of our civilization. It is those who barely escaped with their lives, the Czechs who continued the struggle, the Poles, the Norwegians, the French, above all, the brave British who continued to fight. As for the rest, most of them were, pitiably, the appointed victims of fascism because they thought that their material goods mattered and their bodies were worth keeping alive. That is the conviction of corpses: to that degree, the most brutal fascist who risked his life was still a better man.

What we need, to get to port finally, is the ship itself, a few hands to navigate it, and above all the compass, the chart, the chronometer to give us our bearings. Nothing else matters perhaps. And if the violence and carnage spread, nothing else can be saved. We cannot preserve ourselves against this barbarism and worry about the cost of our effort: we must give beyond the ordinary power of giving. Nor can we ensure seven per cent profits or the eventual redemption of all our bonds and mortgages at par value; nor can we hold fast to a particular patent monopoly or a particular hourly wage scale. Only

one need counts: the need to save the institutions of a free civilization, the institutions of democracy, founded on a profound respect
for the personality of all men, and for a power, not ourselves, that
makes for righteousness.

Too late in the war the British and the French discovered how
great a sacrifice the danger demanded: the French were unprepared
for it until all they valued was indeed churned around and pounded
to pieces in the beating waters; until the plates were buckling and the
water swamping the hold. The ruling classes thought of an easy,
circumspect triumph, which would keep all their smug securities,
their imperial monopolies, their colonies, their landed and City interests functioning as always before for the convenience and comfort
of these classes. American businessmen — at least a very vocal minority — are still making the same mistake: some are even toying with
the earliest of Chamberlain's fatal stupidities, that of making a deal
with the fascists, on Chamberlain's very assumption, that after all
"we must live in the same world." Intelligence that has decayed so
far is almost liquid with putrefaction.

Too late the sleek English rulers discovered, as men discover
when they take to the lifeboats, that the first-class passenger who has
occupied the royal suite has no better chance of surviving than the
poor waif from a third-class bunk: that in fact to save their lives those
who had once been treated with punctilio must relinquish all thought
of place and position and wealth and take their chances with the
ship's company, living on hardtack and water, having even their private flask or private spirit lamp commandeered by the boatswain, in
order to give every member of the boat a fighting chance.

We in America shall not work swiftly enough, ruthlessly enough,
nor shall we have the means of striking back against fascism hard
enough, if we think we can baby ourselves through this crisis. We are
working against a barbarian power that has demanded and exacted
years of bitter sacrifice from every man, woman, and child in Germany, if one excepts of course the fat Goerings and the sleek Hitlers
for whose perverse dreams the sacrifice has been enacted. Fascism's
power is great just in proportion to the unwillingness, on the side of
the nations they threaten, to depart from their comfortable bourgeois

routine. Mr. Walter Lippmann has well called those who think that they must give up no vested interest or privilege whatever, the sleep-walkers; and that is the most charitable name one could apply. Some of these Rip Van Winkles fell asleep before 1933.

The mistakes of Europe, above all, the mistakes of France and England, are a warning to us who survive: *if we cling to the cargo we may lose the ship.* We must strip for action. Nothing is sacred except our ship — our democracy itself — the civilization we share with all men of good will — the ideals that have shaped us — the heritage of immaterial things we hope to hand on to our children. We Americans must struggle for democracy — that is progress, experiment, adventure, innovation: a ceaseless war that brings no promise of security, a war of the spirit against the Caliban [1] in man and old Chaos in nature: a war of the spirit against all that obstructs spirit. Fascism promises peace: *fascist peace, which is death.* While democracy lives, that is the one kind of peace we will scorn to accept.

APPRECIATION HINTS

1. For what reason does the author think our ship is a leaky one?
2. What exactly does he mean by " our ship "?
3. Mention some of the things that will have to be sacrificed if the ship is to be brought into port.
4. How does Lewis Mumford explain the fall of France?
5. How does he explain the mistakes made by the rulers of England before the war broke over them?
6. Who are the " sleepwalkers " in Walter Lippmann's opinion?
7. What does the author mean when he says " if we cling to the cargo we may lose the ship "?
8. There are striking resemblances between this description of the ship of state, and Archibald MacLeish's essay in this section. What are they?
9. Do you think that a majority of American citizens would have agreed with Lewis Mumford in 1940 when this book was written? Why?
10. What reasons do you find for our slow awakening to our peril?
11. Do you think that American citizens are prepared to make the sacrifices which the author believes necessary?

[1] The savage and brutish slave of Prospero in Shakespeare's *Tempest.*

12. What is meant by (a) the ship, (b) the compass, (c) the chronometer, (d) a few hands to navigate.
13. Write a composition on a topic suggested by this essay. Possible titles: London in Ruins, The Ship in the Storm, A Strike on Board, Business as Usual, How I Can Help, Schools and Defense.
14. If you want to read more of Mumford, read the program he recommended in 1939 in *Men Must Act*.

" The world," Dwight Morrow once wrote to his son, " is divided into people who do things and people who get the credit. Try, if you can, to belong to the first class. There's far less competition." Harold Nicolson, *Dwight Morrow* (Harcourt, Brace and Company)

Goodbye, brothers! You were a good crowd. As good a crowd as ever fisted with wild cries the beating canvas of a heavy foresail; or tossing aloft, invisible in the night, gave back yell for yell to a westerly gale. Joseph Conrad: *The Nigger of the Narcissus* (William Heinemann)

The best insurance against old age and disability is an interesting mind. In my life of professional teaching, I have never endeavored to make young men more efficient; I have tried to make them more interesting. I like to hang pictures on the wall of the mind; I like to make it possible for a man to live with himself, so that he will not be bored with himself. William Lyon Phelps, *Autobiography* (Oxford University Press)

ACKNOWLEDGMENTS

The editor of *Essays of Yesterday and Today* wishes to thank the following authors and publishers for permission to reprint the designated selections, all rights in which are in all cases reserved by the owner of the copyright.

The American Scholar: " Education versus Western Civilization " by Walter Lippmann.

Albert and Charles Boni, Inc.: Five definitions from *The Devil's Dictionary* by Ambrose Bierce.

Coward-McCann, Inc.: " The Mystery of Migration " from *Down to Earth,* copyright, 1937, 1938, 1939, 1940, by Alan Devoe.

The John Day Company: " The Importance of Loafing " from *The Importance of Living* by Lin Yutang.

Dodd, Mead & Company: " A, B, and C — The Human Element in Mathematics " from *Literary Lapses* by Stephen Leacock; " Romance " from *Post Impressions* by Simeon Strunsky; " On Running after One's Hat " from *All Things Considered* by G. K. Chesterton. All used by permission of the publishers, Dodd, Mead & Company.

Doubleday, Doran & Company, Inc.: " I Entertain an Agent Unawares " from *Adventures In Contentment* by David Grayson, copyright, 1907, by Doubleday, Doran & Company, Inc.; " Three Days to See " by Helen Keller, copyright, 1933, reprinted by permission from Doubleday, Doran & Company, Inc.

Harcourt, Brace and Company, Inc.: " I Get a Colt to Break In " from *The Autobiography of Lincoln Steffens,* copyright, 1931, by Harcourt, Brace and Company, Inc.; " Great Dam " from *Idle Money Idle Men,* copyright, 1940, by Stuart Chase, by permission of Harcourt, Brace and

Company, Inc.; "A Loud Sneer for Our Feathered Friends" from *My Sister Eileen,* copyright, 1938, by Ruth McKenney, by permission of Harcourt, Brace and Company, Inc.; "The Circus" from *My Name is Aram,* copyright, 1940, by William Saroyan, by permission of Harcourt, Brace and Company, Inc.; "All Hands Save Ship" from *Faith for Living,* copyright, 1940, by Lewis Mumford, by permission of Harcourt, Brace and Company, Inc.; "Words That Don't Inform" from *Language In Action* by S. I. Hayakawa, copyright, 1941, by Harcourt, Brace and Company, Inc.

Harper and Brothers: "Music at Night" from *Music at Night and Other Essays* by Aldous Huxley.

Henry Holt and Company, Inc.: "Town and Country" from *Hillsboro People* by Dorothy Canfield Fisher.

Houghton Mifflin Company: "To Horse" from *Life's Minor Collisions* by Frances L. Warner and Gertrude Warner; "America Faces Tomorrow's World" from *Let the Record Speak* by Dorothy Thompson. Both used by permission of Houghton Mifflin Company.

Winifred Kirkland: "A Man in the House" from *The Joys of Being a Woman.*

Alfred A. Knopf, Inc.: "Pit Mouth" from *Old Junk* by H. M. Tomlinson; "Introduction to the Universe" from *Happy Days* by H. L. Mencken. Both used by permission of and special arrangement with Alfred A. Knopf, Inc., authorized publishers.

J. B. Lippincott Company: "On Unanswering Letters" from *Essays* by Christopher Morley.

David Lloyd: An excerpt from "America's Gunpowder Women," copyright, 1939, by Pearl S. Buck, first published in *Harper's Magazine,* July 1939.

Matson and Duggan: "On ' And ' " from *On* by Hilaire Belloc.

The New Yorker: "Wake Up and Live, Eh?" by James Thurber; "She Did Not Know How to Be Famous" by Clifton Fadiman.

G. P. Putnam's Sons: "Meridian" from *A Book of Hours* by Donald Culrose Peattie; "The Jungle Sluggard" from *Jungle Days* by William Beebe.

Charles Scribner's Sons: "Aes Triplex" by Robert Louis Stevenson.

Survey Graphic: "Look to the Spirit within You" by Archibald MacLeish, as condensed in *The Reader's Digest.*

John R. Tunis: "Who's Catching?" taken from the *Atlantic Monthly.*

The Vanguard Press: "How Has Man Been Made?" from *Out of the Night* by H. J. Muller.

William Allen White: "Mary White."

The National Home Library Foundation: An excerpt from *The New Spirit* by Havelock Ellis.